1975

The American
Historical Novel

THE AMERICAN
HISTORICAL NOVEL

By ERNEST E. LEISY

NORMAN

UNIVERSITY OF OKLAHOMA PRESS

By Ernest E. Leisy

American Literature (New York, 1929)
The American Historical Novel (Norman, 1950)

Editor of

The Scarlet Letter (New York, 1929)
Facts and Ideas for Students of English Composition (New York,
1930, 1939), with others
Major American Writers (New York, 1935, 1945), with Howard
Mumford Jones
Horse-Shoe Robinson (New York, 1937)
The Voices of England and America (New York, 1939), with
others
Mark Twain's *Letters of Quintus Curtius Snodgrass* (Dallas, 1946)

Standard Book Number: 8061-0201-2

Copyright 1950 by the University of Oklahoma Press,
Publishing Division of the University.
Manufactured in the U.S.A.
First edition, January, 1950.
Second printing, March, 1952.
Third printing, October, 1962.
Fourth printing, January, 1970.

To my wife

Preface

THE HISTORICAL NOVEL has enjoyed a wide and continuous favor with the American reading public. At a time when fiction was looked upon as idle entertainment, the historical novel, by offering instruction in patriotism, helped remove the stigma attached to the novel. As a form of art, its relative freedom from rules well adapted it for a cultural instrument in a new world, and its close relation to the mood of the public has helped it keep the popular favor. It has served—to borrow Polonius' phrase—for "historical-pastoral, tragical-historical, tragical-comical-historical-pastoral, scene individable, or poem unlimited." Biographical novels, family sagas, and regional novels, all have merged so variously into historical fiction that border lines are often indistinguishable.

Whatever the mode, the historical novel today is the most popular form of American fiction. Three times in the nation's history the genre has been the dominant form of prose fiction. The first of these periods was during the years of national expansion which followed our two wars with Great Britain. The second was at the turn to the present century. The most important has been that of the last two decades, during which historical fiction has reached its widest and most discriminating body of readers.

In the light of these facts, it is surprising that the form has received little critical attention. Arthur H. Quinn's comprehensive work, *American Fiction* (New York, 1936), described a few historical novels, but made no mention of the species as such. Carl Van Doren's *The American Novel* (New York, 1921, 1940) discussed several historical novels, but devoted no chapter to the genre. Alexander Cowie's recent work, *The Rise of the American Novel* (New York, 1948), considers Cooper and his contemporaries in early historical fiction, but passes over the later writers. Two British compilations, Ernest Baker's *A Guide to Historical Fiction* (London and New York, 1914) and Jonathan Nield's *A Guide to the Best Historical Novels and Tales* (London and New York, 1902, 1929), list mostly ephemeral and juvenile works in the American sections; and Hannah Logasa's outline, *Historical Fiction* (Philadelphia, 1941), was designed for use in high schools.

This book has been written for the intelligent lay reader who is interested in the nation's past and who wants a rather full account of the materials and methods of American historical fiction. To serve this double purpose, the novels are arranged by historical backgrounds. Within each historical period the arrangement follows a topical sequence, novels on a given topic being discussed generally in the order of their appearance. After a novel has been introduced, it is analyzed succinctly, evaluated, and related to others in its category. The term "American" is limited to the United States. Novels by outsiders or about Canada or Mexico are generally excluded. "History Vivified" and the Conclusion seek to define and illuminate the genre as a whole. An extensive list of additional historical novels, which for one reason or another seemed inferior, is given in the Appendix. The Index offers opportunity for cross reference.

The writer is grateful to the Carnegie Foundation and to the administration of Southern Methodist University for assistance in bringing the labor of many years to a conclusion.

ERNEST E. LEISY

Contents

Preface   *vii*

HISTORY VIVIFIED   3

I. COLONIAL AMERICA   21

   1. *The Southern Colonies*   22
   2. *The New England Colonies*   37
   3. *The Middle Colonies*   53

II. THE AMERICAN REVOLUTION AND ITS AFTERMATH   68

   1. *The New England Colonies and Canada*   69
   2. *The Middle Colonies*   76
   3. *The Warfare Beyond the Alleghenies*   88
   4. *The Naval Warfare of the Revolution and of the War of 1812*   94
   5. *The Southern Colonies*   102
   6. *Shays's Rebellion*   112

III. THE WESTWARD MOVEMENT   114

   1. *The Kentucky Frontier*   115
   2. *The Northwest Territory*   121
   3. *The Louisiana Purchase*   126
   4. *The Fight for Texas*   128
   5. *The Far West*   133
   6. *The Slavery Issue*   145

IV. THE CIVIL WAR AND RECONSTRUCTION   153

   1. *Novels of the Civil War*   156
   2. *Novels of the Reconstruction*   179

ix

v. NATIONAL EXPANSION   191

   1. *The Midwestern Frontier*   192
   2. *The Far West*   207
   3. *The Southwest*   211
   4. *The War with Spain*   213

Conclusion   214

Appendix: Additional Historical Novels   219

Index   261

The American
Historical Novel

History Vivified

Historical fiction is often dismissed as mere "escape" literature. It is of course more than that, when it is well written. Even so, whatever takes one away from where he is and brings him back refreshed, has a justification of its own. It is always difficult to make the present transition period add up to something. For that reason it is pleasant to go back to something that is fixed and stable, to rest one's soul in an age in which the problems and perplexities of our day play no part. "A good historical novel," says May Lamberton Becker, "eases strained nerves for the simple reason that whatever happens in it is over. There is nothing now that you can do about it. Besides, though what happened at the time may have seemed the end of the world, the world didn't end. Perhaps the world isn't going to end this time, either."

One reason for the enormous popularity of historical fiction is that it satisfies many tastes. Like any other novel, it satisfies the need of the human mind for a story. It offers suspense and drama. It broadens us by letting us see people more fully in the round than we know them in real life and thus gives us an intensified sense of the happiness and misery which human life encompasses. But the historical novel does more than that. It attracts us to the past, to history. It satisfies the liking for color and pageantry, the love of excitement. A splendid court, remote in time, a dream castle, the "pomp and circumstance of glorious war"—all have their appeal. The picturesque fascinates us. An old sign swinging in the breeze of provincial New York or the passion of a Ramona struggling against overwhelming odds in sun-baked California has power to move us, for this is

3

history touched with emotion. The confined city dweller finds compensation in the adventures which his mode of life denies him. Particularly is this true when he gets, in addition, the factual and informational values of history in fiction. Historical fiction is an excellent introduction to history, biography, and travel. It is an enrichment of our experience, an enlargement of our interests. We feel at one with all that has happened.

Apart from the foregoing, the historical novel satisfies a desire for national homogeneity. It helps us realize the sacrifice for ideas and ideals, the sweat and blood that have made democracy work. We do have a heroic past, and there is glamour in the fact that the heroism was exercised at Yorktown with Washington and at Gettysburg with Lee. It is a usable past, too, one that democracy can profit by. Identifying ourselves with our roots is a form of passion for security. Seeing how our fathers coped with difficulties may help us who have lost our way. It gives us a new perspective, and enables us to project into the past our sense of self-justification. What makes it particularly heartening is the remarkable progress our nation has made in a comparatively short time. Our heritage of memories, then, serves both as a test of the present and as a quickening power for the future.

In the final analysis, however, the value of the historical novel, like that of any other form of fiction, rests on a valid hypothesis of human nature, regardless of locale. If the historical novel enlarges our understanding of the character of human life and of human institutions, it justifies itself beyond the point of therapy and entertainment.

What, then, constitutes a historical novel? On this subject opinions have varied widely. In a sense, all fiction has a preterit quality, a sense of having been lived. More specifically, historical fiction is concerned with historical truth, whatever that is. Whether such truth requires a spectacular historical figure or episode is a matter of controversy, as is the question of whether the term includes novels written contemporaneously with the events. Paul Leicester Ford once said, "An historical novel is one which grafts upon a story actual incidents or persons well enough known to be recognized as historical elements."[1] This definition appears too restrictive, however, for manners, customs, and ideas may suffice to identify a period. Few would dissent from including James Boyd's *The Long Hunt*, or Conrad Richter's *The Trees*, or O. E. Rölvaag's *Giants in the Earth* in the category of historical novels. Owen Wister complicated the problem by asserting that "any narrative which presents faithfully a day and a generation is of necessity historical,"[2] a view concurred in by Brander Matthews when he said, "The really trustworthy historical novels are those which were a-writing while the history was a-making," citing as examples, *Uncle Tom's Cabin* and *The Pickwick Papers*.[3]

But such statements, instead of defining the genre, merely confuse the issues. If novels of contemporary experience are to be regarded as historical, if x equals y, then what is the need of y? A historical novel is a novel the action of which is laid in an earlier time—how much earlier, remains an open question, but it must be a readily identifiable past time. Sir Walter Scott, who in theory and practice laid the foundations of the modern historical novel, set the interval at half a century. But in America—so rapid are changes here—a generation appears sufficient to render a preceding period historical.

Some critics, notwithstanding the fact that Tolstoy's *War and Peace* is widely acknowledged the greatest of all novels, have sought to disparage historical fiction as a bastard art. They shrug shoulders over the hybrid combination of history and fiction, although they accept an art like opera, sprung from music and drama. Homer and Virgil were not averse to min-

[1] Paul Leicester Ford, "The American Historical Novel," *Atlantic Monthly*, Vol. LXXX, No. 482 (December, 1897), 721.

[2] Owen Wister, *The Virginian* (New York, 1902), "To the Reader."

[3] Brander Matthews, *The Historical Novel and Other Essays* (New York, 1901), 18.

gling history and fiction, and they have had a respectable prog-
eny. Surely an art that makes the past come alive and brings it
nearer to its readers justifies itself.

Our standards of what is credible change. History emerged
out of fable. Myth was a preconscious account of significant
experience, which grew up around a kernel of fact and, on recurring, was enlarged by unlettered folk to the stature of legend. As fable became artistic and romantic, it moved away from
history, which became serious and accurate; but the two were
never entirely disjoined. Romance was constantly being trans-
formed by the force of popular sentiment, until History disowned it. Then Romance, believing there were many avenues
to the temple of Clio, did homage to the rising sovereignty of
Realism, and did it not merely as to outline, but in particulars.
It resorted to new devices of language, costume, and sentiment.
Shakespeare's Greeks and Trojans used racy English; Macbeth
never attempted a Scotticism. By the late eighteenth century,
however, came the desire to distinguish fact from fancy: it was
considered undignified for monk or monarch to use the language of the writer's own day. For the sake of verisimilitude,
phrases were picked up out of old plays and chronicles, and
dialogue fell into a stilted jargon, larded with strange oaths
never spoken. Romantic narratives were foisted upon readers
as fabricated history. Scott cast a magical illusion over the large
portions of history that he used. Bulwer-Lytton tried to reconcile history and romance for instructive purposes, even as
Ainsworth and G. P. R. James dwelt on the horrors of history.
Romance today, believing the past beyond bare outlines con-
jectural, has concentrated on depicting those passions which
never change and has provided for them an idiom and a historical setting.

Historians, noting the encroachments of fiction on their
domain, have taken the ground that their art is more objective
and therefore more sound. But does not the historian, if his
work is to be readable, also select and arrange his facts and pass

judgment upon what is worthy of record and what needs emphasis? Whence the many interpretations of Washington and Lincoln, the varying concepts of the Tories, and the discrepant accounts of our Civil War? There is no such thing as objective history.

Historical fiction creates the illusion of a past experience with more particularity than does the historical record. "Given the facts of the past," says Butterfield, "the historian shapes them in one way, squeezes something out of them, hunts out a set of implications in them; the novelist uses them to a different purpose, organises them differently, and turns them over in his thinking with a different kind of logic. Given an event, the historian will seek to estimate its ultimate significance and to trace out its influence; the novelist will seek merely to recapture the fleeting moment, to see the thing happening, to turn it into a picture or a 'situation.' "[4] Whereas the historian looks back to the past in the light of the present, the historical novelist retrojects himself into the period of his choice, and is concerned more with re-creating something akin to the actual experience than with appraising it in the light of what happened later. He is there with the actors, living through the experience.

Generally speaking, the historical novelist is interested less in the many subtle causes of events than in how the spirit of an age is reflected in a place and in a people. Individuals are more important to him than economic movements of goods or of people in the mass. To him the work of women and of wood choppers is as significant as that of military leaders or treaty makers. The everyday relations impress him. He dramatizes social processes, that is, as they bear on the life of the individual, and does it with something of the illumination and the emotional power of the poet. Clifford Dowdey does this in *Bugles Blow No More*, and Leonard Ehrlich, still more definitely, in *God's Angry Man*. As Scott remarked, "Every successful novelist must be more or less a poet, even although he may

[4] H. Butterfield, *The Historical Novel* (Cambridge, 1924), 113.

never have written a line of verse."[5] Elizabeth Madox Roberts produces, in *The Great Meadow*, the effect of illusion through evocative prose-poetry, even as Willa Cather, in *Death Comes for the Archbishop*, begets nostalgia through sensory awareness. It is the peculiar virtue of the historical novel that it can go beyond the evidence—it can display the idealism and enthusiasm of war, for instance, against a background of horror, which, since it is fiction, it can handle with an emotional intensity that the detachment of history cannot recover. It suggests, as Carlyle said of Scott, "that the bygone ages of the world were actually filled by living men, not by protocols, state papers, controversies, and abstractions of men."[6]

History and historical fiction, suggests Hervey Allen, have in common two kinds of truth—the factual and the philosophical. They differ in aim and therefore in art form. The historical novelist differs also from other fiction writers in that "his facts must be congenial to the kind of past he has undertaken to depict." He is not a liar when he departs from literal truth. "His function is to produce a complete illusion in the reader's mind. . . . Neither historian nor novelist can reproduce the real past," but by presenting it dramatically, the novelist may give "the reader a more vivid, adequate and significant apprehension of past epochs than does the historian." The novelist "appeals to the imagination and emotions in full play. He is *under obligation* to alter facts," provided the psychological truth demands it. "But he should not indulge in ill-designed counterfeiting."[7]

The historical novelist's chief difficulties, then, as one successful practitioner sees them, are (1) shaping his story into a design that is part of a grand pattern of historical events preg-

[5] Sir Walter Scott, *The Lives of the Novelists* (Everyman's edition), 109. Stephen Vincent Benét's *John Brown's Body* needs little stepping down of its verse to make it a historical novel, and a good one.

[6] Thomas Carlyle, *Critical and Miscellaneous Essays* (Centenary edition), IV, 77.

[7] Hervey Allen, "History and the Novel," *Atlantic Monthly*, Vol. CLXXIII, No. 2 (February, 1944), 119–20.

nant with significance, and (2) adapting the source material to that design. The argument that the genre cannot be true he considers naïve, and beside the point. Rather, the questions to be asked concerning a historical novel are: Is it convincing? Is it artistically satisfactory? Does it fulfill the requirements of its own aesthetic? If it awakens our imagination to a lively sense of the past it has value, it enriches our experience.

Depiction of the past varies considerably in pattern. Sir Walter Scott, the father of the historical novel, was first of all a novelist, and then a historian. In developing the art of historical fiction, he recombined according to formulas of his own the practices current in the fiction of his day—Miss Edgeworth's flair for local color, Mrs. Radcliffe's fondness for mystery and romantic landscape, and the interest of that period in travel, adventure, and antiquarian lore. He was romantic in his treatment of the past, but he endowed his humble folk especially with flesh-and-blood reality. Scott's American imitators adapted his patterns to local scene and tradition, emphasizing now one element, now another, according as the fashion of the times dictated.

When novel writing began in America, at the close of the eighteenth century, the outstanding native materials were the Indian and the Revolution. Almost a score of years before Fenimore Cooper celebrated the virtues of the guileless savage, there appeared John Davis's *The First Settlers of Virginia*, with the subtitle *An Historical Novel*. But that "glorified memoir" of Captain Smith and Princess Pocahontas merely illustrates the confusion which existed between historical narrative and the historical novel before the advent of *Waverley*.

By 1821, Fenimore Cooper in *The Spy* succeeded in adapting native elements to the sustained method of handling history employed in the then popular romances after the manner of Scott. Cooper used the conflict of guerrilla warfare as background for a household divided by partisan interests, and introduced a mysterious stranger who proved to be none other than the Father of his Country. Cooper also set the plot pattern for most of the novels of the Revolution: a dashing, noble rebel officer loves the daintily feminine daughter of a staunch landed loyalist. As the father wants his daughter to marry a loyalist, there follows a conflict between love and duty. During a series of fights, captures, escapes, hangings, trials, and reprieves, centering in some historical campaign, the rebel exposes the villainy of his loyalist rival, converts the father to the justness of his cause, and wins the beauty. This plot pattern was used over and over by most of the novelists for half a century.

So well was *The Spy* received at home and abroad that Cooper planned a series of historical novels, one for each of the colonies that had participated in the Revolution. Although *Lionel Lincoln* was the only novel in the series actually published, Cooper carried over his technique into other tales of a similar character. *The Pilot* repeated in terms of the sea the general outlines of *The Spy*. In *The Last of the Mohicans* he went a step further, causing his theme to turn upon and be explained by the chief historical event, the savagery of the Indians at Fort William Henry in 1757. So well did he blend research and invention in this work that his treatment of the subject, despite Lowell's jest about "white men daubed red," is our most memorable fiction of race conflict over the possession of a continent.

To appreciate Cooper's outstanding position in historical fiction, one need but compare him with his imitators who now came forward in surprising numbers. Several of them, like James McHenry, Lydia Maria Child, John Neal, and Eliza Cushing, had been bred in the school of Dame Radcliffe; but with "Waverley galloping over hill and dale; the 'Spy' lurking in every closet; the mind everywhere supplied," as one of them put it, "with 'Pioneers' on the land and soon to be with 'Pilots' on the deep,"[8] they tried to adapt their plot and style to the

[8] Lydia M. Child, *Hobomok, a Tale of Early Times* (1824), Preface.

10

kind of romance which Scott and Cooper had made popular.
But this was not easy to do. Mrs. Cheney's two-volume *Peep
at the Pilgrims in Sixteen Hundred Thirty-Six,* for example,
had the common failing of an overcrowded plot. John Neal
out-Heroded Herod in a gory romance of the Mingo chieftain
Logan, and in *Seventy-Six* attempted the preposterous task of
rushing three braggart soldiers and their sighing ladies through
the entire Revolution. James K. Paulding deplored the haste
with which Neal and other novelists were tossing off their
work, but his own historical novels, *The Dutchman's Fireside,
Koningsmarke, Westward Ho!,* and *The Puritan and His
Daughter,* were deficient in action. Characters, too, were commonly drawn only in black and white. Writers of American
historical fiction had yet to learn to draw from history and
tradition the bare outline of their subject, and to embellish that
with the warmth and color of human nature, which, whether
in seventeenth century Massachusetts or in their own day,
were essentially the same.

After 1830 writers of historical romance turned to the cul-
tivation of local history. The larger national themes had been
exploited, and there followed a tendency to use more limited
geographical regions. In the South, where social conditions still
retained many of the conventions of English life, it was easier
than in the more changeable North to contemplate the past in
terms of Scott. The Scottish laird and the English baron were
readily replaced by the aristocratic planter, the vassal and the
serf by the indentured servant and the Negro, while the Indian
and the mountaineer took the role of the Highland outlaw. In
reality the planter was no baron, but a tobacco farmer, his estate
no principality, and his rambling wooden house hardly a man-
sion. Nevertheless, William A. Caruthers in *The Cavaliers of
Virginia* and John P. Kennedy in *Swallow Barn* found it natural
to establish the Cavalier tradition for the Old Dominion. John
Esten Cooke sentimentalized nabobs, baronial halls, and vast
estates. Thus, while the North during this decade was preoc-

cupied with internal improvements and reform, the feudal South, with its planters increasingly on the defensive, dreamed over its Scott of the days of a golden prime. For *Horse-Shoe Robinson,* however, Kennedy used an actually observed local variant of Cooper's scout, a witty homespun blacksmith; this choice, combined with geographical realism and a racy style, produced the best ante-bellum novel in the South.

The most prolific historical novelist of the South, William Gilmore Simms, conceived of his art in terms of the ancient epic:

The modern romance is a poem in every sense of the word. It is only with those who insist upon poetry as rhyme, and rhyme as poetry, that the identity fails to be perceptible. Its standards are precisely those of the epic. It invests individuals with an absorbing interest—it hurries them through crowding events in a narrow space of time—it requires the same unities of plan, of purpose, and harmony of parts, and it seeks for its adventures among the wild and wonderful. It does not insist upon what is known, or even what is probable. It grasps at the possible; and, placing a human agent in hitherto untried situations, it exercises its ingenuity in extricating him from them, while describing his feelings and his fortunes in their progress. The task has been well or ill done, in proportion to the degree of ingenuity and knowledge which the romancer exhibits in carrying out the details, according to such proprieties as are called for by the circumstances of the story.[9]

In practice Simms followed Scott's and Cooper's patterns, but in adapting their technique to the Carolina background he evinced a more realistic portraiture of the Indians and of guerrilla warfare in dismal swamp and luxuriant forest. His own early life on the Mississippi border had familiarized him with the racy speech and highhanded acts of frontier blackguards, and when these appear, his stories sound most convincing. Unfortunately, however, Simms tended naturally to the melo-

[9] William Gilmore Simms, *The Yemassee* (1835), VI–VII.

dramatic and inclined to repeat character and situation in his many novels. He also threw into his work blocks of history, accurate though they were, without blending them into his fiction. The historical romance, however, with its ground plan of fact, afforded the control which his facile fancy needed to produce more memorable works than his romances of the border.

New England in the eighteen thirties showed little taste for the historical novel. It preferred the annuals and gift books found on every parlor table and the songs and stories furnished by its galaxy of poets. Elsewhere, *Evangeline* and *The Courtship of Miles Standish* might well have appeared in the form of historical romance. New England preferred, too, the unvarnished tales which its distinguished historians—Bancroft, Prescott, Parkman, and Motley—were giving it. Motley, to be sure, began authorship with *Merry-Mount*, but it was a conventional romance. Romantic history like D. P. Thompson's *The Green Mountain Boys*, with its dashing exploits of Ethan Allen and his democratic followers, appealed to others, while many enjoyed Sylvester Judd's *Margaret* for its rich storehouse of backwoods manners in early Massachusetts. Harriet Beecher Stowe's *The Minister's Wooing* and *Oldtown Folks* were accepted as faithful transcripts of the cheerful and dynamic aspects of later Puritan life.

Nathaniel Hawthorne, after sharpening his pen on short dramatic episodes in colonial New England, extended his art in *The Scarlet Letter* with a like economy of outward fact, but developed a more detailed, and a correspondingly better-humanized inner drama. As he interpreted the Puritan scene, Hawthorne allowed himself the latitude of the romancer as opposed to the novelist, a difference he elucidated in the well-known preface to *The House of the Seven Gables*. He did not, however, falsify the essential facts. Through the haze of distance he viewed the Puritans with detached understanding. If his story was less pedantically documented than, say, Hoffman's *Greyslaer*, it was nevertheless a more noteworthy piece of historical fiction because it reflected greater insight into human destiny, into man's wrestling with the dark problems imposed upon him by historical conditions.

With the mature art of Hawthorne our earlier period of historical-novel writing comes to a close. By experimenting with various techniques, it succeeded in depicting romantically the cavaliers of the Old South, the somber Puritans, the droll Dutch, the savage Indians, and the noble frontiersmen. Fictional characters were ordinarily from the upper class and were usually drawn in black and white. The American Revolution was the favorite subject, and the patriots always came out on top. Washington and other historical figures were conventionally portrayed and had little obvious connection with the fictional characters; never were any of them vilified. The period was characterized by imitativeness and flamboyance; only at the end was its wealth of romantic material treated with an art that did it justice.

During the Civil War historical fiction was quiescent. So far as it was concerned, the struggle between the states never attained the epic significance of the Revolution, although the complexities and drawn-out hatreds offered material for new analyses of motives as well as new materials for romance. The emphasis now was on partisan issues. John Esten Cooke continued to write in the Scott-Simms-Caruthers tradition, adding the sensationalism of Bulwer, the military gallantry of Lever, and the "historic truth" of Miss Mühlbach. A. W. Tourgée, carpetbagger judge in North Carolina and professional agitator, issued historical novels that were passionate sermons in defense of the radical Reconstructionists, as Thomas Dixon in his novels later rabidly defended the Southern view. Resentment lingered, while sentimental short fiction was written by unreconstructed women and veterans. As the years advanced, tensions subsided. Writers, in a spirit of reconciliation, now favored the theme of divided kinsmen, or better, that of a Union soldier in love with a Southern girl, their many difficulties keeping the reader in constant suspense before passion was rewarded at length in conjugal bliss.

By the seventies and eighties, novels like Edward Eggleston's *The Circuit Rider,* George W. Cable's *The Grandissimes,* and Mary Hartwell Catherwood's *The Romance of Dollard* emphasized realism and local color. William Dean Howells found the creed of realism incompatible with the art of historical fiction, and Henry James looked elsewhere for the background of his novels. With the advance of science, romanticism began to give way to realism in the historical novel. Lew Wallace, for example, was inspired by the animated controversy over the Darwinian theory to make a thorough study of authorities for his widely popular novel *Ben-Hur,* and S. Weir Mitchell, the noted neurologist, kept the ultraheroic out of such books as *In War Time* and *Hugh Wynne.* Characters from now on were motivated more and more by the impulse of the survival of the fittest.

By the middle nineties the novel vied once more with the short story for public favor and in the following decade won supremacy in the unprecedented vogue of historical romance. In England, Stevenson and Kipling revived romance, and in this country the patriotism stirred up by the war with Spain caused historical novels to become best sellers. Writers became interested in depicting costumes and manners in addition to relating an exciting story of love and adventure. Mary Johnston recalled the earliest traditions of Virginia and embellished them acceptably in *To Have and To Hold.* Dr. S. Weir Mitchell in *Hugh Wynne* went into psychological details about how the Revolution affected the Quaker City. Paul Leicester Ford, the historian, drew upon his intimate knowledge of that war in his costume romance, *Janice Meredith,* and Maurice Thompson took his readers across the Alleghenies for a popular romance based on the exploits of George Rogers Clark, *Alice of Old Vincennes.* Ellen Glasgow in *The Battle-Ground* produced the first realistic picture of noncombatants during the Civil War, and Winston Churchill won acclaim with his portraits of John Paul Jones in *Richard Carvel*, of Abraham Lincoln in *The Crisis*, and of George Rogers Clark in *The Crossing*. In these patriotic novels motives were simple and values crystal clear. The triumph of righteousness was seldom in doubt.

Among the historical novels that used foreign settings, the better ones may be mentioned only briefly, as they fall outside the province of this discussion. They include Mark Twain's *Personal Recollections of Joan of Arc*, with its fifteenth century French setting; Booth Tarkington's *Monsieur Beaucaire*, laid in eighteenth century Bath; Arthur S. Hardy's *Passe Rose*, a brilliant romance of the time of Charlemagne; S. Weir Mitchell's *The Adventures of François*, which pictured the turbulence of the French Revolution; Charles Major's heavily embroidered *When Knighthood Was in Flower*, laid in Tudor England; F. Marion Crawford's masterpiece, *Via Crucis*, a story of the Second Crusade, and his tale of Philip II of Spain, *In the Palace of the King*; and Edith Wharton's *The Valley of Decision*, an excellent novel of a late eighteenth century Italian revolution. At the other extreme were the Graustark romances of George Barr McCutcheon, with their easy counters of sword and buckler in imaginary kingdoms. These costume pieces with their pseudoarchaic jargon have long since lost readers.[10]

By 1905 this particular wave of interest in historical romance was over. As the public girded itself for the "strenuous life," writers turned to realism. By the turn of the century novels had made some progress toward the realistic method. Winston Churchill, for example, accumulated data as thoroughly as a historian, Paul Leicester Ford wrote not romance but romantic history, Ellen Glasgow resorted to irony to avoid heroics, and Weir Mitchell used the memoir form of fiction to incorporate the many inconsequential happenings which vivify

[10] Cf. "The 'Pastry' Period in Literature," by Grant C. Knight, in *The Saturday Review of Literature*, Vol. XXVII, No. 51 (December 16, 1944), 5–7.

the daily life of a period. The greatest advance was made by the naturalist Stephen Crane, when in *The Red Badge of Courage* he not only abandoned the structural trappings of historical fiction, but shifted emphasis from "the pomp and circumstance of glorious war" to the ordeal of the common soldier as he faces his first battle. This deglamorizing and personalizing of the historical novel has appealed in particular to recent writers and readers of fiction.

Between 1910 and 1915 historical novels appeared only sporadically. Mary Watts in *Nathan Burke* reverted to the War with Mexico, Mary Johnston restated the Confederate version of the Civil War in *The Long Roll* and its sequel, *Cease Firing*, and Emerson Hough based *The Magnificent Adventure* on the Lewis and Clark Expedition; but in many respects these were old style. Americans were too engrossed in the grim realities of a world war to concern themselves with a romantic treatment of the past. For the historical novelist the war had its compensations, however. After the return of the expeditionary forces, novelists who had seen action abroad could write with keener realism than before of earlier conflicts in the nation's history. If novels of warfare palled, there was always the impressive saga of pioneering.

Beginning in 1925 with James Boyd's excellent novel of the Revolution, *Drums*, and stimulated during the depression by the popular success of Hervey Allen's *Anthony Adverse* and Margaret Mitchell's *Gone With the Wind*, historical novels have appeared in increased number and quality until they now constitute one of the most important types of literature before the public. It would be invidious to single out the more able of the recent writers of historical fiction at this point since their work is soon to be discussed in these pages. Suffice it to say that in the work of these writers history and background are more accurately presented and much better blended with fiction than formerly. The novels are definitely more psychological and sociological than they were, and have less the character of period fiction. They exhibit more frankness and less fustian, the characterization is much better, the action moves faster, and the stories are more alive.

American historical fiction has emerged from the pattern of partisan romanticism in which earlier tales of the Revolution and of the Civil War were enveloped. The romantic adventure pattern is now largely modified by realistic detail. Such details do not necessarily make for a realistic point of view, however, as the partisan history of *Oliver Wiswell* or the thesis novels of Howard Fast demonstrate. Realism is still a matter of degree.

In modern practice, historical novels may be divided into three categories. The first and best type is the historical novel proper, a work like Willa Cather's *Death Comes for the Archbishop*, which admirably integrates character and setting. Then there is the period novel, a work more concerned with detailed background than in presenting the whole of life, as for example, Walter Edmonds' *Drums Along the Mohawk*. Last in importance is the romance of adventure, written by Cooper and Simms in an earlier period, and illustrated at its best by Churchill's *Richard Carvel* and Johnston's *To Have and To Hold*, at the turn of the century.

These distinctions are arbitrary, however, for in actual practice some of the characteristics of one type may be mingled with those of the others. For the purposes of discussion the distinctions may offer some help in the matter of evaluating the novels. The first of these categories shows respect for historical fiction as an art. In the romance of adventure too much emphasis is placed on action for its own sake, as is the case, for example, in the novels of Neil Swanson and Van Wyck Mason. The period novel too often merely exchanges the furniture, the clothes, and the speech of one generation for those of another. And the costume romance, in these days of the more abundant sex life, gives too much attention to "salad dressing." The pattern has become so stereotyped that Robert Ruark in his burlesque, *Grenadine Etching*, quite appropriately provides the hussy with a pet gorilla!

Even in the historical novel proper the relation of fact and fiction may be badly adjusted. In such otherwise excellent novels as James Boyd's *Marching On*, Esther Forbes's *Paradise*, and Kenneth Roberts' *Arundel* a too meticulous use of historical fact impairs the novel as a work of art. On the other hand, Ellen Glasgow's *The Battle-Ground*, Elizabeth Madox Roberts' *The Great Meadow*, and LeGrand Cannon's *Look to the Mountain* really fuse history and life.

Of late, the element of conjecture, always a source of trouble in historical fiction, has been reduced to a minimum that may characterize a fourth form. A historical event is retold in fictional guise, without using plot, but employing instead invented conversation, situations that have their own suspense, and of course truth to fact. Such works as David Garnett's *Pocahontas*, Donald C. Peattie's *Forward the Nation*, and Vardis Fisher's *The Mothers*, differ from the historical novel proper mainly in presenting history with little more contrivance than a chronicle might require, using only actual events and real characters. This type appears to be developing into a favorite as it pleases the modern skeptical temper. What form the historical novel of the future may take remains to be seen. Carl Sandburg has recently finished a novel, *Remembrance Rock*, which aims at no less than a summation of our entire history as a nation.[11]

From these preliminary observations on the nature and the development of the American historical novel, we proceed to a discussion of the novels themselves as they are placed

[11] *Remembrance Rock* (1948) is a thousand-page epic of the American spirit as it unfolded in the life and trials of Plymouth Colony, amid divided loyalties during the Revolution, and in the tensions of the Middle West during the eighteen fifties and sixties. The novel is an extension of the underlying idea of Sandburg's *The People, Yes*, here applied to evoke our "usable past." It is a story of dreamers and seekers, rich in folk sayings and local color—a mixture of learning and naïveté.

against the backgrounds into which American history is most conveniently divided: Colonial America, the American Revolution and Its Aftermath, the Westward Movement, the Civil War and Reconstruction, and the period of National Expansion to World War I. Each of these periods has had authentic legendary appeal for readers of American fiction.

I. Colonial America

THE THEME of how men in hard straits have succeeded has always had a profoundly human appeal. The feeling for the struggles of the pioneers, as they fought along the Atlantic seaboard with the stubborn forces of nature and with the aborigines, is in our blood. We feel somehow that these initial battles were our own. And when the struggle was extended to achieve national self-government, the recital levies directly on our patriotic instinct. Therefore historical novels about colonial America, combining as they do the attraction of difficult new ventures with interest in a great democratic experiment, have for us more than usual significance.

Novels in the modern usage of the term were not written during the Colonial era. It has been the prerogative of the historical novel to tell of that period in retrospect. Efforts to do this have been fraught with difficulty, in the first place, because the records are meager. The Puritans were concerned with inner rather than outward matters, and their accounts take for granted much that the historical novelist would like to know. The problem of how to humanize those stern forebears without exaggerating, and how to avoid over-romanticizing their enemies, the Indians, has had no easy solution.

The difficulty of presenting so remote a period has been further complicated by the fact that among the settlers themselves there was considerable diversity, in their motives for coming, in their adjustment to conditions, and in their worldly fortunes. In the South, the development of a planter economy formed one kind of unity; in New England, the concern with matters of the spirit formed another; and in the Middle Colonies, the adjustments of diverse nationalities constituted a further bond. Accordingly, the novels about to be considered will be discussed under the headings: (1) The Southern Colonies; (2) the New England Colonies; and (3) the Middle Colonies.

1. *The Southern Colonies*

In the colonial South there was an abundance of incidents to invite romantic treatment by novelists. The arrival of the first white settlers in Virginia, the Carolinas, and Maryland; the Smith-Pocahontas romance; the Virginia Massacre of 1622; life in Jamestown under Governor Berkeley at the time of Bacon's Rebellion; events at the capital of Williamsburg; the Yemassee wars in Carolina—these, as well as the romantic careers of Virginia's Governor Spotswood and young Washington, were each the subject of historical fiction at one time or another.

The primacy of the Old Dominion made her a natural favorite among writers of the historical novel. The Virginia depicted in American fiction was a highly romantic land, a land of cavaliers, in contrast to the haven of criminals depicted by Defoe and the Elizabethan dramatists. But the beginnings were hardly genteel. The earliest incident in Virginia history, the story of the settlers of the "lost colony" off the coast of what is now North Carolina, was not treated in fiction until 1923, when Mary Johnston published *Croatan*. The author was a native Virginian, who in her youth had been impressed by tales and legends of early days in the Old Dominion and, after writing a number of historical novels pertaining to various periods of Virginia history, produced in *Croatan* an arresting account of Sir Walter Raleigh's establishment of the first colony.

Under the captaincy of one John White, so the novel runs, three boatloads of colonists set sail in 1587 from Plymouth for the New World and land on the deserted island of Roanoke. After two of the ships have returned to England, the settlement is attacked by Indians, who kill a large number of the colonists, among them the parents of Virginia Dare, the first white child born in this country. The surviving settlers then join the Croatan tribe, with whom they intermarry. Myles Darling, the youngest child on the voyage, grows into manhood among the Croatans and falls in love with Virginia. In the meantime, a Spanish lad, Ruy Valdez, having been shipwrecked off the coast of Florida, finds his way to the Croatans and also falls in love with her. After she is abducted by the Shawnees he helps Myles rescue her and yields him his claims.

Hackneyed as this old-fashioned romance is, it throws considerable light on the hardships of the pioneers in the wilderness. Happily, too, it moves swiftly.

The episode which appealed to novelists more than any other in the early history of Virginia was the rescue of Captain John Smith by the Indian maid Pocahontas. Whether fact or legend (Smith first recalled the story after Pocahontas appeared at the Court of St. James's), here was the essence of romance—the flower of chivalry saved from a cruel beheading by a radiant daughter of nature. John Davis, an English traveler, touched on the theme in *The First Settlers of Virginia* (1802); John Esten Cooke, under the pseudonym Anas Todkill, contributed a "memoir," *My Lady Pocahontas* (1885); and an Englishman, David Garnett, published the most detailed account as *Pocahontas* (1933).

Davis, after a sojourn of several years in Virginia, the Carolinas, and Georgia, briefly mentioned the episode in his *Travels* (1802). He refurbished it in *The First Settlers of Virginia, an Historical Novel* (1802), and expanded it in *Captain Smith and Princess Pocahontas* (1805), with historical material copied almost verbatim from Robertson and Belknap. From the slightness of the plot it is clear that Davis little sensed the dramatic values inherent in his materials. The episode in which

23

Pocahontas intervenes in the Captain's behalf is brief, comes too early, and is treated without suspense. After Smith's supposed death, Pocahontas is comforted by John Rolfe, whom she later marries. The couple leave with their little son for England, where Pocahontas attracts much attention, but soon succumbs to a fever. The book, though it bears the subtitle of "historical novel," is really a plotless chronicle of travel, embellished with romantic sidelights on the Indians and the boundless forests.

Cooke's account of Smith includes glimpses of Shakespeare's England prior to and after the founding of Jamestown. Couched in the semiarchaic style of the Puritan Anas Todkill, the memoir is mainly a love tragedy, a tribute to the devotion of a gentle maid to a courageous cavalier. But dark days are ahead. There are the machinations of three leaders, who, by disputing Smith's authority, force him to go back to England. Pocahontas, supposing Smith dead, assuages her sorrow by serving the infant colony as a protecting deity. But she is seized by the buccaneer Argall, who thus hopes to curb the power of her father, Powhatan. Eventually Rolfe wins her, and takes her with him to England. There she is admired by royalty. On a chance meeting with Smith at the Globe Theater she sees William Shakespeare, who confesses she served as inspiration for his Miranda! Fanciful as this memoir is, it carefully follows Smith's own account in *The Generall Historie of Virginia*, and it conveys the atmosphere of the period.

Garnett's version of the Smith-Pocahontas theme is essentially that of Cooke, greatly amplified by realistic detail. It is almost a day-by-day chronicle of the conflict of two civilizations, with Pocahontas progressing from a primitive forest society to that of the upper class in Jacobean London. Her life runs like a bright thread through the story of the sadistic practices of her countrymen, and of the bickering, bullying, and robbing by the whites. Smith appreciates her loyalty; he has his moments of playfulness as well as of resourcefulness; but he is essentially a bully, who, when glimpsed once more in London, has degenerated into a pitiful blusterer. Powhatan has alternate fits of humor and rage, and is as busy as a country doctor keeping up with various demands upon his time; but his civilization is static, and is therefore doomed eventually.

Garnett's historical narrative, as it alternates swiftly from the idyllic to the sadistic, is full of the tensions of the period, but it does not produce complete illusion. The Indians tend to have the whims and attitudes of white men of the modern era. The amazing vitality of the Pocahontas legend is doubtless due to the sentimental appeal of a tragic love story, particularly when given an epic quality by its relation to the founding of a nation. Strange to say, none of the writers dealing with the story betrays the slightest suspicion that Smith's account of it is open to question.[1]

The Virginia Massacre in 1622 was the next episode in Virginia history to appeal to writers of fiction. It might be observed in passing that "massacre" was a euphemism applied whenever the Indians got the upper hand in combat between the two races; if the reverse was true, it was dubbed a "bloody victory." The "massacre" of 1622, following the period of good will engendered by Smith and Powhatan, came at a time when the settlers around Jamestown had let their fortifications fall into disuse. After Powhatan's death in 1618, his brother Opechancanough felt that the whites should be expelled before it might be too late. Accordingly, he rallied the tribes and raided the outlying plantations, killing some four hundred persons and devastating much property.

This massacre furnished the background of two short romances, *Ruth Emsley* (1850), by William H. Carpenter, and *The Head of a Hundred* (1895), by Maud Wilder Goodwin. In *Ruth Emsley*, the betrothed of George Pierce is taken

[1] See J. B. Hubbell, *Virginia Life in Fiction* (Dallas, 1923), 21. Several dramas were based on the Pocahontas legend between 1808 and 1830, but the only other treatment in prose fiction, *The History of the Female American, or the Adventures of Unca Winkfield* (1814), was a Gothic melodrama.

captive during the general uprising, but is rescued in the nick of time by a young chief—an intervention which enables George and Ruth to be happily united.

The Head of a Hundred resorts to the courtly style of Elizabethan romance in relating the fortunes of a young physician who comes to Jamestown after having been flouted in England by the spirited Elizabeth Romney. Shortly after, she too arrives with a shipload of maids as wives for the settlers. On the voyage she has had the misfortune to break her arm, which offers the physician an opportunity to help her. She spurns further advances, although at his insistence she accepts custodianship of his ancestral ring while he is away on a mission to King Accomac. On the way, his boat picks up John Rolfe and his motherless son. The story comes to its climax during the devastating massacre, when the love of the "head of a hundred" for Elizabeth finally triumphs. Despite conventional plots, both novels blend history and fiction fairly well.

Light as these romances were, they suggested possibilities to a writer of greater competence and with fuller knowledge of the period. Mary Johnston, in *To Have and To Hold* (1900), used the arrival of a shipload of maids and the uprising led by Opechancanough for one of the most popular romances relating to the Colonial period. Ralph Percy, the hero of this tale of conflict and suspended love, is a member of the House of Burgesses. Reluctant to see the maids exchanged for tobacco, Percy is persuaded by Rolfe to go to the lengthy church service in which the suitors are to look over their "prospects." He would return to his plantation wifeless but for his sense of chivalry, which has been aroused by the designs of one Sharpless on a certain high-spirited beauty. After paying his quantity of tobacco to be united to the girl, Percy learns that she is practicing duplicity. She is, in fact, Lady Jocelyn Leigh, a ward of the King, who, in order to avoid being courted by one of his unworthy favorites, has taken passage on the *Due Return* under the name of Patience Worth.

The story, after running through the usual maze of complications, culminates in the arrival of Lord Carnal, her suitor, with orders from the King for her return. Jocelyn and Percy attempt to escape, and, after encountering a band of pirates and being separated by the Indian conflict, are reunited by the antics of Jeremy Sparrow, erstwhile actor and parson. Carnal, seeing that all is lost, ends his base life with poison. Melodramatic as this material is, it is related with compelling interest; the characterization is adequate; and despite a tendency to idealize the Indians, there is truth of atmosphere sufficient for *To Have and To Hold* to rate as the best of the romances about colonial Virginia.

The next group of novels on colonial Virginia center about Bacon's Rebellion in 1676. This rebel attack on excessive taxation and arbitrary government came, significantly enough, just a century before the colonies united in revolt against royal authority. In the course of the long reign of Sir William Berkeley as the royal governor, the conflict between his will and that of the people was heading toward a crisis. The immediate provocation of the uprising was the dilatory policy of the Governor about Indian depredations. Some even accused him of trading with the Indians for personal profit. Whatever truth there may have been in the accusations, the young rebel Bacon, by rallying the people against the forces of despotism, became a symbol of warning for the future in colonial affairs.

In William A. Caruthers' story based on this event, *The Cavaliers of Virginia, or the Recluse of Jamestown* (1834), the Governor is anxious for a leading beauty, Virginia Fairfax, to marry his adopted son, Frank Beverly. This hope is challenged by the young cavalier Bacon, who is leading the people's cause against the royal governor. In the struggle which ensues, Bacon is thrown into prison to await death, but public opinion rallies to his defense, forces Berkeley into temporary retirement, and enables Bacon to win the celebrated beauty.

Although the author based his story on Burk's *History of Virginia*, he adapted his material considerably to meet the requirements of romance. According to the record, Bacon, instead of being awarded the lovely Miss Fairfax, died from a fever at the point of victory. The Gothic subplot of Caruthers' story transfers, on doubtful authority, the regicide Whalley from New England to a cave near Jamestown, where he may serve conveniently as an ally to the cavaliers. The allies of Bacon were really not cavaliers at all, but small farmers. In these respects, as well as in his verbose, rhetorical style, Caruthers was writing under the direct influence of Sir Walter Scott. He deserves credit for managing his double plot with no little dexterity, but it is obvious that he was more interested in his role as storyteller than as historian. His imaginary Virginia, with its absurd mysteries and melodramatic villains, had little basis in reality.

A more realistic version of the Bacon-Berkeley quarrel appeared in St. George Tucker's *Hansford* (1857). Tucker, the grandson of the Revolutionary jurist, tried to reconcile the diverse opinions concerning Sir William handed down by history, but relied mainly on Kercheval's *History of the Valley of Virginia*. He considered Berkeley a brave cavalier who was warped to bloody excesses by his insane loyalty to Charles II. When, after Bacon's death, Berkeley recovered power for a short time, he put to death so many leaders in the rebellion that even Charles, on replacing him, exclaimed, "That old fool has killed more people in that naked country than I have done for the murder of my father."

According to the novel, Thomas Hansford, a rebel friend of Nathaniel Bacon, is betrothed to Virginia Temple, the charming daughter of a member of the House of Burgesses. The Temple family is opposed to the match and favors the courtly Alfred Bernard, a villainous rival. When the temporizing policy of the Governor results in open rebellion, Hansford is dismissed by the family, while Bernard shines at the birthnight ball. Then Bacon's men defeat the Indians; but the Governor rescinds the young man's commission. The attack on the government follows, with the rebels routing the cavaliers and forcing Berkeley to leave. Unable to hold the town for long, they set it afire. Three months later Bacon dies from dysentery, and Hansford's romance ends in tragedy. On a secret visit to Virginia, Hansford is trapped by Bernard, who turns out to be his illegitimate brother. Although Bernard expresses remorse for his brother's execution, he soon sails for England with Berkeley, and dies later in a popish plot. Virginia, another conventionally tragic heroine, accepts her fate.

In summing up his view of the rebellion, Tucker expresses the opinion that Bacon was impelled in his course by his intense desire for fame. In style as well as in point of view, *Hansford* reflects a growing sense of realism in the writing of historical fiction.

Half a century later, Mary Johnston based her romance, *Prisoners of Hope* (1898), on this same uprising of bondservants and slaves against Governor Berkeley. On the plantation of Colonel Verney, the tobacco king, Godfrey Landless, bondservant from Newgate, has fallen in love with the Colonel's daughter Patricia. She is also being formally courted by her cousin, Sir Charles Carew, who has come from England to replenish his fortune, though he is now engrossed by her beauty. After Patricia spurns Landless, he heads an insurrectionary organization. This action leads to his imprisonment and to Patricia's abduction by the Indians. On her recapture by Landless, she confesses her love for him; but her father bans the rebellious bondsman to the forest, while Patricia, in the key of sentimental romance, vows eternal celibacy. The atmosphere of the period is well conveyed, with its laced and brocaded ladies, its silk-stockinged men, its convicts and slaves, and its scenes in the House of Burgesses, at the Governor's ball, and in tobacco fields. Matters of topical interest are discussed, like the Act of Uniformity and the Navigation Laws, and a fresh point of view emerges in the commoner's asserting himself; but the work as a whole is in the romantic manner of an age before realism set in.

Approximately the same period furnishes the background for Mary E. Wilkins Freeman's *The Heart's Highway* (1900). And the plot is not essentially different from that of *Prisoners of Hope*. The Cavendishes, an esteemed family, have just migrated to Virginia when Captain Cavendish dies. His daughter Mary is being tutored by Harry Wingfield, a Cambridge scholar, who is in love with her but is under suspicion for theft of a ring. Mary, pretending to get a shipment of laces and silks, smuggles in ammunition (with Wingfield's connivance), to assist the colony in its tobacco riots against the Navigation Acts. Harry, who tells the story, is put into the stocks for cutting tobacco plants—a sacrifice that hardly seems plausible —but he wins Mary. The story is not well localized, but it does bring out the partisan feelings of the period.

None of the novelists just discussed, however, was truly realistic about the nature of the social upheaval. The planter class, who were jockeying themselves into power, exploited the commoners no less than did the British, who wanted the revenue. Not only heavy taxes, but the overproduction of tobacco was causing economic distress among the small farmers. Indian raids were the result of previous wrongs and abuses. If any of the writers mention these factors, they do so without full understanding. Their concern is with the romantic aspects of a social order that enthroned gentility.

More than any other Virginia novelist, Mary Johnston was conscious of class distinctions. Her Virginia was "the land of good eating, good drinking, stout men, and pretty women." Her knowledge of details of dress and manners was accurate, but it served mainly to make her unreal world seem plausible to the uncritical reader. Her novel *Audrey* (1902) is a romantic story, set in the period of Governor Spotswood and Colonel Byrd. When the Governor, with his group of fifty horsemen, explores the valley now known as West Virginia, he comes upon the Audrey family in the Blue Ridge Mountains. One of his men, Haward, finding the place ravaged next day by the Indians, adopts the waif Audrey. Ten years later, returning from England with Colonel Byrd and Byrd's daughter Evelyn, whom he plans to marry, Haward finds himself strangely attracted to his wood nymph. When Audrey learns that her idol, Evelyn, believes her to be Haward's mistress, she flees to the mountains and joins a traveling show. The death of the primitive dream child, at the hands of a vicious half-breed admirer, seems an unnatural way of removing her from the plot, but is no more unbelievable than her ethereal quality in the light of her daily associates, or her rapid theatrical progress. Even the scenery, about which the author grows lyrical, fails to give the aesthetic satisfaction it was meant to produce, because it consumes too much attention. One cannot deny, however, Mary Johnston's ability to tell a thrilling story of adventure.

During the famous expedition already alluded to, Governor Spotswood took claim to the western valley from the French and Indians, and founded the celebrated Order of the Cocked-Hat Gentry. William A. Caruthers, in *The Knights of the Horseshoe* (1845), built around this episode a series of sketches of horseback journeys over impassable mountain roads, of intrigues, court trials, and political discussion at Williamsburg. For the central episode he employed a favorite Elizabethan device, mistaken identity, to bring together at last Ellen Evylin and her lover. The plot is rather involved, but the narrative is brisk. The most interesting character in the book is the loquacious backwoods scout, Red Jarvis, who owes his inspiration to Cooper, though he appears to have been copied from life. On the whole, Caruthers was less skillful in character-drawing than in reporting pioneer conditions, for which he possessed a real gift.

The valley of the Shenandoah held the greatest romantic appeal for John Esten Cooke, a native of the region. In *The Virginia Comedians* (1854) he drew a mellow picture of its brocaded gentry in the days immediately preceding the Revolution. He depicted such diversions as the earliest theater in the colonies, fox hunts, cavalier balls, the Williamsburg fair, and the Jamestown races. But the center of interest is the love story.

While horseback riding near his ancestral home, Effingham Hall, a short distance from Williamsburg, young Champ Effingham, a blasé Oxonian, meets Beatrice Hallam of Hallam's theatrical troupe, recently arrived from London. He calls on her at the Raleigh Tavern, falls madly in love with her, and even joins the cast. His father naturally is incensed, for Champ might easily marry Clare Lee, a gentleman's daughter. Worse, Beatrice has the hardihood to reject the Byronic young gentleman in favor of the proletarian Charles Waters, who has chanced to save her life when her boat capsizes. Later, in desperation, Champ tries to abduct her, stabs Charles, and is obliged to leave the country. Waters recovers, however, and Beatrice eventually marries him, while Champ, after a sojourn in Europe, returns to marry Clare. In the second volume the interest shifts from Beatrice, who goes into a fatal decline, to the middle-class Waters family. The story closes on the aroused opposition to the Stamp Act, led by "the man in the red cloak," Patrick Henry.

A sequel, *Henry St. John* (1856), notes the strong undercurrent of colonial revolt, in which Virginians were the leaders. "Charles Waters was the *brain*, Henry the tongue, Jefferson the pen, and Washington the sword of the Revolution." St. John, a great-grandson of Pocahontas, expresses the general opposition to Lord Dunmore after the haughty governor dissolves the House of Burgesses. Following a duel over the beautiful Bonnybel Vane, and following Dunmore's refusal to give him a commission, St. John in final desperation leaves for the frontier. The novel, based on Campbell's *Virginia* and on early files of the *Virginia Gazette*, blends history and romance better than its predecessor, but it is too attenuated for the modern reader. As romancer and historian, Cooke did "more than any other to popularize the legendary view of Revolutionary Virginia. His intimate knowledge of historical details did not correct his view of colonial life, but only served to make his picture of it seem more real to those who read him. Not only has he impressed his conception of colonial life upon untrained historians like Page and novelists like Mary Johnston and Hallie Ermine Rives; he has even influenced so well trained a historian as John Fiske, who in his *Old Virginia and Her Neighbors* betrays the influence of Cooke's *Virginia: A History of the People* (1883)."[2]

Mary Johnston's novel set in the Shenandoah during the French and Indian Wars, *The Great Valley* (1926), is mainly one of dislocated domestic life. The story opens in 1735 with the long journey of the Selkirks from Scotland to their new home in the wilderness. Their daughter Elizabeth marries Conan Burke, son of the chief landowner in the valley, and undergoes all the hardships of a woman in those troublous times. Two of her children are slain by the Indians, her husband is struck down before her, and she and her little daughter are taken captive. Although she bears Long Thunder a child, she has an intuition that she must escape to Burke's Land; and after an arduous flight through the wilderness she is finally united there with her husband, who has not been killed after all. The only historical character to appear, and that briefly, is the young surveyor, Washington. He warns the outpost of Indian trouble—a warning that with Braddock's defeat should have been mandatory, but is forgotten, and disaster results. The characters seem real, especially Elizabeth; the natural background is faithfully presented; and the narrative flows smoothly.

[2] Hubbell, *Virginia Life in Fiction*, 26.

The beginnings of another colony, Maryland, are the theme of *Sir Christopher* (1901), by Maud Wilder Goodwin. This romance of a Maryland manor in 1644 pictures the life of the immediate descendants of the people in her earlier book, *The Head of a Hundred.* Sir Christopher Neville, a Roundhead, after being refused by the young widow Elinor Calvert because of religious differences, comes to Maryland as overseer of a seven-thousand-acre estate given by Lord Baltimore to Mrs. Calvert and her young son. Neville further incurs the dislike of the Calverts, who are fairly hospitable to persons of other faiths, when he is thought to have killed Father Mohl. Then the pirate Ingle on his deathbed confesses the murder, and the way is open for Elinor and Sir Christopher to wed. Among the historical characters introduced are Giles Brent, deputy governor, Councilor Claiborne, and Sir William Berkeley. The work is one of few on the Papist-Protestant conflict along the border between Maryland and Virginia, but it has barely survived the generation that produced it.

An earlier and much livelier novel of colonial Maryland, *Rob of the Bowl* (1838), by John P. Kennedy, pictures the conflict between Protestants and Catholics at a slightly later date (1681) than in *Sir Christopher.* When King Charles orders all Catholic officers in the province to be replaced by Protestants, there is a flare-up. Blanche Warden, however, has troubles of her own, for she is loved by Albert Verheyden, Lord Baltimore's secretary, as well as by Cocklescraft, member of a smuggling ring. A duel fails to materialize, but one rainy night Albert loses his way and arrives at a deserted house on the seashore, known as the Wizard's Chapel. At this smugglers' rendezvous he is taken captive, but the mysterious cripple Rob, who transports himself on a bowl, recognizes Albert as his own long-lost son and helps him to escape. Later, when Rob publicly confesses his paternity and repents his smuggling activities, the council forgives him and jails Cocklescroft. As the story closes, Blanche and Albert are to be married.

Clearly the importance of this book does not lie in originality of plot or characters. The introduction of the smugglers, and the author's manner of alternating history with fiction and then blending the two, mark Kennedy as a devoted follower of Scott, although his style is more brisk. There are overtones, also, of Elizabethan drama. Garret Weasel and his wife, keepers of the Crow and Archer, are well realized, and the scenes at the fisherman's hut are excellent. Albert appears too saintly, but the proprietary, Lord Calvert, is well portrayed. He is tolerant toward Protestants, even though their active antagonism is shown to underlie much of the trouble in the colony. The things, then, that make *Rob of the Bowl* a satisfying work for the reader of historical romance are a beautiful heroine, a hero with clouded ancestry, smugglers plying their trade, picturesque tavern scenes, an abduction and a rescue, excitement, and a happy ending. All this is presented in a style that knows no lassitude, and the story is readily enjoyable today.

The beginnings of South Carolina have been ably described by her leading novelist, William Gilmore Simms. In *The Yemassee* (1835) the theme is the conflict between the early settlers and the powerful Yemassee Indians, abetted by designing Spaniards in Florida. The setting of the romance is Pocota-ligo, ancient seat of the tribe, headed in 1715 by Sanutee and his wife Matiwan. Their son, Occonestoga, has been bribed into betraying the tribe to the encroaching whites, after which his mother in a moving scene kills him rather than have him publicly dishonored. The love story centers about Gabriel Harrison, who is really Governor Craven, and Bess Matthews, daughter of a Puritan preacher. This use of an "unknown" character Simms borrows from Scott, while the exciting attack upon the blockhouse comes from Cooper. His Indians, like Cooper's, lament their unhappy fate in metaphorical language, but they are more realistic, more ferocious, and shrewder than Cooper's. Some of the incidents come from legends told Simms by his grandmother, but the vividness of the setting is the result of the author's alert personal observation. *The Yemassee* is a thrilling story, as is natural where men surrounded by danger battle for survival. Simms, in telling it, displays unusual gifts of narrative.

Some twenty years later, Simms wrote another colonial romance of South Carolina, *The Cassique of Kiawah* (1859). The narrative skips lightly over an Indian insurrection to describe pioneer life and smuggling activities in and about infant Charleston in 1684. The scene shifts from the deck of a privateer to the low drinking houses on the Ashley and then to the fashionable masquerades of the town. The cassique, Sir Edward Berkeley, brother of the Virginia governor, has built a spacious house at Kiawah for his family, consisting of his wife Olive, his infant son, and his domineering mother-in-law. Olive has been in love with his younger brother, Harry, a buccaneer of the Drake and Cavendish school, and has married Edward only after being assured that Harry has been lost at sea. Tortured by the realization that she cannot love her husband and nagged by her mother, she becomes a melancholiac with visions of her lover at night. When Harry returns as the Captain Calvert who supplied the colony with Spanish booty, he brings with him his Spanish wife, Zulieme, who before long becomes the belle of Charleston society. One night Sir Edward and Olive meet Harry, but before the old love is revived, Olive dies in an Indian attack, and Harry and Zulieme have an heir.

Although the history is of subsidiary interest and the action drags in places, there is a skillful contrast of personalities in the fun-loving Zulieme and her matter-of-fact husband, as well as in the idealistic cassique and his pensive wife. The Indians are not so well individualized as in *The Yemassee*, but the corrupt governor in his relation with smugglers is well characterized, and the early life of Charleston is ably depicted. Simms, despite his fondness for the melodramatic, was a true raconteur.

2. *The New England Colonies*

Life in colonial New England presented a bleak contrast to the gay, sophisticated round of activities in the southern colonies. The northern colonists were interested in the salvation of men's souls, rather than in social frivolities or business, although they seem not to have been averse to driving a shrewd bargain with the Indians or with one of their countrymen. Themes which have stirred the imagination of novelists are: Puritanism, with its religious conflicts; Indian life and insurrections; the trouble with the regicides; the loss of the Connecticut charter; and the witchcraft frenzy. Besides these subjects from the seventeenth century, there were others, such as smuggling, the land-grant controversy between New York and New Hampshire, and the French and Indian Wars, which led up to exciting events in pre-Revolutionary Boston.

Puritan life is glimpsed in an early novel entitled *A Peep at the Pilgrims in Sixteen Hundred Thirty-Six* (1824), by Mrs. Harriet V. Cheney. Her two-volume "peep" is fairly comprehensive, extending from Plymouth to Boston, New Amsterdam, and Hartford, as it follows the romance of a newly arrived Anglican and a Puritan maid. It enables the reader to meet the affable Miles Standish and the waggish Peregrine White, as well as to hear Governor Winslow and Governor Winthrop discuss political and religious dissensions; and, for good measure, it lets him attend Governor Kieft's ball with the hero, before assisting Captain Mason in a hairbreadth rescue of the heroine from the Pequods. Obviously, Mrs. Cheney was trying to incorporate in her plot too much history, gleaned from Morton, Neal, and Irving, and it impeded the progress of her narrative. A plethora of historical matter was a problem that was to plague novelists for many a year.

A thorn in the side of the Plymouth colony was the roisterer Thomas Morton. When he was not annoying them with selling rum and firearms to the Indians, he appears to have been in league with Sir Philip Gardiner in some of his dark schemes. John Lothrop Motley, before becoming a famous historian, wrote a fantasy about these men of mischief and their conflict with the colonists, which he called *Merry-Mount* (1849).[3] According to this account, the cavalier Morton had been obliged to leave England because of indiscretions involving love and money, and, dissatisfied on reaching Virginia, had come up to Plymouth, where with a set of lawless resolutes he lords it over the Pilgrims at Merry-Mount near by. The merrymaking this spouter of Horace and his greenwood crew indulge in is at such variance with the austere code of his neighbors that Morton soon finds himself in the hands of Captain Standish. But the good-humored man frees himself and once more commands his roisterers in a greenwood fortress before he is finally deported. Meanwhile, Sir Philip saves the heroine from a wolf, but is prevented from winning her hand, even though he fights a duel in her behalf. Clearly, the grim Puritans were winning the day, and the most intolerant of all was Governor Endicott at Naumkeak.

Motley had Morton's own account, *The New English Canaan* (1637), as source. Evidently, too, he had read the Stratford playwright, not only for the hawking scene and the scene in the fortress, but for such low comedy types in the ribald crew as the sprawling Rednape, the clumsy Bootefish, Canary Bird, and Peter Cakebread. The Elizabethan period was not remote, and these characters and scenes might be transferred with slight change of atmosphere. Rich as the story was in local color and vivid factional strife, it never attained the compact force of Hawthorne's contemporary tale, "The May-Pole of Merry Mount."

Of late, there has been a disposition to reinterpret the Puritans, less as saints than as human beings absorbed in making a living. Helen Carlisle's *We Begin* (1932) is in large part such

---

[3] In the *North America Review* for 1846 Motley had gone on record as opposed to sermonic fiction and in 1847 he had defended the realism of Balzac.

an attempt. The author traces the story of the Pilgrims from their obscure beginnings in Scrooby, England, through their difficulties in Holland, the hazardous voyage of the *Mayflower*, and the encounters with the Indians, to the establishment of Plymouth as a permanent settlement. It is a swift-moving narrative of inner and outer adjustment, told in a sensitive prose style that skillfully hides its careful documentation. The conflicts with English laws, with nature, with greed, and with the Indians, and various other tensions—all are made freshly real. Governor Winthrop, Captain "Shrimp," and the renegade Morton are seen from the Plymouth point of view; Bradford, Brewster, and Winslow and their barter economy have a minor role. The romance is a psychoanalytical triangle. The lusty John Dester lives happily with Anne, his wife, but is envied by his brother Eleazar, a sex-frustrated preacher, who finally rapes Purity, a London waif adopted by Anne, and is thereupon promptly hanged by the Puritans. The author errs in making a stock figure of Freudian romance so central as to give the age a neurotic temper. There were sex-repressed Puritans in New England at a later date, but at this time everyone was occupied in merely keeping alive.

The outstanding romance about colonial New England is of course Hawthorne's *The Scarlet Letter* (1850). This distinction belongs to it by virtue of a thorough assimilation of historical fact, together with the unfolding of a perennially interesting human story, one motivated at every point by the conditions and circumstances of the times. Minister Dimmesdale's sin of concealing an adulterous relation with Hester Prynne is set against the reverence of the populace for the man of God. Adultery is conceived of not as an affair of the civil order, but as a problem that concerns the immortal soul. The minister can find peace only through expiation; Hester, because of the public ignominy she has endured, is prepared for a larger view.

The Scarlet Letter, as a tale of human responsibility in terms of Calvinistic preoccupation with the problem of evil, possesses the very stuff of Greek tragedy. Three scenes of communal coloring outline the drama. The opening tableau shows the condemned adulteress led to the scaffold to receive the magistrates' sentence. Then, at the Governor's Hall the magistrates seek to take Hester's child from her while she is confronted by both the minister and her fiendish husband. Finally, after seven years of penance, climaxed by the holiday scene and the election sermon, it is clear that conformity is better than nature's lawless law. The story owes its somber understanding to the author's latent Puritanism—an insight modified by the critical perspective of a fourth- or fifth-generation descendant. To Hawthorne passion was of a higher order than intellect; even the church, disregarding the very nature of man, had relied too much on laws and on learning. As a work of art, this gaunt, powerful romance demonstrates that it is not necessary for a historical novel to be cluttered up with historical names and events in order to be effective. If it is true to the spirit of the times, that is sufficient; if, in addition, the action delineated is universal and timeless, the work is a masterpiece.

Before Hawthorne wrote *The Scarlet Letter*, he had made a number of short excursions into the New England of the seventeenth century. In one of these, "The Gentle Boy," he introduced the theme of sectarian conflict by depicting the fate of a winsome Quaker child left helpless among the Puritans. A number of minor novels dealt with sectarian strife. Eliza Buckminster Lee's *Naomi* (1848), although evincing no conspicuous creative ability, is a fair and accurate story of Quaker persecution. *Margaret Smith's Journal* (1849), by John Greenleaf Whittier, is in the form of a pretended diary of an English girl visiting her relatives in the Bay Colony during 1678–79. The main thread of the narrative tells of Rebecca Rawson's jilting a noble youth in favor of a baronet's son. The baronetcy proves spurious, however, and the husband a bigamist who deserts her in England. Interpolated in the diary are various historical references: to the persecution of Quakers and witches, to Sir Christopher Gardiner, John Eliot, Cotton Mather, and Michael Wigglesworth. In general, historical and fictitious elements are interwoven in much the style of Hawthorne's "The Gentle Boy."

Joseph Banvard's *Priscilla, or the Trials for the Truth* (1854) tells of a girl who escapes to America in order to avoid proselyting by Anglicans, only to discover Puritans equally intolerant. With her family, she finally takes refuge among the Baptists of Rhode Island. *The Knight of the Golden Melice* (1856), by John Turvill Adams, connects the mysterious Sir Christopher Gardiner with plans to establish Catholicism in 1630 in the Massachusetts Bay Colony. Governor Winthrop, though he differs from Gardiner in creed, respects him highly, and trusts his relations with the Pequots. In other versions, as for example, Miss Sedgwick's *Hope Leslie*, Sir Christopher is regarded with suspicion. In Motley's *Merry-Mount* he appears a Puritan saint in Plymouth and a worldly plotter at Merry-Mount.

Yet another novel to bring out Puritan intolerance was J. G. Holland's *The Bay-Path* (1857). At Agawam (Springfield), about 1650, Magistrate Pynchon is banished by Cotton and Norton for writing an unorthodox book about Puritanism, and a young woman whom he has befriended is accused of witchcraft and executed. Holland, editor of the *Springfield Republican*, and later the first editor of *Scribner's Monthly*, knew local legend thoroughly but chafed under the restrictions imposed upon him by history, and he wrote rather verbosely.

The second generation of Puritans, according to Esther Forbes's *Paradise* (1937), were not altogether pious and gloomy, but were earthy men and women, contriving, eating, lusting, and, on occasion, warring with the Indians. In the novel, Jude Parre, gentleman, in 1639 acquires from the Indians a large tract of land some twenty miles inland from Boston. Here he founds the town of Canaan, builds his estate, Paradise, rears his family of five children, and is looked up to by the community. But troubles are ahead, both in the family and with the Indians. Fenton, Jude's lusty son, brings home a siren, Bathsheba, causing the gawky Salome, who admires him, to commit adultery with his brother Christopher. The public branding of the couple hurts Jude, who serves as justice for Canaan, and he dies. Bathsheba develops into a mad schizophrenic, while Fenton goes on to martial and amatory exploits as a squire extraordinary. His fine-grained, passionate sister, Jazan, has a frustrated marriage with a fanatical preacher, Forethought Fearing, who dares, however, to defend Bathsheba in public. The Indian troubles, culminating in King Philip's War, hurl the community into a maelstrom of death, from which the group at Paradise emerge, though not without scars. In this fast-moving story, history and romance are deftly interwoven, with due regard for social, political, and religious tensions, and without a trace of sentimentalism. But the characters are typed, and considering their apparent sophistication, undermotivated. A story pivoted on adultery and branding unfortunately courts comparison with *The Scarlet Letter*, a classic that not merely interprets the past, but illuminates human nature regardless of fashions in psychology.

Most of the novels about early New England revolve about the relations of the whites with the Indians. By the eighteen twenties, when the first of these novels appeared, red men in that region were no longer a menace. As a result, there developed a sentimental attitude toward them. Young women novelists speculated on what kind of husband an Indian would make. That is the question in Lydia M. Child's *Hobomok* (1824) and in Catharine M. Sedgwick's *Hope Leslie* (1827). Young Hobomok, living at Naumkeak (Salem), is so "unwarped by the artifices of civilized life" that he gives up his white wife and infant upon the unexpected return of her betrothed, long mourned as dead. This is probably as well, for the author's picturing of domestic life is better than her handling of her noble red man.[4]

Miss Sedgwick, a preceptress and distinguished literary lady of western Massachusetts, conceived of her task in *Hope Leslie* as illustrating for juvenile readers domestic manners in the seventeenth century. Hope is an orphan, the ward of her uncle Fletcher, with whose son Everell she falls in love. Magawisca, an Indian maiden of high lineage, and also a member of the Fletcher household, becomes so attached to Everell that, during an Indian raid, when he is about to be executed by her tribe, she outdoes Pocahontas by catching a blow which lops off her arm.

Seven years later the scene shifts to Governor Winthrop's household in Boston, where the villain, Sir Philip Gardiner, abetted by Thomas Morton of Merry-Mount, has designs on Hope; but when he attempts to abduct her, his "page" warns her of her danger from the Papist and notorious bigamist. In the further development of this overinvolved plot, Hope almost loses the man she really loves, but the end comes out all right. Aside from presenting the trials of the young people, this highly moral tale depicts the persecution of the Indians by the Puritan oligarchy. The author consulted the leading authorities, Hubbard, Trumbull, and Heckewelder, with a view to illustrating, as she says, "not the history, but the character of the times." She has succeeded in doing this without impeding her narrative. *Hope Leslie*, though diffuse and sentimental, is plausible; it rightly enjoyed wide popularity in its day.

The strained relations between the Indians and the whites in New England culminated in King Philip's War, 1675–76. This conflict marked the final desperate effort of the Indians to preserve their hunting grounds and to keep the whites from imposing their form of civilization upon them. James Fenimore Cooper, in *The Last of the Mohicans*, had dealt with the red

[4] This novel was inspired by J. G. Palfrey's notable article in *The North American Review* in 1821, calling upon novelists to use our early history.

man's final stand in New York, and he now undertook to picture the tragic fate of this race in New England. *The Wept of
Wish-ton-Wish* (1829), based in the main on Trumbull's *History of Connecticut*, was laid in the infant settlement of Hartford. The outpost of the stalwart Puritan, Mark Heathcote, is
attacked and his daughter Ruth taken captive by the Indians.
She is long wept for, but when, years later, hope for her return
has been abandoned, she is discovered to be the wife of Conan-
chet, sachem of the Narragansets, to whom she has borne a
child. Her life ends in tragedy, for after disowning her family,
she loses her husband at the hands of Uncas, the Mohican
chieftain. Cooper was quite in his element in this novel in depicting the Indian raids on the defenseless villages and farms,
in particular the attack on the blockhouse. The leader of the
villagers against the Indian attack is Goffe, the regicide, who
figures in several romantic novels thereafter. Unfortunately,
the author had a deep-seated antipathy for the Puritan character, and in this novel harps on their absurdities, especially the
hypocrisies of one Rev. Meek Wolfe. So constantly is this
worthy made to reprimand his followers that some readers have
thought him intended as a caricature of Cotton Mather, but
Mather is referred to in another connection. *The Wept of
Wish-ton-Wish* is not one of Cooper's best efforts.

Two other early novels which concentrated on King
Philip's War were *Mount Hope* (1851) by G. H. Hollister, a
Connecticut lawyer and diplomat, and *The Doomed Chief*
(1860) by Daniel P. Thompson, a Vermont novelist of the
mid-century. Hollister focused attention on King Philip rather
than on the regicides, but lacked imaginative power to bring
out the dramatic aspects of his tale. Thompson was hardly more
successful. In *The Doomed Chief*, Deacon Mudridge of Plymouth orders some Indians hanged for a crime they did not
commit—an act which so incenses Metacom (King Philip) that
he threatens bloody warfare. Meanwhile, the zealous Deacon
attempts to have his nephew Snifflin marry Madian, a girl be-

loved by Vane Willis. In the warfare which follows, Vane, be-cause he is stigmatized as a Quaker, is unable to obtain a com-mission. Mudridge even accuses him of having made away with Madian. Finally, Vane helps inflict a severe defeat upon the Indians, pushing them as far as Mount Hope and confusing them to the extent that King Philip is slain and Queen Weta-moo drowns herself. Madian is found at last, and the Deacon punished. Thompson appears to have regarded the war an in-fliction from God for decadent manners. Despite his use of Mather's *Magnalia*, Sparks's *Life of Eliot*, Thatcher's *Indian Biography*, Carver's *Travels*, and possibly Mason's *History of the Pequot War* and Hubbard's *Narratives*, he could not draw a fair picture of the Puritans. His portraits of King Philip, John Eliot, and Roger Williams are acceptable, but in general he lacked imagination to transmute the events of history.

The fate of the regicides in New England was the sub-ject of several works of fiction. Cooper's *The Wept of Wish-ton-Wish* and Caruthers's *The Cavaliers of Virginia* have al-ready been mentioned. Upon the restoration of Charles II after the Commonwealth period, three men who had signed the death warrant of Charles I—Goffe, Whalley, and Dixwell—fled Eng-land and spent the remainder of their lives hiding in Puritan havens in the New World. The first novelist to use the regicide theme was Sir Walter Scott in *The Peveril of the Peak* (1822). Doubtless the popularity of this work inspired one of his ardent disciples, James McHenry, but lately come from Ireland to Baltimore, to use the theme in *The Spectre of the Forest* (1823). His pictures of Goffe's activities in Connecticut were spectral, however, rather than historical, and were designed to heighten the Gothic effects of his narrative. The few historical events—Sir Edmund Andros's attack upon Frontenac and the witch-craft episode (which McHenry asserted had been suppressed by Connecticut historians), as well as the escapades of Goffe—were employed merely to vary and complicate the machinery of horror in a rather slight novel. Writers in other media did comparatively better. Delia Bacon's "The Regicides," Hawthorne's short story "The Grey Champion," and J. N. Barker's play *Superstition* (1826) certainly were in no way inferior to the novels on the theme of the regicides.

The loss of the Connecticut charter in 1687 was the subject of one novel, *The Romance of the Charter Oak* (1871). Its author was William Seton, a military officer and scholar. After creating interest in Lydia Goffe, the author turned aside to show how the Connecticut colony sought a union with Massachusetts rather than with New York. At the request of James II, Governor Andros demanded that the people of Connecticut return the liberal charter which Charles II had given them in 1662. He was unable to obtain the document, however, since the people had hidden it in the hollow trunk of an old tree. The story, based on colonial records, Palfrey's *History of New England*, and Bulkeley's *Will and Doom*, combines with an account of political events, interesting observations on the costumes, furniture, and architecture of the period. The narrative lacks animation, however, and is mentioned here only because it memorializes an episode which other novelists overlooked.

A more popular subject for writers of fiction was the witchcraft delusion. Superstition had long been a scourge in Europe, and the mania found its way into Massachusetts and Connecticut toward the end of the seventeenth century. Salem was the principal seat of the delusion. In 1693, after nineteen victims of the craze had been hanged, a revulsion of feeling led to the liberation of all accused persons. The first novel to treat witchcraft in New England was *Rachel Dyer* (1828), by John Neal. This "North American Story," written for English readers, was not a narrative so much as a series of violent, incoherent accusations, and refutations made by Mather, Phips, and Sewall during the trials of Martha Cory, Samuel Parres, Sarah Good, Elizabeth and Rachel Dyer, and the hero-victim, George Burroughs. The author conceded the sincerity of the

Puritans, but charged their gloomy state of mind with facili-
tating belief in witchcraft; once hallucinations sprang up, they
quickly multiplied.

Neal declared that "the time was at hand for a Declaration of Independence in the great Republic of Letters," and
that knowing that in the view of Englishmen, Irving was only
"the American Addison" and Cooper had "just enough reputation not to hazard it by stepping aside into a new path," he,
who had too little respect for authorship to risk anything,
thought he might call the attention of American "novel writers
to what is undoubtedly native and peculiar." Instead of gaining
American followers, however, the egregious Neal, who had recently "exposed" American writers in *Blackwood's Magazine*,
attracted the attention of those English critics who were only
too ready to accept his assertion that roughness and turgidity
were distinctive characteristics of American writers and his
grotesque characters truly representative of American life. The
most distinct impression left by *Rachel Dyer* is of a too liberal
peppering of dashes and exclamation points.

John W. DeForest, a well-known novelist of the mid-
nineteenth century, dealt with the Salem delusion in a novelette, *Witching Times*, which appeared in *Putnam's Magazine*,
1856–57. Henry More, after fighting the superstition of the
period, is executed for his zeal. His daughter Rachel is also
condemned, but is rescued by her husband in a realistic scene.
Among the historical figures introduced are Elder Noyse,
with his passion for Rachel, the "tyrant" Elder Parris, Judge
Hathorne, ancestor of the novelist, and Cotton Mather, who
seizes his opportunity for advancement among the clerical oligarchy then in power. DeForest's sense of the historical is not
sufficiently imaginative to keep the narrative from dragging.
The scene in which Giles Corey is executed by being pressed
to death is the only vivid episode in the book.

In effective contrast to these earlier attempts to depict the
atmosphere of witchcraft, stands Esther Forbes's *Mirror for*

Witches (1928). Mrs. Forbes preserves the speech rhythms and catches the devout spirit of piety of rural New England. She also manages to convey the mental processes of a witch. The story relates the misfortunes of a girl whose parents in Brittany are burned to death for witchcraft, after which a friendly sea captain brings her to Salem. Here her foster mother talks her into believing herself bewitched. The narrative moves swiftly from her downfall with her demon lover to the horrible death which cheats the gallows. The simple plot is told with a candid warmth and a detached irony that admirably convey the unearthly mood of that strange period in our annals.

A fairly recent story based on the witchcraft furor during the last chapter of Puritan supremacy in Massachusetts is Frances Winwar's *Gallows Hill* (1937). As the story opens, there have been strange whispers of goings-on, and these sparks are being fanned by further gossip. The grim and portentous Cotton Mather says the Devil is loose in the country. Suspicion appears to center on Bridget Bishop, the innkeeper, and her daughter Mary. Bridget is worldly, preferring to worship in the woods, and has been seen there with Martin Downer; Mary is in love with the seagoing Starry Lane. Excitement mounts until the mother meets her doom on Gallows Hill, while the daughter finds happiness with her lover. The author has produced a colorful and vigorous pageant, with an approach to verisimilitude in diction, but has not fully digested her source material. Her sexually repressed Salemites exhibit Freudian rather than Puritan psychology.

This discussion of seventeenth century New England may come to a close with *A Candle in the Wilderness* (1930), by one of the well-known writers of historical fiction, Irving Bacheller. In this book the reader is given glimpses of both the Massachusetts and the New York colonists through the eyes of the two young English comrades who arrive in Boston in 1635 to escape Stuart oppression. While one of the heroes associates with such worthies as Governor Dudley, John Endicott, the Cottons, and John Winthrop, the other visits the Lake Champlain area, including Indian lodges and trading posts along the Hudson as far down as New Amsterdam. This arrangement enables the author to reveal the relations not only of the English and the Indians, but of the French and the Dutch, and their estimates of one another. The plot contrasts the severe Puritans with the roistering Dutch, who enjoy such pastimes as "goose-pulling" and "clubbing-the-cat"; it also introduces the savages with their sports and hunting expeditions. The author appends a list of authorities used, a matter about which previous novelists had been extremely reticent. A rather pretty love story runs through the book, but the final impression is that this novel is erudite rather than inspired.

One of the best stories to convey the effect of actually living on the colonial frontier is Grace Stone's novel of the Deerfield massacre and its aftermath, *The Cold Journey* (1934). One night in January, 1704, the stern Massachusetts village of Redfield is attacked by a party of French and Indians, and most of its inhabitants are forced to trek, with property on back, through the snow to Quebec. Behind the plodding little band the reader observes the interplay of French, Puritan, and Indian cultures. A gentle Jesuit priest softens the coarse sternness of the Reverend Mr. Chapman (alias John Williams, author of *The Redeemed Captive*), while the attractive life of the colorful city beguiles others. When the ransomed Americans return home after three years, they are no longer austere Puritans but mellow backwoodsmen. The strong feature of the novel is the happy fusion of thought and emotion, particularly manifest in psychological crises requiring subtle spiritual adjustments. The story as here related reveals not only thorough historical knowledge, but a skill and dignity in narrative art that mark it a finished product.

The eighteenth century found New England either in conflict over boundary disputes, as in the quarrel between Vermont and the York gentry over the Hampshire Grants, or

engaged in the French and Indian Wars of the pre-Revolutionary struggle. One novel, *Agnes Surriage* (1886), by Edwin
L. Bynner, may serve as a transition between those novels already discussed and those about to follow. It touches on witchcraft, but has more to do with smuggling. In the main, however, it is a love romance, based on the legend of Sir Harry
Frankland, previously used by Oliver Wendell Holmes in his
ballad "Agnes." According to the story, the young collector of
the port of Boston in 1745 falls in love with a beautiful servant
at an inn in Marblehead. Agnes, this daughter of a poor fisherman, apparently lives with him for a while in sin, but after they
go to Europe and she helps him escape from the wreckage of
the earthquake at Lisbon, he marries her in gratitude. John
Fiske praised the book as "one of the greatest of American historical novels."

For generations Yankees and Yorkers contested with each
other for control of the borderlands between the Connecticut
and the Hudson, Yankees contending that Yorkers were sloven-
ly, uneducated, godless folk, and Yorkers convinced that Yankees were pushing, miserly hypocrites. As a matter of fact, Yankees did penetrate into the lands of the Yorkers, and honey-
combed upstate New York with their ideas and institutions. By
the time of the Revolution the boundary dispute had turned
into a class war between landlords and tenants engaged in an
agrarian struggle. This controversy over the land was joined
with the Revolutionary campaigns of Ethan Allen and Seth
Warner in a very popular novel, *The Green Mountain Boys*
(1839), by Daniel Pierce Thompson.

Judge Thompson, Vermonter born and bred, considered
these episodes in the early history of his state in themselves
romantic "with the use of little more fiction than was deemed
sufficient to weave them together and impart to the tissue a
connected interest." According to his racy account, the Ver-
monters drove the York state men from the Grants, but the tool
of the land-jobbers vowed he would take revenge on the green-

wood hero's sweetheart. While her lover was away helping heroic Ethan Allen take Fort Ticonderoga, the villain won over the girl's neutral father, and by calumny secured the defection of the daughter. After Allen was captured, the hero, Seth Warner, joined St. Clair against Burgoyne, who was then descending from the north. During this expedition the young man vindicated himself by rescuing the girl and her father.

Thompson was able to relate his story with something of the animation and suspense which actually characterized the strife because he had the story directly from aged participants. Ethan Allen, St. Clair, Seth Warner, Schuyler, Benedict Arnold, and others move through these scenes freely and humanly —an important advance in historical fiction over such stiff and shadowy portraitures as Cooper's Washington and John Paul Jones. Perhaps the greatest charm of the narrative lies in the piquancy of its provincialism, which triumphs over occasional lapses in idiom. These mountaineer kinsmen of Thompson were fighting, not for adventure merely, but for defense of home. It is only natural that such a stirring appeal to patriotism should have caused the book to run through many editions.

The French and Indian Wars, 1754–63, were fought largely outside the borders of New England. But in *Haverhill, or the Memoirs of an Officer in the Army of Wolfe* (1831), James A. Jones linked mid-eighteenth century Yankee manners with the conflict when he told of the rise of a humble youth from Cape Cod. When Lynn Haverhill's love for Mary Danvers is thwarted by the girl's aristocratic father, who wants her to marry her wealthy cousin Charles, the unhappy youth seeks to prove his worth by going to sea. After rescue in a storm and a period of imprisonment in an Indian camp, he joins Wolfe's army at Quebec. Following the victory on the Plains of Abraham, he comes home to find his mother and his brother dead and his wayward sister gone—reportedly to the West Indies. During his fruitless search for her, he becomes infatuated with a Creole, Margaretta, only to find that his former rival Charles has prior claims, which leaves him free to marry his first love. In spite of its use of the long arm of coincidence, the book is still worth reading. The fact that the narrative is in the first person gives the reader a sense of actual participation in the events. General Wolfe is shown as unpretentious as a clerk in banter, but unsurpassed when energy and decision are required, and noble in the hour of death. No previous author has related with such detail the manners of a New England community—its shooting matches, husking bees, quilting frolics, sleighing parties, wrestling matches, horse races, favorite dishes, court-ships, gossip, and superstitions. The style is fluent and seasoned with homely wit, and for once the characters are not impec-cable.

Wolfe's defeat of Montcalm at Quebec was only one of the three objectives for which the French and Indian Wars were waged. The others were Louisburg and Ticonderoga. In the Champlain region there fought a romantic American hero, Major Robert Rogers, whose exploits have been recorded by the historian Francis Parkman, and in fiction by Sir Gilbert Parker in *The Seats of the Mighty* (1896). It remained for Kenneth Roberts in *Northwest Passage* (1937) to re-create the brilliant story of Major Rogers and his rangers from the pro-vincial point of view. While Sir William Johnson in the Mohawk Valley schemed for an inland empire, and most officers of the Crown viewed native efforts against the Indians with contempt, Rogers and his two hundred men left Crown Point in 1759 for a hazardous expedition against St. Francis. The ob-jective was the headquarters of the French and Indians, who had ravaged the English settlements for years. The journey back was complicated by further hardships because of misun-derstanding about supplies.

Langdon Towne, camp follower and Indian painter, is made to chronicle this anabasis. After a brief interlude in Lon-don, where Towne sees the great, he meets Major Rogers try-ing to get money for a scheme to find a short cut across America to the Orient, a northwest passage. When Rogers is given the post of governor of Michilimackinac, he takes the painter with him. But the straightforward governor is unable to cope with politicians, and the overland expedition comes to grief. Rogers is put in irons on charges of treason and malfeasance. After he is acquitted, he drifts about as a shifty adventurer. The story, based on Rogers' own journals and on contemporary histories, and strengthened by the author's own military experiences, admirably recreates the atmosphere, especially of the first of the two episodes. True, Rogers glows a bit, at the expense of Sir William, who was hardly so low as he is here represented. The minor characters and the Indians, however, are magnificently realized; the cupidities and stupidities of the period have never been better exposed in fiction. With this excellent recreation of a notable element in the American legend, Roberts stepped into the forefront of our historical novelists.

Willa Cather's story of the French colony under Count de Frontenac, *Shadows on the Rock* (1931), goes back to an earlier period and lies outside the province of this discussion. It is mentioned here, however, because Miss Cather is fundamentally right in believing that historical, as well as other, fiction should be stripped of its excessive furniture. However, in this pictorially rich idyl of lonely winters and wilderness perils in and around Quebec, the story is thin and the background hardly substantial enough to compensate in artistry for what it has lost in firmness.

3. *The Middle Colonies*

The Middle Colonies—New York, Pennsylvania, Delaware, and New Jersey—had a more mixed population than either the New England or the Southern colonies. Perhaps because of the more placid nature of the people, or because of a more cosmopolitan spirit, there were in this area fewer episodes to stir the imagination of writers of romance than in either of the other sections. The stolidity of the Dutch and the Swedes and the sobriety of the Quakers offered little excitement in an outwardly prospering community. As the century unfolded, the landlord-tenant problem engendered by the patroon system became sufficiently acute for the leading novelist of the area, James Fenimore Cooper, to rise to the defense of the landed gentry.

The chief source of inspiration for the historical novelists, however, was the race conflict with the Indian. William Penn at the outset had established a tradition of friendly relations with the red men, but by 1750 there had been so many outrages that the Five Nations went on the rampage, not only in central New York, but in the Wyoming Valley of Pennsylvania and around Fort Duquesne in the western part. These conflicts grew out of a gigantic struggle between the French and the English for the possession of North America. And novelists were not slow to see the dramatic implications and possibilities of this great struggle.

The first of the chronicles of the Dutch colonists, *A History of New York by Diedrich Knickerbocker* (1809), was neither the serious history its title might suggest nor a novel, but a masterpiece of fictional humor. This heroicomical story was supposed to have been written by "a small elderly gentleman, dressed in an old black coat and cocked hat," who had mysteriously disappeared and left the manuscript behind him. Washington Irving, the author of this clever hoax, originally designed the work as a parody on Samuel Mitchill's ponderous "Picture of New York." Not to be outdone by that worthy antiquarian, the mythical Dutch historian went back in his account to the days of Noah and the creation; but by the third book he gave up the idea of parody and described in his own best comic vein the customs of the Dutch during the reign of Wouter Van Twiller, William the Testy, and Peter Stuyvesant. The author gloried in that golden age, nonchalantly celebrating the virtues of indolence and stupidity. The rotund Wouter smoked and doubted by turns the livelong day; William was as testy as he pleased; and the volatile Kieft, when he heard that the English had taken Good Hope, vowed he would have nothing to do with such blackguards. An invasion by the Swedes, described as "the most horrible battle ever recorded," was in reality quite bloodless. A mixture of wit and nonsense made the book widely popular. Incidentally it satirized various forms of pedantry and even propounded theories of statecraft. Its importance to historical fiction was the warmth of life it breathed into the meager outlines of colonial history. It created a romantic legend that has become a part of our national heritage.

Two novelists who continued the Knickerbocker tradition, though with diminished skill, were James K. Paulding and Paul H. Myers. Myers' three novels, *The First of the Knickerbockers* (1848), *The Young Patroon* (1849), and *The King of the Hurons* (1850), were uniformly romantic and but slightly based on history. More significant was the work of Paulding, who had been Irving's collaborator on a *jeu d'esprit* of their youth, *The Salmagundi Papers*.

Paulding's novel, *The Dutchman's Fireside* (1831), based on Mrs. Grant's *Memoirs of an American Lady* (1808), sketches the "Doric days" along the Hudson in the years immediately preceding the French wars. The openhanded living of the Dutch, their picnics and barn theatricals, their fashions in clothes, their dialect, and their matchmaking mammas are all depicted with sympathetic humor. Sybrant, an awkward young Dutchman in love with his cousin Catalina, whom he saves from drowning, gains some measure of self-confidence when, on a hunting trip to a frontier settlement in the Mohawk Valley, he meets Sir William Johnson. On his return he ingratiates himself with his fastidious cousin by saving her from a degenerate savage, although when she becomes the belle of New York, his bashfulness returns. He develops manly valor in the campaigns of Sir William against the Indians, in particular the defense of old Ticonderoga. After a false report that he has been killed, he returns and marries Catalina.

The portrait of Sir William accords with history in showing him a fair-minded gentleman, considerate of the welfare of the whites, but concerned also with the proper treatment of the red men. *The Dutchman's Fireside* combines the attractive features of a frontier novel by Cooper with something of the mellow style of Irving. The novel is loosely organized and seldom rises to high occasion, but its decidedly national point of view, dramatized in the victory of rags over riches, pleased the popular mood and helped to emancipate American fiction from European prototypes.

The scene of Paulding's *Koningsmarke* (1823) was the Swedish settlement on the Delaware during the governorship of Heer Peter Piper. As an artist, Paulding was jealous of the enormous vogue of Scott, and, fearing its adverse effect on American novel writing, he burlesqued parts of *The Pirate* in this work, substituting, for example, the ominous Negress Bombie for Norna of the Fitful Head. In terse, satiric essays scattered throughout the book, he condemned the haste and inaccuracy of historical novelists of the time. His own plot was rather melodramatic.

The hero of the work is a tall young Finn who is jailed for passing English coin. When the jail catches fire, Koningsmarke is injured in escaping, but he does not mind, since the governor's lovely daughter nurses him back to health. The course of their love does not run smooth, however, because the two are taken captive in an attack by the Indians and inducted into the tribe. The hero refuses to marry an Indian woman and is about to be executed, when an emissary of William Penn ransoms the couple. Later, when the English seize the "long Finne," his sweetheart secures his release through the governor of New York.

Diversified as the appeal of this book was, the story was of less importance than its mocking criticism of contemporary American fiction. Paulding realized that the noble heroes of Scott could not readily be translated to a democratic country:

> Even Indian monarchs, provincial governors, nay our good friend William Penn himself, though the illustrious founder of what may almost be called an empire, are but poor substitutes for dukes and earls, whose very titles tickle the fancy so delightfully, that the reader seems all the while swimming in an ocean of peacock's feathers.

To improve these conditions he advertised that he had "six historical novels on the anvil and each shall have one legitimate tyrannical king at least, provided enough remain unhanged at that time, or an Irish peer." Paulding's satire was evidence that better standards were being considered for historical novels.

The most important transcripts of colonial life in the Middle Colonies were those left by James Fenimore Cooper. Cooper lacked the antiquarian sense of Scott, but so varied was his personal experience and so rapid were changes in American life that he was not obliged to get up with infinite toil the social life of an earlier day. American history in general, and New York history in particular, he knew thoroughly. His love of action fitted him well to write the historical novel of adventure. In the preface to *The Pioneers* (1823) he stated his theory of the fictional treatment of history: "Rigid adhesion to truth, an indispensable requisite in history and travels," he said, "destroys the charm of fiction." He followed the beau ideal.

In *The Pioneers,* Cooper sharpened his pen on frontier material, the memories of his boyhood among the forest-clad hills in central New York. With such Cooperstown characters in mind as the hunter Shipman and the motley nationalities of the settlement, the author leisurely recalled the town as it had been forty years before: its raw street of wooden houses, the snowy congregation crowding around the fire at church, the drunken old Indian at the inn, the seasonal sports on the lake and in the wilderness, and the forest fire ushering out with grim reality the period of romance. American empire-building and American prodigality were here set before the world, with a word of caution, however, about squandering our natural resources. There was dramatic tension, too, when the old hunter and the Great Serpent, sons of nature both, bowed to the encroachments of civilization and took their departure toward the setting sun. It was the legend of Daniel Boone with but a difference in locale.

The noble-presenced frontiersman appeared again in *The Last of the Mohicans, a Narrative of 1757* (1826), Cooper's best novel, and the one in which he gave fullest attention to the habits of the red men. Cooper lived too late to know many Indians personally, but he studied such works as Heckewelder, Cadwallader, Colden, Penn, and others; and although he romanticized the Indians, he did not essentially falsify them. What Cooper noted in the red men was their acute senses, developed through woodcraft and warfare, their belief in omens, their mummery, their stoicism when undergoing torture, their "gift" of revenge, their war dance, their love of baubles, their respect for the feeble and the aged, their funeral customs, the crafty eloquence of their orators, and their fierce tribal pride. For contrast Cooper made Uncas a noble savage and Magua a treacherous one. No doubt, also, he emphasized certain barbaric virtues in order to reprimand the crude democracy of his countrymen.

The historical episodes of this novel center about the siege of Fort William Henry, on Lake George. Thither Cora and Alice Munro, daughters of the British commander, are bound, escorted by Alice's betrothed, Major Heyward, and accompanied by David the psalm-singer and the deceitful Magua. The scout Hawkeye, with his Mohican companions, Chingachgook and Uncas, thwarts Magua's attempt to capture the girls before the surrender to Montcalm. For the massacre which follows, Cooper blames the French. Incidentally, Montcalm is his best-drawn historical character. Munro typifies the British incapacity to cope with the Indians, later fatefully illustrated in Braddock's defeat. After the surrender, the girls are taken captive. Adventure follows adventure. Alice is later rescued, but Cora, Magua, and Uncas are killed. The death of the mysterious Uncas is made to typify the pathetic history of his race, and lends the work an epical significance.

The Last of the Mohicans is a better historical novel than many others because the central theme, the conquest of the Indian by the white, turns upon and is explained by the chief historical event, the savagery of the red men at Fort William Henry. When readers wish to know what it was to live when the aborigines were in power, it is to this story of "disastrous chances, of hair-breadth 'scapes, and moving accidents by flood and field" that the imagination naturally turns.

The Pathfinder (1840) and *The Deerslayer* (1841) continue Cooper's interest in the Indian, but without the supplement of historical suggestion. The former is a sylvan romance with a notable admixture of sentiment, and the latter is a tale of adventure purely for adventure's sake. Both are well told, but they do not classify as historical novels.

As a wealthy landholder, Cooper was so disturbed by the antirent difficulties of his day—the attempts to stop continuous leasing of land to tenants and to sell it outright—that he resolved to trace their history through three generations of the Littlepage family. He devoted *Satanstoe* (1845) to the first generation, *The Chainbearer* (1845) to the second, and *The Redskins* (1846) to the third. Only the first is historical, and not objectionably encumbered by its thesis.

Cornelius Littlepage, the young squire who lives on the family estate, Satanstoe, is accompanied by the young Dutch aristocrat Dirck and the Yankee schoolmaster Jason on his first visit to New York. Here he stays with the Mordaunts, Dirck's cousins, who have a lovely daughter, Anneke. Among the social affairs with which the visit coincides is the Pinkster frolic, an annual festival among the Negroes of Manhattan. Cooper thus brings the black man as well as the red man into his fiction. During the festival, "Corny" wins Anneke's admiration by saving her from the paw of a caged lion. Soon thereafter the young men leave for Albany to survey large grants of land on which their fathers plan to settle tenants. The Mordaunts also come there, and the mischievous Albanian, Guert Ten Eyck, falls in love with Anneke's companion, Mary Wallace. The French and Indians now approach from the north, and the men, led by a well-drawn Indian scout, Susquesus, join the forces at Ticonderoga. Historical characters, like Montcalm, Abercrombie, and Howe appear in the story, and Fort William Henry is the scene of some of the action.

Cast in the form of a memoir, *Satanstoe* naturally reflects a reminiscent mood. The descriptions lack the freshness of those in *The Last of the Mohicans*, perhaps because they owe something to Mrs. Anne Grant's *Memoirs of an American Lady*, which was the basis also of Paulding's *The Dutchman's Fireside*. The most exciting scene is the near catastrophe to the young people one night in their sleighs when the ice in the Hudson begins to break up. The round of social gaiety among the patroons is so well presented in this book that *Satanstoe* is still unsurpassed as a document of colonial manners in New York. Its sequel, *The Chainbearer*, is a counterblast, from the York state point of view, to Thompson's *Green Mountain Boys*, but the feud between owners and squatters can hardly be called "historical."

Colonial Pennsylvania had much the same material to offer novelists as her neighbor New York. The dealings of William Penn with the Indians did not catch their fancy so well, however, as did the Wyoming Massacre in 1778. The English poet Campbell, in 1809, had drawn attention to the romantic possibilities inherent in the subject by his popular poem, "Gertrude of Wyoming." Then, with the rising vogue of historical fiction in the eighteen twenties, two novelists, Nicholas M.

Hentz and James McHenry, each based a novel on the episode.

Tadeuskund, the Last King of the Lenape (1825), by Hentz, is in the style of Cooper's novels of Indian warfare. It even antedates *The Last of the Mohicans* by a year. When the story opens, the tribe of the Lenape, which has been at peace since the days of William Penn, is being incited by the Mingos against the whites through the designs of a handful of white renegades aided by the Demon Rum. The Indian-hater Rogers, who has been scalped in an earlier raid on Mount Hope, for a mysterious reason threatens the Quaker Burton, whose daughter disappeared during that raid. Livingston, the hero, tries to keep peace between the two, but is captured by the Indians as Rogers calls out, "Remember Mount Hope!" In time Livingston is liberated by the friendly chief Tadeuskund and is nursed back to health by the king's stepdaughter Elluwia. At a council meeting a Mingo conjurer in bearskin tries to incite the Lenape against Livingston, but his wiles are annulled by Burton, who came to America from France to seek "romantick purity and golden-age virtues" among the aborigines.

Livingston, accompanied by Conrad, his humorous Prussian squire, now makes a hazardous journey to Philadelphia to assure the government of the peaceful intent of the Lenape. On the way back he runs into the Paxton Boys, who at Rogers' instigation are drinking themselves into a mood to fight the Lenape. As the travelers approach the valley, they are greeted by a scene of dismay. The massacre is on in fury, Tadeuskund is dying, and even the villain Rogers is mortally wounded. He dies with his secret, but a locket discloses the information that Elluwia, the elf-maiden who has sought to restrain the malcontents with her witchery, is none other than Burton's long-lost daughter. Elluwia is killed by a stray shot from the Indians who are celebrating the massacre and is in death reunited with her magnanimous Tadeuskund.

Fantastic as some of the incidents are, and circumlocutory as the style is, this story is still pleasant reading. The brusque

Indian-baiting frontiersman is realistically conceived. The comic Prussian soldier, despite his long-winded recital of his campaigns, is an interesting variant from the comic Irish squire in Hugh Brackenridge's well-known frontier book, *Modern Chivalry*. The direction of the story is not always clear, but all told, *Tadeuskund* is no mean contemporary of Cooper's Indian novels.

The closest corollary to *Tadeuskund* is *The Bethrothed of Wyoming* (1830), by James McHenry, author of *The Spectre of the Forest*. While her lover is away seeking reinforcements for the outpost threatened by the Indians, the betrothed undergoes harrowing advances from the ruler of the little colony, who is in secret alliance with the notorious half-blood leader Brant. Her only help against the villain's importunities is a friendly hermit who mysteriously appears from time to time. At length, in the final melodramatic scene the lover returns at the head of the Wyoming Volunteers and puts an end to the bigwig's villainy. The author gives evidence of having gone over the historical ground thoroughly, and exhibits a certain ability at creating suspense. Such incidents, however, as the rescue of the heroine on the balcony, the death of Isabella by a random shot, and the movements of the hermit rescuer are imitated directly from Cooper and Scott.

McHenry dealt with the Pennsylvania frontier in another novel, at a period slightly later than that depicted in *The Betrothed*. This book, *The Wilderness, or Braddock's Times* (1823), introduces an Irish family living under pioneer conditions near Fort Duquesne, in western Pennsylvania. With this domestic scene the author connects the episodes in which young Washington wins his spurs by his hazardous journey to the outpost of the French commandant on the Monongahela, and his subsequent retrieval of Braddock's disastrous expedition. Using as his basis the slight reference to these events in Marshall's *Life of Washington*, the author shows the nation's idol in love. Young Washington is represented as finding in the settler's ward (really Mary Philipse) a person whose attractions and tastes, thanks to her tutelage by an Indian prophet, he declares "better than any met with in society." He sues most eloquently for this elegant lady's favor, presents her with a copy of Shenstone as a token of his affection, and, in the guise of an Indian chief, saves her from the villainous Frenchman at Fort Le Boeuf, only to learn that she has been previously betrothed to a young man of the wilderness. He thereupon resolves, high-minded gentleman that he is, to devote himself to his country.

Naïve as such mythmaking appears, it had been going on since soon after Washington's death, when Parson Weems caught the popular fancy with his cherry-tree story. The plot formula, with its chief feature an Indian prophet who mysteriously appeared from time to time to give counsel to the lovers in moments of distress, and who, in the penultimate chapter, was discovered to be the father of the heroine, was one to be employed with slight variation by most of the novelists of the decade. It was doubtless a graceful compliment to the father of the historical novel, but it can hardly be said to have improved the form among his American imitators.

Whether another form that is lately being projected will find favor with the public remains to be seen. In 1933 Hervey Allen conceived a historical novel without taboos and on a grander scale than any American historical novel before it. *Anthony Adverse*, though it touched American history only slightly, was a popular and a financial success. Almost at once Neil Swanson set out to write, in thirty novels, "a continuous narrative of the advance of the American frontier from the Atlantic to the Mississippi."

His epic begins in *The First Rebel* (1937) with the story of James Smith and the unruly Scotch-Irish of Pennsylvania, who, by opposing the British policy toward the Indians, annoyed the ruling classes of the province during King George's War, 1744–48. The grim story of Smith's captivity is projected against the Pontiac uprising, Braddock's defeat, the butchery by the Paxton Boys of the harmless Conestogas, and the attacks on Fort Loudon and Fort Bedford. *The First Rebel* is well documented for an adventure story, but hardly makes its case of the events preceding Lexington and Concord. *The Judas Tree* (1933) has as the subject of its intricate, thrilling plot the siege of Fort Pitt in 1763. The tantalizingly long-drawn-out love story outdoes *To Have and To Hold* in that the bond-servant turns out to be no less than a duchess. Its sequel, *The Silent Drum* (1940), continues the account of the struggle between the traders and the settlers of the province, and *The Forbidden Ground* (1938) extends the picture from Detroit to the fur-trading region northwest of the Great Lakes. It emphasizes the ruthless rivalry of the fur barons, but says little of the hard daily routine of the trade. *Unconquered* (1947) is yet another rushing narrative about Pontiac's uprising. The scene is laid at the Forks of the Ohio in 1763, and the story is spiced with a hussy and a gratuitous bit of sadism. Swanson's novels are full of action in the Sabatini manner and call for little mental effort. Plot and characters are stereotyped in the Hollywood tradition, and the rudimentary prose evidences increasing haste.

Undertaking a project not quite so grandiose as Swanson's, the redoubtable Hervey Allen has conceived an elaborate series of novels on the same theme. This massive work, to be called *The Disinherited*, is expected in its five volumes to trace the advance of the frontier across the Alleghenies to the time of the Civil War.[5] *The Forest and the Fort* (1943) is the preface to the saga. The setting, which extends from western Pennsylvania to the Ohio Valley, is impressive by its very size. In the Delaware Valley, during Pontiac's conspiracy against the encroaching whites, young Salathiel Albine has been snatched into captivity and reared to be a Shawnee warrior; but at seventeen he deserts the redskins and joins the defenders of Fort Pitt

[5] Allen has illuminating comments on his art in "History and the Novel," *Atlantic Monthly*, Vol. CLXXIII, No. 2 (February, 1944), 119–21.

against the French. In time he becomes the trusty aide of Commander Ecuyer, who superimposes the rudiments of civilization on Sal's "noble savage" qualities. Meanwhile, there is trouble at the fort. Because of personal ambitions St. Clair has let things get out of hand; he has, in fact, connived at Quaker Japson's selling arms to the Indians.

In *Bedford Village* (1944) Allen continues Salathiel's adventures during the year 1763–64, when the debris of the French and Indian Wars is being mopped up. The siege of Fort Pitt has been lifted, but Pontiac's uprising is far from scotched. As scout for Captain Ecuyer, in charge of Fort Bedford, which holds the supply line for Fort Pitt, Sal helps to ready Bouquet's expedition to pacify the Indians of the Ohio and while so employed sheds some of his Indian ways and learns others from the frontiersmen. One of the seven who assist Captain Fenwick in fighting the Indians, he discovers that the new nation is founded by "the disinherited," rugged individualists, for the first time free to act on their own responsibility. He too indulges in some of the garrison's deviltry, falls in love, and in the end sets out with his refugee bride for the settlements. If the story is somewhat loosely organized and lacks some of the excitement of *The Forest and the Fort*, it moves, nevertheless, and overflows with pageantry and local color. The third panel, *Toward the Morning* (1948), continues Salathiel's eastward course from the wilderness as it merges with the relative refinements of colonial society.

Pennsylvania has had few novelists treat her early period. Carl Van Doren's statement about the imagination recurring often to such a theme as Penn's liberality and tolerance[6] has little evidence to support it in historical fiction. In *Nancy Lloyd, the Journal of a Quaker Pioneer* (1927), Anna L. B. Thomas has given a sympathetic interpretation of Penn's character in connection with a simple, vivid account of the first twenty years of the Pennsylvania province. Nancy Lloyd be-

[6] *The American Novel* (New York, 1940), 18.

gins her journal in 1681, shortly before her family is persuaded by William Penn to help him govern his new province across the sea. It requires little urging for these staunch Quakers, who are suffering persecution in England as heretics, to come to this new country with its promise of freedom. But all is not well. Domestic troubles alternate with sectarian problems, rumors about the Indians, political fears, and disquieting news from abroad. On the death of her mother, after the birth of the tenth child, Nancy takes her place in the home. Her hand is sought in marriage by John Delaval, a good man, but the virtuous Nancy refuses until the Captain of the militia becomes a devotee of the Quaker faith. Her story ends on a note of pathos, for her husband and children are taken by a ravaging fever. She retains her inner composure, however, and in the end is to marry an upright Quaker.

The *Journal*, while not cast in the form of a novel, is fictionized. It states with characteristic simplicity and directness both the material and the spiritual attitudes of a people whose every act was motivated by their religion. The author, a descendant of the Lloyds, used, in addition to family papers, Watson's *Annals of Philadelphia*, Janney's *Life of William Penn*, and Bowden's *History of Friends in America*. Nancy mentions the distresses of William Penn, suffered because of his faith, and comments on the ruthless treatment given him for fifteen years in England. She further points out that during the war with England, the Quaker colonists, believing that good will was better than military stratagem, had a difficult time. They boldly denounced the importation of slaves, flatly condemned the exploits of war, and lamented all dishonesty. Theirs has been a quiet but pervasive influence on American life.

On the whole, the Colonial period of American history has been least frequently and least adequately treated by novelists of ability. Often it has been left to writers of juvenile fiction, whose representation of that early life has been quite innocuous. The first experimenters with Colonial material were rank amateurs who tried in one way or another to adapt the technique of Sir Walter Scott to native subjects. Not all attempts to deal with Colonial history were trivial, however. Among romantic writers, Cooper and Simms devoted their best efforts to the period, and Hawthorne in *The Scarlet Letter* produced a masterpiece. In the twentieth century, Mary Johnston continued the romantic tradition, while Helen Carlisle and Esther Forbes have applied the technique of psychoanalysis. Greatest hope for the future lies in the direction which Kenneth Roberts has so ably explored in *Northwest Passage* and Hervey Allen in *The Disinherited*.

II. The American Revolution
and Its Aftermath

THE BIRTH OF THE NATION in the uncertain days of the Revolution has been from the first the favorite theme of American historical novelists. It has enabled writers to identify themselves with an authentic tradition close to the hearts of their readers. The shaping of the principle of individual liberty and of the sovereignty of the people is a story that cannot too often be told. Now that the Revolution can be seen in perspective, it emerges as the most important single step in the rise of the common man in world history. Whatever the immediate causes assigned to the struggle, they reduce to a shortsighted policy on the part of the mother country in dealing with her lusty offspring. Frontier conditions and a half-century of warfare with the French and Indians had engendered a spirit of self-sufficiency which caused the colonists to seek a new way of expressing themselves politically. When the policy of imperial rule and commercial exploitation became economically intolerable, back-country agrarians, assisted by merchants and tidewater planters, threw off the parental yoke and evolved a new political philosophy based on individual freedom.

The Revolution was hardly, however, the unanimous uprising against the mother country which Whig historians once made it appear, and it is to the credit of the novelist James Fenimore Cooper that in the first American historical novel, *The Spy*, he presented the war as distinctly fratricidal. All early treatments of the subject were of course highly romantic.

The redcoats were made villains, while Washington and his men were heroized. By 1835 the apotheosis of Washington had reached a point which caused Catharine M. Sedgwick to feel at mention of his name "a sentiment resembling the awe of the pious Israelite when he approached the ark of the Lord."[1] More critical standards came with the rise of realism in the eighteen eighties, although the costume romance of the nineties still displayed bombast and fustian. Recent novels have been sounder psychologically; they have been more frank in picturing the ignoble as well as the heroic aspects of the war; they have sought out neglected episodes for treatment; and there has been a tendency to show a case for the Tories and the English.

The war swept through the colonies in a generally north-south direction. The novels about to be considered are therefore arranged according to the backgrounds of the war, the three principal ones being the New England Colonies and Canada, the Middle Colonies, and the Southern Colonies. In addition, there is a group of novels on the warfare beyond the Alleghenies and one on the naval warfare of the Revolution. Since both the War of 1812 and Shays's Rebellion were aftermaths of the Revolution, they are included in this division.

1. *The New England Colonies and Canada*

The novels laid in New England and Canada center about such early events of the war as the battles of Lexington, Concord, and Bunker Hill, the Boston massacre and siege, the defense of Ticonderoga, and Arnold's march to Quebec.

The first novel to treat Boston before the Revolution, Lydia M. Child's *The Rebels* (1825), had its inspiration in the young Republic's semicentennial. Prominent in the story were the aggrandizing Governor Hutchinson, the Tory punster Dr.

[1] *The Linwoods*, Preface.

Byles and the pacificator Samuel Adams. An imaginary speech by James Otis and a sermon by George Whitefield soon passed for genuine in the school readers and books of declamation. As the political episodes seemed "only too familiar" to her readers, the author concentrated interest on "the domestic annals" of her fictitious characters. The heroine, a ward of the Governor and a prospective heiress, gives her hand to a proud redcoat but, through a consumptive rival, discovers his duplicity in time to turn to the less flashy but devoted patriot. The conventional Gothic touch is supplied by a vengeful sibyl, the grandmother of the heroine, who is mysteriously connected with a dying miser on his treasure island near Boston. Although the novel is overwritten, it has a winsome brashness at times. Its chief historical value is its graphic picture of the stamp tax agitation.

By the fiftieth anniversary of the battles of Lexington, Concord, and Bunker Hill, the spirit of nationalism had become tense. Daniel Webster in his Bunker Hill oration eloquently voiced the popular mood. The Monroe Doctrine was promulgated amid this "era of good feeling." Lafayette came back from France and was enthusiastically received by the country which he had helped to gain its independence. His friend, James Fenimore Cooper, in the first flush of popularity, projected a series of historical novels to be called *Legends of the Thirteen Republics*—one for each colony, to show what that colony had contributed to the Revolution. Although the project never went beyond the first of the series, *Lionel Lincoln, or the Leaguer of Boston* (1825-24), Cooper began with great industry and enthusiasm. He pictured the state of unrest among the citizenry of Massachusetts and gave a spirited account of the battles of Lexington and Bunker Hill. He mentioned Warren, Gage, and Putnam, but did not try to portray them. As in *The Spy*, his sympathy with the losing side equalized the contest and made it a worthy struggle. When the attempt to blend a complicated plot of domestic intrigue with historical research proved irksome, he shifted attention to the melodramatic fortunes of his

Byronic hero, a British major. A mélange of murder, morbidity, and sudden death gave the book a contemporary appeal which has been lost in an age of different critical standards, but this should not obscure to us its penetrating psychological analysis.

Whenever Cooper was obliged to substitute painstaking research for personal experience, he was in trouble. His followers were even less successful, whether they accepted his adaptations of the technique of Scott to local history, or imitated the Wizard of the North directly. When Catharine M. Sedgwick wrote *The Linwoods; or "Sixty Years Since" in America* (1835), she obviously had *Waverley* in mind, although her plot more nearly resembled that of *The Spy*. In imitation of Scott, her domestic tale opened with a visit to a sibyl. But the setting, like Cooper's, was the highlands of the Hudson with their bands of Skinners and cowboys; and the hero, as in *The Spy*, was entrapped in his father's house. He was disowned for joining Washington's army and was not restored until the end. All this while a Tory friend flirted with all the pretty girls. Miss Sedgwick, a preceptress, was more interested in the moral tone of her story than in its art; nevertheless, she exhibited unusual gifts in characterization and in handling dialogue. Since she had a wide personal following, her adaptation of history for juvenile readers proved highly popular.

During a wave of interest in historical fiction in the eighteen nineties, Colonel John W. DeForest, pioneer realist, wrote a thumpingly patriotic tale of the Revolution, *A Lover's Revolt* (1898). The plot is negligible, but the battles of Lexington and Bunker Hill are ably described, the jealousy among the colonial forces is well brought out, and the picture of Prescott is excellent.

One of the most authentic and appealing stories of events about Boston that led to the Revolution is *Gilman of Redford* (1927), by the historian William Stearns Davis. The narrator, a Harvard man by the name of Roger Gilman, is enabled to learn about developments at first hand since he is secretary to

Samuel Adams and later to John Hancock. Incidentally, he learns, through secret parleys of his Whig friends, how the germ of independence takes hold and flourishes. His activities include participation in the Boston Tea Party and in the battles around Boston, about all of which he keeps a record. After his escape from impressment, Roger learns from the underground of plots against the Adamses, Hancock, Franklin, and other leaders. He falls in love with Emilie Rivoire, cousin of Paul Revere, and wins her affection by rescuing her from the black-hearted Captain Prothero of the British navy. As backdrop to the story appears a well-drawn picture of family and social life. *Gilman of Redford* is an uncolored and uncensored statement of the occurrences in and near Boston that are dear to the heart of every red-blooded American. It is lively and entertaining.

The campaign north of Boston has repeatedly attracted writers of fiction. D. P. Thompson seems to have had enough material left over from his colonial romance, *The Green Mountain Boys,* for a novel of this period. In *The Rangers; or, The Tory's Daughter* (1851) he used the Battle of Bennington and the massacre at Westminster in the older, southern part of Vermont, where he asserted the first blood of the Revolution was drawn. The story opens with a bitter feud between Whig and Tory over fraudulent voting, and with the confiscation of cattle and farms by unscrupulous lawyers. Two years after the fight over the county court, Ticonderoga falls, and savage hordes attached to the British army ravage the countryside. Then Vermont becomes a state; its founders at once authorize a regiment of rangers to act with General Stark against Burgoyne and Riedesel. The forays of doughty woodsmen bring out the intensity of fratricidal strife. The love plot, though of minor importance, capitalizes on the tragic interest in the hapless Jane McRea, whose abduction by the Indians has been celebrated in song and story.

A more powerfully imagined romance of pioneering and fighting in the Hampshire Grants from 1769 to 1777 is Le-

Grand Cannon's *Look to the Mountain* (1942). This simple story of Whitfield Livingston and Melissa Butler, hewing out a home in the White Mountain wilderness, growing their crops, fighting weather and beasts and poverty, and developing their holdings as other settlers join them, has a universal and timeless theme. It is realized with a freshness and a fullness of knowledge that has seldom been equaled. The trek of the young couple to the mountains and the return of the protagonist from defeating the Hessians at Bennington are especially well dramatized. So overshadowed by local doings are the events of the Revolution—Concord, Bunker Hill, Burgoyne's invasion—that they are barely noticed. Little things hold attention—such things as making a sledge or a chimney or a canoe, the gift of a puppy, the ownership of oxen, a scene at the forge, or the salty speech at the tavern. With never a sentimental note, the book, like *Giants in the Earth*, faithfully illuminates the basic human virtues which carved out American homesteads in the wilderness. This is the way it must have been.

The most satisfactory account of the Revolution in New England and Canada is found in two novels by Kenneth Roberts, *Arundel* (1930) and *Rabble in Arms* (1933). Both deal with the Northern campaign: *Arundel* picturing Arnold's arduous march against Quebec, and *Rabble in Arms* the retreat down Lake Champlain and the defeat of Burgoyne at Saratoga. In *Arundel*, Steven Nason, the narrator, serves under Colonel Benedict Arnold on the secret expedition that goes up the Kennebec and across forests and swamps to the St. Lawrence. Here the poorly clad, ill-fed troops have a long wait for Montgomery, who is to come down the river from Montreal. Then follows the ruinous assault on the snow-clad cliffs of Quebec on New Year's Eve, 1775, the death of Montgomery, and defeat. Steven has a personal stake in this expedition because he has secretly enlisted the aid of the Indians against the British after his sweetheart, Mary Mallinson, is taken captive to Quebec.

The plot is conventional, but not the telling, which evinces knowledge of woodcraft, vivacity, humor, and originality. Outstanding characters of fiction are the Falstaffian Cap Huff, dainty Mary Mallinson (who turns into the heartless Marie de Sabrevois in *Rabble in Arms*), the villainous preacher, and forthright Phoebe Nason, who, despite her disappointments, holds true and wins Steven's admiration for her unconventional honesty. The atmosphere is redolent of rum and roast pork, wood smoke, and pine forests. Especial attention is given to the Indian lore and to the primitive folkways of earthy people. But the real novelty of the book lies in the unconventional portrait of Benedict Arnold. Instead of drawing him as the despicable character of legend, the author shows the acrobatic Arnold as a really capable leader.

In *Rabble in Arms*, Steven and Phoebe, Marie, and Cap Huff are put into minor roles, and Doc Means is added to help in the escape from some very credible Indians. The center of interest is in two brothers, Peter and Nathaniel Merrill, one a rebel and the other a Tory. Peter relates the story of the starved and diseased rabble that retreat from Canada—of their hastily building a fleet on Lake Champlain, the delaying engagement against the British flotilla at Valcour Island, the flight from Ticonderoga before Burgoyne's confident advance, and the Battle of Saratoga, in which the ragged rebels under Gates cut to pieces Burgoyne's finest regiments. While Peter worries and starves during the terrible summer he is building ships, the weakling younger brother is in the web of the spy Marie. Each in turn is made prisoner by the hostile Indians, and Peter escapes only in time to retreat from Ticonderoga and to share in the defeat of Burgoyne. The romantic episodes appear somewhat stereotyped, but the author's vivid prose sweeps the reader from incident to incident while entertaining him with irony and humorous epithet. A new standard in historical fiction has here been set, one that does not gloss facts or attempt to soothe national pride. Arnold's wisdom and courage are seen to have been responsible for the success of the campaign; the solemn officialdom of the Continental Congress is the real villain of the piece. If the record shows that Arnold had another side— a domineering nature and a habit of running up bills without knowing how to pay them—nevertheless, history as here presented is convincing and unforgettable.

In *Renown* (1938)—a first novel by a former sergeant of marines, Frank Hough—Benedict Arnold is also the central figure. Hough is not blind to the fact that Arnold was a frustrated opportunist. His desire for renown, even if he had to cheat for it, was his undoing. Where Roberts tried to make Arnold's treason seem a fundamental, if mistaken, act of patriotism Hough shows Arnold from the first to have been an indifferent revolutionist and does not attempt to vindicate him. The story begins when Arnold, as military governor of Philadelphia, was at the peak of his fame. Devoted as he was to Washington, who reciprocated the feeling by regarding Arnold his most valued general officer, he lacked the fortitude of his chief. When Congress, made up of small-town autocrats, promoted five brigadier generals over him without consulting Washington, and when no decisive victory seemed possible, he saw no point in carrying guerrilla warfare further and favored the generous peace offered by the British in 1778. One misfortune now led to another. Bankrupt, he misappropriated funds, for which he was court-martialed, and mildly reprimanded. He suffered from a wound gained in the patriot cause. In a fit of passion he married Peggy Shippen, whose Tory connections influenced his decision to conspire with Major André against his countrymen. When, soon after, André was captured, Arnold was obliged to take flight from West Point. After his act of treason the proud man for a time put up a brave front. Disappointed in the British army, which did not appreciate his energy, he sought new fortunes in Canada and saw service in the West Indies, finally dying in poverty and despair. The author has written a fine and discriminating novel. Realizing that readers are too astute to believe in a storybook villain, Hough admits Arnold's dark and magnificent heroism, yet notes at the same time the General's wrongheadedness.

The New England phase of the Revolution has been adequately dealt with in fiction. Particularly the novels of Roberts, Hough, Cannon, and Davis, in their diversity of approach, their faithfulness to history, and their general liveliness, rank well with the fictional treatment of any period of American history.

2. *The Middle Colonies*

Historical novels laid in the Middle Colonies have dealt with the conflict on the Neutral Ground of the Hudson highlands; with the campaign around New York, followed by Washington's retreat to New Jersey; with the Hessians and the activities of Howe around Philadelphia; with the Battle of Oriskany in the Mohawk Valley; with the terrible winter at Valley Forge; and with the Battle of Monmouth—a series of episodes beginning in 1776 and extending to 1778, or roughly speaking, through the first half of the war.

When James Fenimore Cooper laid the foundation for American historical fiction in 1821 with *The Spy*, he builded better than he knew. He could easily have yielded to the temptation to furnish a strongly biased picture of the Revolution. Instead, he showed the Wharton family as a house divided against itself, and, by causing the spy to be harassed as much by bands of Skinners as by freebooting cowboys, kept his readers in suspense to the last. Especially to be commended is his emphasis on the fratricidal nature of the war, for only recently has the fog of patriotic legend lifted from the tradition of Whig historians who misrepresented the Revolution as a united uprising against the mother country.

Cooper knew the locale of the Neutral Ground north of New York City from having resided for years in Westchester

County. The tale of the spy came from John Jay, his neighbor, and Cooper may have been struck by its plot value after seeing the play *André* by his friend William Dunlap. The idea of making the peddler-spy the hero may have been derived from Scott's *The Antiquary*, as was undoubtedly the idea of the mysterious stranger who proved to be none other than the venerated General Washington. The protracted pursuit-rescue scheme of the plot was ideally suited to Cooper's genius. Romantic adventure was always more attractive to him than antiquarian lore, and in this case he could depend on the information of eyewitnesses beyond his own very full knowledge of the history of New York. So fair was his rendering of partisan warfare that it appealed to English readers as well as to patriots. Even Puritan readers, who winced at fiction as mere fabrication, could enjoy its sugar-coating of piety. So well, in fact, had Cooper estimated the taste of the public that his experiment in native fiction was from the first a success. No longer might a Sydney Smith sneer, "Who in the four corners of the globe reads an American book?" The reception of *The Spy* at home and abroad heartened Cooper and his contemporaries, and it created a vogue for historical fiction which lasted well into the eighteen thirties.

The immediate result of the popularity of Cooper's *The Spy* was to inspire James A. Jones, writing under the pen name of Captain Matthew Murgatroyd, to produce a tale of the war around New York City, *The Refugee* (1825). Gilbert Greaves, a gay young blade and son of an English Tory, in attempting to enlist recruits for the King's cause, barely escapes being tarred and feathered by his rebel neighbors. Gil cares less for nobility than for sport, and when his dissolute general attempts to seduce Ellen Keith, he changes his allegiance to the American side. After serving valiantly in the Battle of White Plains, he is captured by the British and saved from execution only by a timely reprieve from Sir Henry Clinton, the new commander-in-chief. The style is witty and forthright. The vignettes of Washington, De Kalb, Jones, Howe, and Clinton are interesting, and the conflicting loyalties are well dramatized. The book is as readable as one of Irving's.

In 1846, James K. Paulding, Irving's friend, laid *The Old Continental* in the no man's land of *The Spy*. A young man, left alone with his grandparents, joins his father's company in the highlands in order to win the favor of the "old Continental," his sweetheart's father. Some mutinous soldiers try to clear themselves by accusing him of treason. At one time he barely escapes execution as a spy. When he is finally captured by the British, his desertion seems confirmed, but the Colonel, on a quixotic journey to American headquarters, learns of his innocence. After several other escapades, including some months aboard a pestilence-ridden British prison ship and conflicts with bloody outlaws, he assists in taking the spy Major André (as Paulding's own cousin John actually did), and wins the "old Continental's" daughter. The book is remarkable for its time in that the center of interest is the common soldier.

The territory of bitterly divided loyalties presented in *The Spy* has recently interested two novelists, Frank Hough and Burke Boyce. Hough's *If Not Victory* (1939) and its sequel, *The Neutral Ground* (1941), use Westchester County as the background of our first civil war. In the former, Enoch Crosby appears as he did in Cooper's story, and so does Washington, but the center of interest is a green country lad who achieves patriotism little by little. Inclined at first to side with the loyalists, he comes to the conclusion, midway in the war, after having been captured by both sides, that the young nation struggling for survival is his country, and he is prepared to fight for revenge "if not victory." The story is more episodic than Cooper's and is quicker-paced. Some of its characters reappear in *The Neutral Ground*, but the burden of that story rests on two friends, Rob Trowbridge and Sam Hilton, who, divided by the conflict, try to force the neutrals into one party or the other. After five years of patrolling, espionage and counterespionage, pitched battles, and bitter suffering, it is clear that neutrality is out of the question. While the loyalist Hilton with Rogers' Rangers loses all save honor, the young rakehell Trowbridge develops into one of Montgomery's efficient officers, succeeding Burr in 1789. Between these friends stand the Van Drusens, whose neutrality is shattered when the wife gives in to the sinister Maxwell Bartlet. Hough agrees with the author of *Oliver Wiswell* that the greatest harm to the loyalist cause was rendered by the British generals through their contempt for the raw colonial troops on either side. He relates with exceptional knowledge of strategy Washington's brilliant retreat from Long Island, André's capture, and the guerrilla fighting in Westchester. Burr, Arnold, Rogers, and Washington all appear as very natural human beings. Washington, in particular, is well drawn, and Rogers is more fairly presented than by Kenneth Roberts, but the story as a whole, despite its excellent telling, lacks Roberts' driving force.

The Perilous Night (1942), by Burke Boyce, is laid in the narrow valleys across the Hudson from Westchester. Asa Howell, a country gentleman who has two sons and a spirited daughter, is prospering and feels sure that warfare will not reach his peaceful acres. He willingly endures taxation and regulatory acts, but is incensed when the redcoats take a farmer's pig. Pillage and bloodshed follow, and Asa's house is not free from attack one perilous night. His daughter Tempy Ann is the victim of several love tragedies. One son profiteers and is held in contempt by the patriots; the body of the other is brought home from Fort Montgomery for burial. Asa doggedly plants crops and accepts depreciated Continental notes in payment, realizing that in war one has everything to lose and nothing tangible to gain. Out of such stubborn Americanism the new nation was born.

The fiercest fighting of the Revolution seems to have taken place in the Mohawk Valley of New York. The first novelist to be attracted to the Battle of Oriskany was Charles

Fenno Hoffman, editor of the *Knickerbocker Magazine*. Hoffman had protested from time to time against the flood of ephemeral American imitations of Scott. In *Greyslaer* (1840) he followed precept with example when he undertook "to blend the historical novel with the domestic love tale, and stamp the whole with the unity of a dramatic poem." Contending that Whig and Tory enmity burned more fiercely among the mixed nationalities of central New York than elsewhere, he kept his readers on the rack with his terse recital of the rise of border warfare, the inroads of Brant and his Iroquois cohorts, and the fierce Battle of Oriskany. In the love plot, too, he kept readers in suspense. Greyslaer's sweetheart Alida was abducted by a Tory suitor and forced into a sham marriage, from which, however, she is promptly saved. The author introduced, although briefly, such historical figures as the self-seeking Sir William Johnson, Herkimer and his gallant Yaegers, St. Leger, and Burgoyne. From Cooper he borrowed the hunter in the primitive forest and from Scott the hag, the subterranean chapel, and the youth of dubious parentage; but his woodsman was less poetic than Leatherstocking and could "not abide a Redskin." Hoffman documented his work, and deftly wove history into transitional paragraphs; his characters, though stock figures, were well individualized; but he admitted that romance had fallen upon an evil day and awaited another Scott "to revivify the dry bones which it is our humble task to collect."

By 1840, after publishing several novels on European themes, Cooper had returned to writing about his native New York. After picturing Natty Bumppo in love in *The Pathfinder*, and on his first warpath in *The Deerslayer*, he put into *Wyandotté* (1843) material which he had gathered for a novel on the Revolution. Into it went also his very evident pleasure in commencing the labors of civilization, as reflected, for example in the settlers' securing "patents" to their land from the Indians. The main action centered in an outpost held against an untrustworthy tenant in league with a treacherous Indian. So strong was Cooper's sense of property that when he wrote of the eddies· of war reaching this frontier estate, he turned the sympathy of the reader in favor of the Tory lord of the manor and against the Yankee bigots with designs on the "patent." Here, a century before *Oliver Wiswell,* Cooper moved toward realism and brusquely censured "patriots" for confiscating loyalist property.

In 1890 the Mohawk Valley was used as the setting of a novel which went considerably beyond Cooper in utilizing economic and racial issues. Harold Frederic's *In the Valley* was also the first realistic picture of the bloody campaign around Oriskany against the forces of St. Leger. During Sir William Johnson's last days as governor of the territory, a growing discord has arisen among commoners, aristocrats, and Indians. Soon after General Herkimer has driven off the Indians, the narrator, Douw Mauverensen, is sent by his patron on a fur-trading mission to the West. During his absence a young aristocrat, Philip Cross, alienates his sweetheart, whereupon Douw accepts an appointment as government agent at Albany. Here he meets genteel folk like the Ten Broecks, the Van Rensselaers, the Gansevoorts, and the De Lanceys, and is impressed by such leaders as Cadwallader Colden and Philip Schuyler. In the Valley, meanwhile, Philip Cross and Walter Butler have become violent Tories, and have organized the tribes against their neighbors. Douw becomes Schuyler's aide in the expedition against Quebec, and is later sent to the Valley to help wipe out the conspirators there. Because of intercolonial jealousy and severe financial stringency, Congress sends only two hundred men to aid the five hundred colonists against St. Leger's invasion; but plucky General Herkimer, with the aid of the friendly Oneidas, manages to stem the tide, although he loses half his men. The Battle of Oriskany is regarded by the author as the turning point of the war. His book is carefully written, and still well deserves to be read.

Not until Walter D. Edmonds published his popular novel,

Drums Along the Mohawk, in 1936, however, was the effect of the campaign upon the Valley farmers fully realized.[2] For them the war was New England's war, carried on by an inaccessible and misunderstanding Congress. The frontier was concerned with its own conflicts. The great landowners, the Johnsons and the Butlers, had been driven out, some of them finding refuge in Canada. Races were in conflict: the Scottish settlers resented the presence of the Palatine Germans, and the old Dutch disliked both, while all feared the Indians. Life was not romantic, but a grim everyday struggle. When in the summer of 1776 Gilbert Martin takes his young bride to this wilderness, the Indians burn his crops. Next year he and the militia are obliged to fight Brant with his Mohawks, Butler with his Tories, and St. Leger with his regulars. They fight the indecisive Battle of Oriskany, but give such a good account of themselves that St. Leger is unable to join Burgoyne as he moves southward. In this way, as Harold Frederic, too, pointed out, the battle determined the outcome of the Revolution.

In the Valley stops with the victory at Saratoga; *Drums Along the Mohawk* describes the remaining years of the war, in the course of which the whole region was so devastated that the people were obliged to live in forts and farm in posses. The particular virtue of this novel lies in making the ordinary people come to life. Their earthiness and their stubborn will may be overemphasized, but at least the odds are made clear against which they returned again and again to their dismantled homes. The narrative has little plot, and there are few strongly individualized characters, especially among the women, but the book does convey a distinct sense of a countryside full of human beings. The author's active imagination has generally triumphed over his careful documentation and has here produced an exemplary historical novel.

[2] In "How You Begin a Novel," *Atlantic Monthly,* Vol. CLVIII, No. 2 (August, 1936), 189–92, Mr. Edmonds tells in detail how he composed this novel.

It is but natural that Philadelphia should have served as setting for a number of novels of the Revolution, for it was "the cradle of liberty." Some of the greatest clashes of the war took place in this vicinity. *The Quaker Soldier* (1858), by John Richter Jones, deals with the period of British occupation of the city. The story itself falls into two parts, relating the career of a young Quaker, Hazlewood, who, despite the opposition of his tyrannous father, enlists against the British, and subsequently serves as a colonel in the Virginia army; and the career of young Hazlewood's villainous English cousin. The young Quaker, by gathering information for Washington, manages to serve his country best by helping to foil the Conway Cabal. Although this novel is written in too heroic a key to have much merit, its general plan directly anticipated that of one of the greatest of Revolutionary novels, *Hugh Wynne, Free Quaker* (1897), by Dr. S. Weir Mitchell.

One reason for the superiority of *Hugh Wynne* over most novels based on the Revolution is the care that was lavished on its preparation. For seven years the author studied his materials —the topography, the costumes, the speech, and other aspects of the period—in order to give his story the effect of actuality. Finding Watson's *Annals of Philadelphia* inaccurate, he supplemented it with Marshall's and Shoemaker's diaries. The hero tells his own story, devoting much space to his boyhood and youth in Philadelphia amid conflicting ideals of brotherhood and general strife. As in *The Quaker Soldier*, there is rivalry in love and in war between cousins. Following the Battle of Germantown, Hugh is taken captive, and the reader is given a vivid description of life in a British prison. Later, Hugh is attached to Lafayette and becomes a lieutenant colonel on Washington's staff. In connection with the "Mischianza," given in honor of Howe on his departure for England, the author sketches André and analyzes Arnold. Historical events are properly subordinated, as befits a memoir, to the account of the private fortunes of the hero; the atmosphere is always in keeping with that of Philadelphia gentlefolk. No novel before it quite so vividly dramatizes the ongoing of daily life amid the turmoil of war. None better illustrates that a historical novel is first of all a novel and only secondarily a history.

What a distinguished historian might make of the war was illustrated by Paul Leicester Ford in a costume romance which became at the turn of the century a best seller. *Janice Meredith* (1899) opens with the inertia of a New Jersey community just prior to the Revolution. Squire Meredith is a Tory who is in the predicament of having to look to the Whigs for protection, a fact which obliges the Meredith family to be friendly to both sides. Suspense is enhanced by the mystery which hangs over the status of their impertinent bond servant, Charles Fownes, with whom (as Colonel John Brereton) Janice is in love. Soon the action becomes so brisk that the heroine, who has many admirers in both armies, is rushed from one dramatic episode to another, and Colonel Brereton once narrowly escapes being hanged as a spy. After frequent misunderstandings, the capricious Janice and her patriot lover are married and receive the blessings of General and Mrs. Washington. Readable as this book is and true to the history and general atmosphere of the Revolution, especially its political intrigues, it is too highly romantic to be a novel of real distinction. Its chief value lies in its rapid survey of the outstanding events of the war.

A similarly comprehensive picture of the Revolution, but one centered upon the many-sided Franklin, appears in Irving Bacheller's novel *In the Days of Poor Richard* (1922). The action covers Franklin's richest period, the years of his multitudinous labors in the colonies, in England, and in France. The romance brings out the best qualities of the English and the American people; Marguerite Hare is the daughter of an English aristocrat but is imbued with rebel principles; Jack Irons personifies the American spirit, refusing the allurements of the British to tempt him to desert the cause of freedom. The author indicates much sympathy in England for the American cause, not only among men like Chatham, Burke, and Fox, but among the rank and file; on the other hand, he is not unmindful of divided feeling in the colonies. A very human Washington rides in and out of the story, and there are glimpses of Putnam, Hancock, Adams, Jefferson, and Patrick Henry, as well as of Arnold, Lord Howe, Stanhope, and General Herkimer. The climax occurs when Arnold almost succeeds in surrendering both West Point and General Washington. The author stresses Arnold's greed more than his resentment of unjust treatment. Franklin's wisdom and the humor of Solomon Binkus, another of Bacheller's rustic philosophers, enliven the tale—a tale rather ordinary in talent, yet offering a colorful and illuminating panorama of the men and events, the motives and forces, which established the nation.

The desperate winter of 1777–78 at Valley Forge has not greatly appealed to novelists. They like action, whereas that was a period of paralysis and exhaustion. The genteel school of writers did not care for it because its shabby aspects seemed too terrible to contemplate. Modern realists, however, are not averse to depicting scenes of privation, filth, gangrene, thievery, and licentiousness. They like to reverse conventional opinions of the past, including traditionally held opinions of men like Benedict Arnold and Tom Paine. To this school belongs Howard M. Fast, author of *Conceived in Liberty* (1939), *The Unvanquished* (1942), and *Citizen Tom Paine* (1943).

Fast, like Stephen Crane in *The Red Badge of Courage*, used the subjective method of narration in *Conceived in Liberty*. Alan Hale, a private from the Mohawk, goes to war for fun, but undergoes incredible hardships during the memorable winter at Valley Forge. Some eleven thousand troops, after retreating across New Jersey, are camped by the Schuylkill that December—a rabble of farmers, half-trained militia, and boys. The Commissariat mismanages, and Pennsylvania farmers profiteer by selling food to the British while refusing it to the starving rebels. Congress fails them, and jealousy, weather, and disease do the rest. Grumbling, foraging, fighting, and hysteria make up the daily round. In this darkest moment, it is the fortitude of Washington that keeps alive the flame of liberty. So severe is the ordeal that Alan deserts, but he is soon caught and severely flogged. He has a sordid love affair with a camp follower, but at length achieves self-respect in the Battle of Monmouth the following summer when, after Von Steuben has drilled the rabble, Wayne rallies the disordered forces of Lee. Hamilton, Wayne, Lafayette, and Lord Sterling are seen at close range. The book, written in a tense, emotional style, inclines toward the use of modern ideological sentiments.

The Unvanquished sets out to humanize George Washington with no more fictional additions than a little conversation here and there. In place of the lifeless Father-of-his-Country portrait offered by Cooper and his imitators, this novel pictures an indecisive Virginia fox-hunter developing gradually into a great military leader. In this respect, Washington is a happy contrast to the professional soldier Charles Lee, whom he venerates but who has ambitions of his own. Washington's genius in commanding a quarrelsome rabble is illustrated in the miraculous evacuation of New York, the retreat across Jersey, the second crossing of the Delaware, and the rout of the Hessians at Trenton. There are glimpses of Nathan Hale, Greene, Putnam, Knox, ragged Tom Paine, and Alexander Hamilton, but the picture that stands out is that of the lonely man whose wisdom takes the colonial forces through the dark night. With Congress divided in policy, his soldiers deserting in droves, and Lee's surrender, it is all Washington can do not to feel that the cause is lost. A reading of his diaries and letters suggests, however, a more resourceful and self-reliant Washington than the one here presented.

Fast's *Citizen Tom Paine* is a fictionized biography rather than a historical novel. The author dwells on the propagandist's idiosyncrasies to such an extent as to make Paine a swashbuckling roisterer, seen against a stormy background of appeasers, heroes, and profiteers. Fast writes sensitively, but trims his stories always to a proletarian thesis.

Nations do not like to face unpleasant facts. Even after the lapse of a century and a half, readers dislike to hear of the rascality of some of the patriot leaders or of the brutality of Tory-baiting mobs. Yet that is precisely the conception of the Revolution which the iconoclastic Kenneth Roberts displays in *Oliver Wiswell* (1940). This novel is, in short, an apologia for those colonials who remained loyal to the Crown. They were in the majority, and their battalions fought valiantly; but they had the misfortune to be caught between the regulars, who refused to consider them competent, and the rebels, who regarded them as traitors. Cornwallis and Rawdon were efficient generals, but were outranked and overmatched by Howe, whose conduct is still inexplicable, and by Clinton, who never took advice. Besides, in faraway London was the ineffectual Lord Germain, trying to direct the war in his own way.

The setting of *Oliver Wiswell* has enormous scope, extending from Bunker Hill to Yorktown, with scenes in London and Paris thrown in for good measure. Oliver is a Tory refugee living in Boston until that city is evacuated; then he becomes a British spy in advance of the Battle of Long Island; next his work as a secret agent takes him to London and Paris; finally, as a captain of dragoons under Arnold, he goes on an undercover mission to the Southern Colonies. In this connection Arnold is conceived of as more heroic than Carl Van Doren's *Secret History of the Revolution* proves him to have been. John Hancock, on the other hand, appears as a smuggler, Patrick Henry, a rabble rouser, and Samuel Adams, a snob, mistrustful of the Sons of Liberty. The British come in for their share of debunking also. The Battle of Charlestown (Bunker Hill) is bungled by both sides. The Battle of Long Island is a draw because of Howe's dalliance with Mrs. Loring. The London and Paris episodes show that the Whigs pretend sympathy for the rebels only because they regard this as a Tory war. Washington appears a general of questionable competence, and the smug Franklin a gull to spies, and worse. In the admirably dramatized siege of Ninety-Six the loyalists really show their mettle, but because the stupid British generals fail to protect and utilize the Tories, they lose the war and are forced to migrate en masse to Nova Scotia.

Oliver's star-crossed love affair is relegated to a minor position. Salley Leighton is barely mentioned, and is less memorable than Printer Buell or forthright Mrs. Belcher Byles, who also appear in minor roles. Oliver's preference of action over analysis of causes does not prevent him from disparaging the Continental side. As a loyalist he is not to be blamed for this, nor is his author. But in his preoccupation with the struggle of the city mobs against men of property, Roberts quite overlooks the importance of the revolt of the agrarians. He does not overstate the case for the Tories, however, and in that respect *Oliver Wiswell* is a refreshing book. For, at this late day it can be admitted that the rabble rousers brought the colonies to the very brink of social disaster, a tragedy from which they were fortunately saved by the intelligence of the men who framed the Constitution. Kenneth Roberts' passion for justice, as much as his vivid narrative talent, serves to make *Oliver Wiswell* a memorable historical novel.

3. *The Warfare Beyond the Alleghenies*

The principal events of the Revolution had been related in historical fiction by 1900. After that, writers sought less familiar episodes. Among these none had greater attraction than the warfare beyond the Alleghenies. The Northwest Territory, as it was called, was thrice-won, first from the Indians, then from the French, and finally from the English. The conflict with Pontiac has been described in an earlier chapter. The duel now was between George Rogers Clark and General

Hamilton, and the centers of interest were Kaskaskia and Vincennes. The outcome was the winning of the Wabash country for the new American government. In Ohio, however, the Indians caused further trouble, until subdued in 1789 by General Wayne in the Battle of Fallen Timbers. In the War of 1812 the duel between Tecumseh and William Henry Harrison brought these various uprisings to a conclusion in the Battle of Tippecanoe and the Battle of the Thames.

Mary Hartwell Catherwood, with the approval of the great historian Francis Parkman, whose findings she followed implicitly, first called attention to the riches of this material in three novelettes: *The Romance of Dollard* (1889), *The Story of Tonty* (1890), and *Old Kaskaskia* (1893). The first book related how Dollard and his devoted Hurons repulsed a horde of Iroquois in 1650. *The Story of Tonty* showed the frustration of La Salle and his lieutenant in their dreams of an empire extending from Fort Frontenac to the Illinois country in the sixteen eighties. *Old Kaskaskia* dealt with fur trading and politics in 1818, when Illinois was demanding statehood. Miss Catherwood did genuine research in her material, but her character-drawing was negligible and her romance too "sweetly refined" for modern taste.

Few single exploits have influenced more profoundly the course of our later history than George Rogers Clark's expedition from Kaskaskia through the Wabash country in 1778. One of the best-selling novels at the turn of the century, Maurice Thompson's *Alice of Old Vincennes* (1900), was based on this exploit. Clark does not enter the story until the last third of the book, but his personality pervades it, since Lieutenant Beverley, the hero, is under his command and expects him hourly. Alice Roussillon, reared by a Creole trader but daughter of an old Virginia family, it develops, is the spirited belle of the sleepy town of Creoles and Americans at the time it is taken by the British. General Hamilton, the "Hair Buyer," as he is dubbed for his sinister dealings with the Indians, pays unwelcome attentions to Alice, which induces Lieutenant Beverley to break parole and set out to seek reinforcements. He is overtaken by Long-Hair, a cruel but grateful Indian, who, mindful of past favors, sets him free. By the time Clark with less than two hundred men arrives, after marching through icy waters and subsisting on little food, the entire fort, tired of the overbearing Hamilton, is ready to capitulate.

In the narrative, history and romance are forwarded alternately by a racy style. Alice and Beverley conform to the pattern of romantic patricians whose only faults are those of headstrong youth in love. Of the other characters, Father Beret, the ubiquitous priest who looks after Alice, resembles a priest in Longfellow's *Evangeline*. Laconic Oncle Jazon recalls Natty Bumppo, without Natty's vindictiveness. Jazon's friend Simon Kenton, here as elsewhere, adds the right frontier touch. Clark appears as a blunt but kindly frontiersman, an example of heroic efficiency, taken from W. H. English's *Conquest of the Northwest and Life of General George Rogers Clark* (1896).

The epic quality of Clark's conquest of the Territory has been best brought out by Winston Churchill's *The Crossing* (1903). This book maintains that the triumph of the small band of Americans over the large force of Indians and British in this area decided the fate of a continent. The story begins in North Carolina during the early stages of the Revolution and concludes with the cession of New Orleans and the purchase of Louisiana in 1803. The hero, David Ritchie, relates his adventures from the time when as a forlorn waif he fled from Mrs. Temple, his aunt in Charleston, who despised him, until his marriage in New Orleans many years later. As a youth Davy accompanies Polly Ann and Tom McChesney on their honeymoon across the mountains into Kentucky. In the Wilderness Campaign he meets Sevier, Boone, and Kenton, and wins the friendship of Clark. As Clark's drummer boy Davy goes with the Long Knives that capture Kaskaskia, Cahokia, and Vincennes. After studying law in Virginia, Davy returns to Kentucky, where he meets Andrew Jackson. He now finds his admired Colonel Clark an embittered old man, neglected by the nation he has served so nobly, plotting with General Wilkinson and with the French of New Orleans to secure the West for France. The richness and romance of *The Crossing* are largely inherent in its materials. Its triple plot widened the scope of historical fiction to a notable extent, but the work lacks the unity and cohesion of Churchill's earlier novels. The style is spirited, the history accurate, and the story informed with moral earnestness, but the narrative lacks edge. The character-drawing is adequate, although David Ritchie is not a vital symbol for the outreaching young nation.

The extension of the fur trade north and west of the Ohio aroused the Indians of that area to fear the loss of their lands. When General St. Clair, the military governor, sought to restore order, his troops were ambushed on the upper Wabash in 1791. This disaster, the first under the new government, was retrieved three years later by Mad Anthony Wayne and his forces in the Battle of Fallen Timbers. These events were the subject of James B. Naylor's *In the Days of St. Clair* (1902) and *Under Mad Anthony's Banner* (1903), both trite and unconvincing accounts. *The Heritage* (1902), by Burton Stevenson, was a more plausible rendering of the events, despite its wooden characters; it was not until 1928 that the episode had its due in Thomas Boyd's *The Shadow of the Long Knives*. The impression left by this work is that the British government was hardly aware of a war beyond the Alleghenies until it was over. The protagonist, Angus McDermott, hardly knows it either, for during the quarter-century before the Revolution most of his days on the Ohio frontier are spent traveling among the Indians. Reared by the Senecas, he is well fitted to serve as intermediator between them and the British at Detroit. Later, domestic ties further this happy relationship. As one of Governor Dunmore's men, Angus rescues from the Shawnees a girl who yearns for the settlements; he marries her and tries to instill in her his own friendliness toward his foster brothers. However, when the Indians, grown restive over broken promises, are betrayed by the British and massacred by the Long Knives, Angus is bewildered and beaten by changing conditions. Not until Simon Kenton calls him a traitor does he realize that the British are gone, and not until his son George, prompted by his mother, joins Anthony Wayne's Legion does he fully comprehend there is a new order. The author has thoroughly absorbed his material and, although he has not fully blended fact and fiction, has written about it in a natural, unaffected style.

The young government had a second embarrassing situation to cope with. In the Genesee Valley in western New York, the Scotch-Irish were rebelling against Hamilton's excise law during the seventeen nineties. This rebellion was the subject of a lively novel, *Genesee Fever* (1942), by Carl Carmer. Nathan Hart, a young teacher, and a tippling companion, after siding with the farmers in the Whiskey Rebellion, continue the fight of the ragged democrats against an English aristocrat, Colonel Williamson, who, with Robert Morris and Aaron Burr, wishes to establish landed estates in the Valley. Other characters taken from history include Wayne, Red Jacket, Colonel Wadsworth, and Mary Jemison. The love story hardly lights up the factual history, but the picture of the motley assortment of settlers, still awkward in their newly acquired freedom, is carefully wrought with the background of fairs, horse racing, and political conflict, and is presented with deep and subtle understanding.

Wayne's conquest of Ohio was followed by a series of treaties by which the Indians ceded their valuable lands along the Wabash. When some of the tribes became alarmed over the relinquishment of their ancestral lands, they rallied around two able brothers, Tecumseh and "The Prophet," in the hope of putting a stop to the encroachments of the whites. The settlers, in their turn, believed that Tecumseh and his league of Indian tribes were being encouraged by British agents in Canada, and felt justified in calling on Governor Harrison to drive them out. It was Tecumseh's misfortune to be away rallying tribes in the south when his tribesmen lost the Battle of Tippe-canoe. Worse, driven into an alliance with the British, he was killed the following year, and his ally fled in disgrace.

James S. French, in a now almost forgotten novel, *Elks-watawa* (1836), took the position that our government brought on the conflict because it refused to recognize Tecumseh's con-tention that Indian lands were a common possession that could not be ceded by or purchased from individual tribes. French, who had hunted with the Shawnees, paid tribute to The Pro-phet, whom Harrison had lured into the disastrous Battle of Tippecanoe. The delineation of the Foreman family near Shawneetown was a deliberate protest against previous "bur-lesques of Western manners." The narrative paused from time to time to bring up history gleaned from Tanner's *Indian Nar-ratives*, Hunter's *Manners and Customs of Several Indian Tribes*, and Thatcher's *Indian Biography*. Unfortunately, two subsequent novels that dealt with Tecumseh and his tragic death, *Kabaosa* (1842) by Mrs. Anna Snelling, and *The Sign of the Prophet* by James B. Naylor, were no improvement on *Elkswatawa*, and to date there has been no adequate treatment of the subject.

Fenimore Cooper devoted the last of his wilderness stories, *Oak Openings* (1848), to the flight of a pioneer Michigan family from the pro-British Potawatomies after the fall of Mackinac, during the War of 1812. Most of the story is laid along the Kalamazoo River in southern Michigan, although before the whites escape their enemy, they circumnavigate the entire lower peninsula in a canoe. As the plot unfolds, Cooper relates in his characteristic style, with much moralizing, how the bee-hunter Boden assists the wife and the attractive sister of Waring, the drunkard, to escape the treachery of Scalping Pete and encirclement by the Indians. All in all, *Oak Openings* is a better picture of the primitive wilderness than some of

Cooper's other books, though its prolixity is hardly attractive to modern taste.

Modern readers who have been brought up on comprehensive "outlines," should find to their taste Louis Zara's panoramic treatment of the period from 1755 to 1835, *This Land Is Ours* (1940). Following a description of Braddock's defeat and of Pontiac's uprising, it includes, as the best feature of the narrative, Clark's conquest of Vincennes. The fiction begins with the hackneyed device of a hero taken captive in youth by the Indians and married into their tribe. When he again takes up his white life, he, like Chaucer's Knight, is present at every battle in the Territory. He is at Detroit to expose the conspiracy of Pontiac, at Kaskaskia when Clark takes it from the British, and with St. Clair when he is defeated by the Indians; he participates in Wayne's march to the battle at Fallen Timbers, and fights with Harrison at Tippecanoe. In rheumatic old age he sees the tribes under Black Hawk making vain efforts to hold their lands. All this, of course, is preposterous; but amid its tall adventures the novel conveys a strong sense of physical reality, the historical characters are alive, and both Indians and whites, though strongly possessive, act from mixed motives. Actually, none of them hold the land, for as this book ironically suggests, there is a blind destiny which impels men to move onward. *This Land Is Ours*, although it has a good grip on frontier psychology amid merrymaking as well as fighting, lacks the pioneering depth of less sprawling works, say, Carl Carmer's *Genesee Fever* or Conrad Richter's *The Trees*.

4. *The Naval Warfare of the Revolution and of the War of 1812*

One phase of the Revolution previously neglected by historians, the naval warfare, first appeared in historical fiction in Cooper's *The Pilot* (1823) and *The Red Rover*

(1827). Having spent some ten years before the mast, Cooper knew the sea as well as the forest. In *The Pilot* he meant to leave no doubt of his sailors' knowledge of seamanship as compared with the nautical data in landlubber Scott's *The Pirate*. By choosing the northeastern coast of England as the locale of his story, he had the twofold advantage of exploiting sea maneuvers, which *The Pirate* had lacked, and of complicating it with a love story in the "Abbey" of Colonel Howard, a self-expatriated American loyalist. The over-all plot pattern was not new: Cooper converted the land skirmishes of *The Spy* into chases between frigates and men-of-war; he found a parallel for the devotion of Harvey Birch in Long Tom's love for the sea; and he substituted for an incognito Washington an incognito John Paul Jones. Such economy of creative effort enabled Cooper to concentrate on the peculiar argot of the sea, in knowledge of which he was unsurpassed, and to lavish his expert attention upon the details of handling a ship. The pilot guiding his ship through the channel in the face of a biting northeaster presents a graphic little drama, as do the wreck of the *Ariel* and the frigate's escape from the British fleet. Long-drawn-out love scenes alternate with short episodes, as the Tory captain and Jones are captured, released, and recaptured; finally the elder Howard is wounded and consents to the marriage of his attractive ward to a Yankee. Throughout the story the personality of Jones, the privateer, is wrapped in mystery. He is a moody Highlander, a lover of freedom, something of a notoriety-seeker, but mercurial when action is needed. Although he gives his men a sense of quiet confidence, he hardly dominates the action. Reader affection goes instead to the resourceful old salt from Nantucket, Long Tom Coffin. *The Pilot* was to have many imitators, but none surpassed its exciting action on the sea.

The Red Rover, too, has its setting in the period of the Revolution, but its scene is entirely on water. During the lawlessness preceding the Revolution, American sailors still served on English men-of-war, and piracy was rampant, especially in the West Indies. The story opens with Lieutenant Ark sailing from Newport, on the lookout for the Red Rover, a freebooter. When his faulty ship sinks, his superstitious crew leave him with two passengers, Gertrude Grayson and her governess, Mrs. Wyllys, to be picked up by the Rover. The gentlemanly pirate explains that he deserted the Royal Navy because of his affection for the colonies. In a stirring sea fight, interrupted by a storm, Ark is taken and is about to be hanged as a British spy, when he is disclosed to be the long-lost son of Mrs. Wyllys. The Rover now frees his prisoners, burns his ship, and disappears. Twenty years after the war he comes to the home of Ark and Gertrude, and on his deathbed discloses that he is Mrs. Wyllys' brother and that he has given his best years to the patriot cause.

John Paul Jones figures prominently in Herman Melville's one historical novel, *Israel Potter* (1855). This book, based on an anonymous biography, relates the story of a Yankee youth who, after being captured at Bunker Hill, is taken as prisoner from an American cruiser to England and, after making his escape, engages there in rebel activities. In time his travels take him to Paris, where he meets Benjamin Franklin, Horne Tooke, and John Paul Jones. He assists Jones in the *Bonhomme Richard's* thrilling defeat of the *Serapis*. Returning to England, Potter associates with Ethan Allen, now in exile after his disastrous expedition against Montreal. Forty-five years later Potter returns to America, applies for a pension, but is refused and dies in poverty. The story has possibilities, as shown in Israel's meeting the King and in the interlude with Franklin, but Melville seems not to have been in a mood to develop them.

One of the most popular novels of the Revolution, Winston Churchill's *Richard Carvel* (1899), was largely about sea warfare. The author, as a graduate of the Naval Academy, had been indoctrinated with the legendary beginnings of the United States Navy. In this story, Richard, the rebel grandson of a truculent Maryland Tory, relates in the idiom of the period how he was kidnapped through a villainous uncle who desired the youth's estate, and was put aboard a slaver. After being rescued by John Paul Jones, Richard goes to England, where he hopes to see his old Maryland playmate, Dolly Manners; but her father refuses him admittance, his drafts are not honored, and he and Jones are thrown into debtors' prison. Eventually Dolly repels her suitor, the Duke of Chartersea, and liberates the two men. Jones returns to America immediately, while Richard lingers in the coffeehouses of Georgian London. There he meets Horace Walpole, David Garrick, and Charles Fox, and learns how political winds are blowing before returning to America. Soon after that, he joins his old friend Jones and has the misfortune to be wounded in the famous encounter with the *Serapis*. He is again brought to England and nursed to health by Dolly, is smuggled out of the country by Fox, regains his American estate, and eventually marries Dolly.

Although much of the action of the war is omitted from *Richard Carvel*, the feeling of the time is accurately and fully recorded. Some parts of the plot are patterned after *Henry Esmond*, and the London episodes, as well as the idiom, are indebted to Boswell's *Life of Johnson*. Churchill's portrait of Jones, like Cooper's, is of a lover of fame and fine apparel, but Churchill's is a much more human picture. By rewriting the story five times, the author managed to weave history neatly into his pattern of fiction. The chief shortcoming of this patriotic story is that it has been shaped by the demands of romance rather than by the issues of the war, but it is, nevertheless, well worth reading.

Jones is not the hero of Sarah Orne Jewett's *The Tory Lover* (1901), although as in *Richard Carvel* he is the most dynamic character in the story. He agrees to take Roger Wallingford as a lieutenant on the *Ranger* to France where he expects to fit out a warship. After getting no aid from the patriarchal Franklin in Paris, Jones determines to harry the coasts of England. At Whitehaven he is betrayed by a rival for the hand of Mary Hamilton, and when he sees that his hopes with Mary are futile, he quietly slips away to the *Ranger*. Unfortunately, this story of the lonely and disillusioned lover shows little grasp of historical background. The war is regarded as a fight against English commercial policy, rather than against England herself.

A bolder recreation of the life and times of the Father of the American Navy appears in Clements Ripley's *Clear for Action* (1940) and in Edward Ellsberg's *Captain Paul* (1941). Ripley's terse novel includes backgrounds of French court life, Virginia estates, and naval intrigues, figuring Franklin, Washington, Jefferson, Henry, and others. It barely mentions Jones's amorous adventures as it concentrates on his turbulent military decade. It pictures him a whimsical sea raider, ready to fight for any cause, and ready to pay his men out of his own pocket. It concludes with his immortal words during the clash with the *Serapis*: "Struck my colors? I've just begun to fight!"

Commander Ellsberg's dynamic narrative of the beginnings of the American navy is a story of complacent bungling and treachery, as much as of high endeavor. It shows how Jefferson's embargo strangled commerce for fear of embroilment with Europe. Jones, a dashing figure when luck is with him, mingles with the Virginia gentry, but is jilted by Dorothy Dandridge, a Tory. After his battles with the *Drake* and the *Serapis*—graphically described by the seaman author—even the women of the court in Paris are mad about him. To the protagonist, who tells the story, Jones is a born leader. He is not merely an alert and resourceful captain, but serves his adopted country despite the jealousy and the incompetence of his superiors. The author, by dint of tense description and virile narrative, has made a hackneyed subject come magnificently alive. None of these authors makes clear, however, why mishaps constantly pursued Jones and why insubordination persistently occurred on the fiery Scot's ships. He had a violent antagonism to the caste system in the British navy, but also inclined to nurse personal grievances. Doubtless this fascinating figure will always be shrouded in something of a mystery.

F. Van Wyck Mason, who began as a writer of mystery and adventure stories, has written four lusty historical novels on the naval warfare of the Revolution. *Three Harbours* (1938) is based on events during 1774–75 as they affected Norfolk, Boston, and Bermuda; *Stars on the Sea* (1940) takes up the next two years of our infant navy, and ranges from Newport to Charleston and the Bahamas; *Rivers of Glory* (1942) begins in Boston, two years after the evacuation, and advances the action to Tory New York, Jamaica, and Savannah. *Eagle in the Sky* (1948) relates the plight of three young surgeons during the last two years of the war.

Each of these novels has a different set of characters, although there is continuity both historically and geographically, and in the fact that the major figures in one appear as minor characters in the next. *Three Harbours* may be considered typical of Mason's art. It centers its interest in the Ashton family, Norfolk traders, who feel they have little to gain by a war. While Rob Ashton tries to keep neutral, his brother David smuggles contraband for the Boston colonials into Rob's ship. David is captured and, when set free, fights at Breed's Hill, in one of the finest scenes in the book. Rob takes refuge with a cousin in Bermuda, and now willingly smuggles arms to the Revolutionary troops in Philadelphia. Two women, Andrea Grenville, a social butterfly in London who loses her fortune and becomes a governess, and Kate Tryon, a blonde tavern wench, who both love David, enliven the story and suggest that it was evidently designed for the jaded reader of romance.

Of the sequels, *Stars on the Sea* is a rousing companion story of privateering, *Rivers of Glory* has a similarly dizzying succession of adventures along the Atlantic coast, and *Eagle in the Sky*, full-bodied romance though it is, somehow fails to endow its research with meaning. Ostentatious period pieces they are, full of subplots and violence, but the history is slight.

During the period between the Revolution and the War of 1812 military matters were in the hands of incompetents, with the result that they deteriorated badly. Despite the brave soldiers, pompous leadership was responsible for the horrible massacre at Fort Mims and the shameful surrender of Detroit by regular army officers. The ignominious defeat at Bladensburg was due to a lack of army discipline. But for Jackson's rousing victory at New Orleans, the exploits at sea, and the weariness of the Britons over the war, it would have been a tragic era for the young Republic.

The impressment of American seamen which led to the War of 1812 has been dealt with in Irving Bacheller's *D'ri and I* (1901). In the guise of a memoir, Colonel Ramon Bell, U.S.A., relates his experiences in company with D'ri, his father's hired man, from the time in 1803 when they leave Vermont for the West until the close of the war. D'ri, with his shrewd, laconic observations, is the chief contribution of the book. The two comrades, Bell and D'ri, a modern Damon and Pythias, float down the St. Lawrence on a raft and narrowly escape capture and impressment by the British. Later, aboard Perry's flagship, Bell intimately describes the Battle of Lake Erie. The novel comes to a stirring close as the troops are being reviewed by President Monroe.

The naval action on Lake Erie is related with color and spirit in Robert S. Harper's *Trumpet in the Wilderness* (1940). The protagonist, Jubal Johnson, joins an Ohio regiment of volunteers, is present at General Hull's disgraceful surrender of Detroit to General Brock, and participates with Commodore Perry in the Battle of Lake Erie. His romance with the daughter of a frontier doctor is properly subordinated to some excellent pictures of frontier life in northwestern Ohio.

The best sea tales laid in the period of the War of 1812 are *The "Lively Lady"* (1931) and *Captain Caution* (1934), by

Kenneth Roberts. The story of the *Lively Lady*, a sloop captained by Richard Nason, a son of the hero of *Arundel*, is mainly one of privateering and imprisonment, bound together by a slender thread of romance. Richard slips out before the embargo is put into effect and harries British shipping on the Atlantic. As he sails for Cadiz, he loses some prizes, but wins others before he is finally captured and incarcerated in the darkest dungeon of Dartmoor prison. With Emily's assistance he escapes, but is recaptured and put into the Black Hole. Here he undergoes the hardship and torture of the infamous massacre which took the lives of some seventeen hundred American naval prisoners. The author's strong feeling for liberty, couched in vigorous and colorful prose, makes this a vivid story.

In *Captain Caution*, Daniel Marvin, another mariner from Arundel, Maine, is returning from China in the *Olive Branch*, an armed merchant ship, when the bark is captured by the British. Captain Dorman is promptly killed and the men are impressed into the British service. By surrendering the craft, Dan incurs the scorn of the captain's headstrong daughter, Corunna. The rest of the story is devoted to his attempt to win back the *Olive Branch* and Corunna against the wiles of the lustful Argendeau and the American slaver Slade. The characters are eccentric but are ably delineated, and, while plot and characterization are restricted in scope, the action and suspense are excellent. The portrait of the one historical figure introduced, Talleyrand, is accurate.

The foreign policy of President Monroe, with its attempt at securing hemispheric solidarity, is the theme that underlies *Call the New World* (1941) by John E. Jennings. During the War of 1812, Peter Brooke, a likable soldier of fortune, is court-martialed because an order miscarries. He then joins in the wars of liberation in Venezuela, Chile, and Peru. The action begins with the Battle of Bladensburg, a muddled enterprise which did little to hamper the British from burning Washington or laying siege to Baltimore. After Peter's dismissal, he fights a duel and quarrels with Judith Mason. Generally embittered, he accepts a captaincy in Bolívar's army and later crosses the Andean passes to help liberate Chile. His passion for freedom is rewarded by a diplomatic commission from the Peruvian government asking him to persuade London to recognize the South American republics. The twenty crowded years of military and diplomatic history here given offer a rich canvas of romantic background for the Monroe Doctrine.

5. The Southern Colonies

The last phase of the Revolution was fought in the Southern Colonies. During these closing years, Gates was at Savannah and Charleston, and denizens of the cypress swamps under Marion and Sumter fought against the Tories under Tarleton. After the loss of Camden, Greene took command and hastened the end. The battles of Kings Mountain, Cowpens, and Guilford Court House came in rapid succession, and the war ended with the surrender of Cornwallis at Yorktown.

James Boyd's *Drums* (1925) is an excellent novel to connect the warfare on the sea with the events of the Revolution in the Southern Colonies. It is laid in North Carolina and is related as well to the career of John Paul Jones. The Frasers, although they live in a cabin among the hills, belong to the tidewater gentry. They send their son John to Edenton to study, but in the polite society of Eve Tennant, daughter of a British captain, he mainly acquires the habits of a gentleman. North Carolina is loyal to the King, although there is an occasional upsurging of democracy as economic interests divide the people. When the war breaks out, the father, expecting the British to win, sends John to England. There he meets again the Tennants, but he sees also Charles Fox and the raffish and gallant sea-fighter John Paul Jones. He goes with Jones on his marauding trips in the *Ranger* and the *Bonhomme Richard*, and becomes a fervent patriot. The high point of the book is the graphic description of the battle with the *Serapis*. In this encounter, Fraser's arm is shattered by a bullet and he goes home to recover. Later, he joins Morgan's troops and sees several engagements against Tarleton in North Carolina. When he is again wounded, he has to be invalided home, but he is happy in the love of his childhood sweetheart Sally. In this work the atmosphere of a precarious decade in the national history is treated with true imagination. The exciting adventures carry their burden of research lightly; incidents are subordinated to competent characterization; the hero, despite the wealth of detail, is always in focus; the everyday hopes and tribulations of the common people are fully realized—*Drums* is social history in the best sense.

The Albermarle district of North Carolina has been the subject of five very good novels by Inglis Fletcher. *Roanoke Hundred* (1948), a tale of adventure that goes back to the founding of the first English settlement in the New World, begins the series. It includes such Elizabethan sea dogs as Walter Raleigh, Philip Sidney, Richard Hakluyt, Francis Drake, and the valiant hero, Richard Grenville.

Four of the novels have their setting in the eighteenth century. *Men of Albemarle* (1942) depicts the fight for gubernatorial power among Hyde, Glover, and Cary from 1710 to 1712. Confusion reigns until a calm-minded official recalls to the small society on the village green the imperativeness of our common law. *Lusty Wind for Carolina* (1944) deals with the attempts of the Huguenot settlers on Cape Fear to ward off the buccaneers that harassed the coast after the Treaty of Utrecht.

Raleigh's Eden (1940), spanning the period of the Revolution as it does, is representative of the series. It shows that although the feudal society of Albemarle Sound was closer to England than to the Northern Colonies, there was class dissension within the province itself. Some saw a need for breaking with the mother country and drew up the Mecklenburg Declaration, the first organized demand for American independence. This narrative, which extends to Cornwallis' surrender, has the common fault of overcrowding. Alongside unusually well-drawn minor characters—pirates and Highlanders, planters and slaves, Whigs and Tories—there clamor for the reader's attention historical figures like John Paul Jones, General Greene, Flora Macdonald, Hewes, Iredell, Tarleton, and Cornwallis. The story centers on Adam Rutledge, wealthy slave-owner, who is indifferent to politics until his back-country neighbors groan under their burden of taxes and persuade him to represent them in the provincial assembly. Later, he takes his stand with Washington at Valley Forge and against Cornwallis. His querulous wife Sara is no match for Mary Warden in vying for his love, even though out of sheer jealousy Sara would ensnare him with the Moslem princess and the slave Agizi. The story, while colorful, is dignified; it reads better as history, however, than as fiction.

Toil of the Brave (1946) slightly overlaps *Raleigh's Eden* in time, as it begins in 1779 and covers the Southern campaign of the Revolution. After depicting the leisurely life of country families, their sports, parties, and balls, and an occasional duel, not to mention spy activities, the colorful pages come to an effective climax in the Battle of Kings Mountain. Mrs. Fletcher's novels, compounded of romance and gallantry, and shrewdly laced with derring-do, are full, vividly evocative pictures of their times.

The earliest and most extensive treatment of the Revolution in the South was by William Gilmore Simms. Conceiving of historical romance as the modern equivalent of the ancient epic, Simms turned to the heroic age of his native South Carolina and wrote a series of seven Revolutionary romances with the "Swamp Fox," Francis Marion, as the Agamemnon of its wars. The first of the series, *The Partisan* (1835), begins at the lowest ebb of Carolina's fortunes, the fall of Charleston during the spring of 1780, and ends with the temporary defeat of Gates by Cornwallis at Camden. At the time the Tories under Tarleton are patrolling the highways and annoying the countryside around Dorchester. The Whigs (Partisans) in retaliation are harrying the British by seizing supplies, cutting off foraging parties, and engaging in ambush fighting. The principal action of the tale centers around Major Robert Singleton, patriot leader. Singleton is helping a young provincial to win the innkeeper's daughter from a British officer, while his own affair with his patrician cousin, Katherine Walton, encounters opposition from a British major. As the war progresses, Singleton, accompanied by the gourmand Porgy and others, goes with Marion to assist Gates and De Kalb. Gates, who is an opportunist, rebuffs the crude swamp-fighters and so badly misdirects the Battle of Camden that he is defeated.

Several of the characters met in *The Partisan* reappear in *Mellichampe* (1836), which describes the conflict between Marion and Tarleton in the low country from the time of Gates's defeat to Greene's taking over the command. The real sequel to *The Partisan*, however, is *Katherine Walton* (1851), a romance of manners set in Charleston under British rule. Balfour, the British commandant, confiscates the elder Walton's estate and tries to bring Katherine, a typical gentlewoman of the times, to terms by threatening to hang her father. He succeeds so far in foiling Singleton as to exact her promise to marry, but when he bungles the affair, Katherine is freed from her promise.

The Forayers (1855) and *Eutaw* (1856) continue this history with new personal complications. The Tory Inglehardt has the Travises under his thumb, which abundantly worries Bertha's rebel lover, Sinclair. Besides, the house of Sinclair's Tory father is raided by Inglehardt's henchman, Hellfire Dick, who with his outlaw band abducts Bertha Travis. Sinclair, with the aid of Hurricane Nell, is able to rescue his beloved after the Battle of Eutaw Springs, but Inglehardt kills her father. Marion, Greene, Gates, Lee, and Horry are introduced in the accompanying scenes of fratricidal bushfighting. Although these battles were not decisive, they helped break the power of the British in Carolina.

In *The Scout*, originally called *The Kinsmen* (1841), two half brothers, Whig and Tory, are involved in a feud over a highborn damsel at a moment when the patriot cause is at a low ebb. The siege of Ninety-Six is the chief historical episode, and it, together with the outrages, arson, and murder by partisans and irresponsible banditti, is well authenticated; but the novel contributes little to the advance of the series. The last of these romances, *Woodcraft*, originally named *The Sword and the Distaff* (1853), has several well-drawn characters in its double plot. The "sword" part shows Greene triumphantly entering Charleston at the close of the Revolution, but ungraciously patronizing the Swamp Fox and his shabby partisans in the victory procession. In the "distaff" part, Porgy, with his scout Frampton, returns from the wars with a sad heart. He is heavily in debt, largely because of advantages taken by his overseer in selling slaves during his absence. Also, he makes love to two widows at the same time, and, like his prototype Falstaff in *The Merry Wives of Windsor*, is jilted by both; but easygoing as he is, he resolves not to be nettled by these rebuffs.

Simms's plots are broken up to a great extent by minor incidents. Porgy lends some unity to the various fictional parts, as Marion does to the historical parts. The background of Carolina history and local tradition, which Simms knew thoroughly, further helps to hold the loosely constructed fiction together. For his romance, Simms borrowed from Scott and Cooper stock figures and incidents that would enhance the interest, making such adaptations to locale as seemed necessary. Since he tended naturally to multiply episodes of horror, it was salutary for his art that his facile fancy was subjected to the organized ground plan of fact afforded by history. Even so, his stories give the effect of having been written in unrelated moods; also they lean heavily on coincidence. They are the work of a true raconteur, however, and picture the intricate play of motives in the bush warfare which finally proved too much for the British. No one else has written so intimately of the colorful denizens of the Southern swamps and their contribution to American independence as has William Gilmore Simms.

In the year of *The Partisan* there appeared a much better unified novel on the Southern campaign, John Pendleton Kennedy's *Horse-Shoe Robinson* (1835). The urbane Baltimorean had had his ideas of romance and chivalry nurtured in the skirmish at Bladensburg, and later served with national distinction as a Whig. He was an intimate of Irving and most of the literary men of his day. *Horse-Shoe Robinson* opens with Gates taking command of the army against Cornwallis and ends dramatically with the triumph of the yeomanry at Kings Mountain. Kennedy introduces, in the manner of Scott, such figures as the conservatively neutral lord of the manor, Mr. Lindsay; his rebel daughter, the victim of a scheming loyalist; British officers harried by Marion and Sumter, who dash out of woodland retreats; Tarleton and his guerrillas, thieving and burning; a rustic maiden and her lover; and aged noncombatants facing ruin. Kennedy's own contribution is the resourceful blacksmith, the titular hero. Albert Butler, Mildred Lindsay's lover, is taken captive early in the story and thus forfeits a hero's attention. Horse-Shoe, with right good will and mother wit, then squires the distressed heroine through the tightening net of a Tory admirer and restores her at last to her beloved in the exciting affray at Kings Mountain. Horse-Shoe, like Leatherstocking, is a thoroughly indigenous character and, though less poetical than his prototype, is far more companionable, good-humored, and patriotic. He is one of the better-drawn characters in our fiction. The chief historical value of the book lies in its vivid picture of guerrilla warfare and in its excellent description of the Battle of Kings Mountain.

The early aftermath of the Revolution is the subject of *Balisand* (1924) by Joseph Hergesheimer. The story is laid in tidewater Virginia, between 1782 and 1801, when the Federals receded into the background and the Jeffersonians came to the fore. The central figure is Richard Bale, owner of Balisand estate, who has always been an ardent Federalist and who, when he is swept aside by the new forces of democracy, finds he cannot change. At a house party to celebrate the engagement of his Jeffersonian friend, Gawin Todd, to Lavinia Roderick, the fiancée and Richard fall in love. He is challenged by Gawin to a duel, but before it can be fought, Lavinia dies from an accident. In the next sixteen years—years filled with politics, drinking, gambling, racing, and cockfighting—Richard wins Lucia Matthews from Todd and becomes the father of three daughters. Then he and Gawin meet again in a tavern and renew their quarrel over Lavinia and politics, with the result that they have their duel and both men fall. The atmosphere of the changing times is well brought out in the gay assemblies as well as in the personal situations and in the frequent references to Washington, Adams, Jefferson, and Hamilton. The stubborn and petulant Bale appears rather saturnine in the clash of the Federal minority with the increasing numbers of Jeffersonians, but his struggle with destiny has something of Elizabethan romantic magnificence also, as episode and atmosphere blend splendidly in this late eighteenth century pageant.

The conflict between French and English sympathies during Washington's administration is the background of *The Red City* (1907) by S. Weir Mitchell. The hero is a French *émigré*, René, Vicomte de Corval, who, after the father was murdered in the French Revolution, came to Philadelphia with his mother. The irony of social contrast is well brought out when the Vicomtesse objects to her son's marriage to a Quaker gentlewoman. René soon finds opportunity to avenge his father's death when Carteaux, the Jacobin responsible for the murder, arrives as the secretary of Citizen Genêt. In the duel in which they engage, René is wounded, but he achieves satis-faction later when in a second duel he shoots his man. Carteaux's death brings on international complications, since the French-man was the bearer of important dispatches—complications that involve Edmund Randolph, the secretary of state. The author of *Hugh Wynne* introduces that well-known character again and adds a most human picture of Washington the statesman. The full background is re-created from diaries with Mitchell's usual skill.

The conflict between Jeffersonians and Hamiltonians in the young nation has best been brought out in Elizabeth Page's *The Tree of Liberty* (1939). An appended bibliography of 240-odd items testifies to the author's thorough research before she set out on her five-year period of writing the story. The principal setting is Virginia, and the action extends from the time of Braddock's defeat in 1755, when the French still oc-cupied the Ohio Valley, through the period of Jefferson's ad-ministration to his re-election in 1804. The story concentrates on several generations in the fortunes of the Howard family. Matthew Howard, a Blue Ridge frontiersman and rugged in-dividualist, argues every democratic point with Jane Peyton, his planter wife from the tidewater. She thinks the frontier rude and horrible. Jefferson, the commoner, is to her no less than a renegade. Naturally, their two sons have divergent poli-tical leanings, James becoming an aide to Hamilton and later the owner of cotton mills, and Peyton, like his father, running afoul the law—in his case, the Sedition Law. One of Peyton's sons is lost in fighting the Barbary pirates; the other carves out a home in the Ohio Valley. The daughter Mary weds an ordi-nary farmer, but for compensation her daughter marries an aristocratic cousin, and thus reunites the family.

The political conflict presented in *The Tree of Liberty* brings glimpses of most of the important characters of the period—Washington, Adams, Jefferson, Hamilton, Madison, Monroe, Burr, Gallatin, Marshall, and Patrick Henry. The narrative includes such dramatic episodes as Dunmore's inciting the Indians, Patrick Henry's rebel-rousing speech, the signing of the Declaration, the fighting at Trenton and Saratoga, the wrangling over the Constitution, the XYZ Affair, the Whiskey Rebellion, the organization of Jacobin clubs, and Burr's plot for federal expansion. It also describes the yellow fever epidemic in Philadelphia, the fitfulness of early transportation, the terrorizing of seamen by pirates, Shays's farm riots, jealousies over trade barriers, and the dawning of the industrial revolution.

In particular this book brings out the significant issues of the day—liberty versus order, progress versus tradition. The author is an admirer of Thomas Jefferson, of whom she gives an unsurpassed picture. He dominates with his ingratiating manner every scene in which he appears. Though a democratic liberal, Miss Page does not pass over the excesses to which democracy is exposed. The Revolution, she makes clear, was won by a relatively small group of radicals. Miss Page's thorough understanding of that complicated half-century sets *The Tree of Liberty* apart, and makes it, despite crowded scenes and somewhat ubiquitous stock types, a graceful, straightforward account, a thoroughly informed, unsentimental historical novel of a high order.

Another soundly informed novel laid in the stirring era of our early independence is *Holdfast Gaines* (1946), by Odell Shepard, prize-winning biographer, and his son Willard Shepard. This novel begins in the last years of the Revolution, and, after an interim packed with many historical episodes, battles, massacres, and seafights, ends shortly after the War of 1812. It includes in its panoramic sweep the immense territory extending from the Atlantic seaboard to the Mississippi and the Gulf Coast. Holdfast Gaines, the Mohegan giant who has been reared by whites, is ideally fitted for his self-appointed role as mediator between reds and whites, since he combines in himself the mellowing culture of an old civilization and the religious bent of primitive man. He fails in his peace efforts, but his many movements serve to bring out the interplay of good and evil during those exciting times.

Shocked by General Arnold's massacre of his people at Fort Griswold, Holdfast leaves his lovely foster sister Rebecca behind, leads some of his tribe to Western Waters in search of independence, trades fur on the Mississippi, shares fortunes with the firebrand Andy Jackson, goes to the Pacific Coast with Lewis and Clark, tracks down a conspiracy between American and British officers, matches oratory with the vengeful Tecumseh, and witnesses the terrible massacre at Fort Mims. Later, he ships on a privateer which delays, in the far Azores, a part of the British squadron sent to take New Orleans. He hurries back, fights the mysterious villain "The Knife" in a Natchez tavern, meets Lafitte, and assists his friend Jackson in the Battle of New Orleans.

Incredible as this saga may seem, it skillfully evokes events and interprets them. It is alive with individuals like Lieutenant Reid and his son Sam, who designed the present American flag; lusty Russell Bean, backwoods rifle maker and dandy; Jake McNab, who killed for red flannel underwear; Parson Blandison, aging gambler, who is fleeing from a shady past; Andy Jackson, cockfighter, duelist, and general; and many others, including Tecumseh, Jefferson, Nathan Hale, Lewis, and Clark. There are dramatic scenes, notably the Indian council at which Holdfast argues with Tecumseh, the massacre at Fort Mims, and the duel in the Natchez tavern. So far as love is concerned, it is a long gamble whether Rebecca or the "Beloved Woman" of the Choctaws is to be the one woman in the hero's life; but the reader hardly minds, since he is offered many scenes of rousing action. Although a good deal of dialect spots the narrative, and antiquarian details threaten it, the story not only marches on, but frequently offers glints of poetry. *Holdfast Gaines* is a rewarding fantasy on many early themes.

6. *Shays's Rebellion*

At the conclusion of the Revolution there occurred an uprising in west-central Massachusetts known as Shays's Rebellion. This insurrection developed in protest against a variety of grievances of which the sorest was the heavy taxes inflicted by a high protective tariff. Ralph I. Lockwood wrote early an amusing story, *The Insurgents* (1835), about the former Revolutionary captain and his "broomstick army." He followed Bradford's account of the uprising rather closely and was not too successful in interweaving with it a romance between members of the opposing Talbots and Eustaces. His discussions of the town meeting, the militia, and other local groups were seasoned with Yankee dialect, rather better than John Neal's, and with an anecdotal style that had something of Paulding's satiric vigor. From the time of this account the episode lay fallow until 1879, when Edward Bellamy, after intensive research, treated it with due reference to social contrast in *The Duke of Stockbridge*. Although the collectivist author of *Looking Backward* sympathized with the oppressed farmers, he kept a fair balance between the insurrectionists and the representatives of the law. *The Duke of Stockbridge*, though somewhat bleak in style, was finely imagined and true to the facts.

William Degenhard has recently dealt exhaustively with the subject in *The Regulators* (1943), endowing it with the sweep of a minor classic. In his lively account the period seethes with all the ancient grudges which the Revolution brought into the open and left unsolved. Shays's Rebellion, as he sees it, was a protest against foreclosures—a popular uprising which stopped most of the courts from sitting and challenged the stiff-necked Boston government before being subdued by troops from the arsenal at Springfield. Unfortunately, the vocabulary of the participant who tells the story is drawn from an age of gasoline motors, night clubs, and western movies.

It is apparent from the illustrations above that the ramifications of the Revolution have been given varied and sustained attention by writers of fiction. Early novelists saw the Revolution purely as a military incident and busied themselves with a résumé of its strategy and a glorification of its heroes. Recent writers have reconstructed its social and economic atmosphere and have given the civilian element greater attention. Because its events are fairly well known to readers, novelists have not dared to take so many liberties with it as with more obscure subjects. Some recent novelists have chosen episodes of unsettled fact rather than those associated with great names. In some instances the complications of a later day have been imposed on the plot; that is, modern concepts of which the forefathers were unaware have been read into the struggle. Nevertheless, greater perspective has developed with the passing years. Common folk have been given more attention. The seamier aspects, formerly avoided, have come into view. In fact, a deliberately revisionist attitude has developed in regard to complex figures like Benedict Arnold, George Rogers Clark, Thomas Jefferson, Robert Rogers, John Paul Jones, Tom Paine, and George Washington. The sense of bewilderment over changing conditions now enters the register, and the bungling on both sides of the conflict has been exposed from a smart journalistic angle. This penetration into the life of the times that tried men's souls has produced a number of novels of the Revolution that are truly works of art.

III. The Westward Movement

T HE EPIC SUBJECT in American history has been without question the winning of the West. Westward migration had, of course, been going on ever since the founding of the colonies; but in this chapter the phrase is applied to the great movement toward the west which took place between the Revolution and the Civil War.

Several distinct phases of this larger movement have appealed to the imagination of novelists. In the latter half of the eighteenth century, before the young Republic was established, Daniel Boone blazed a trail into the Kentucky wilderness, and other restless spirits followed.[1] But the Indians stubbornly held on to their lands, and Kentucky and Tennessee became in popular idiom "the dark and bloody ground." The migration into the Northwest Territory opened under more fortunate auspices. Those pioneers, coming upon the scene after the Ordinance of 1787, were able to invoke the might of the new federal government in their collision with the aborigines. Such conflicts as the Battle of Tippecanoe and the Dearborn massacre were soon over, and no further opposition was encountered by settlers of the Middle Border than the abortive Black Hawk War.

After Jefferson, bargaining with France for New Orleans, obtained Louisiana through the caprice of Napoleon, he sent Lewis and Clark to explore the frontier beyond the Rockies, with the result that settlers soon flocked into that vast domain.

[1] Robert L. Kincaid's *The Wilderness Road* (1947) describes the history of this adventure for the "American Trails Series." John Bakeless' *Daniel Boone* (1939) is authoritative.

Meanwhile the Kentucky frontier was expanded into the Southwest, partly through Burr's and Wilkinson's scheme for personal aggrandizement, partly through efforts to extend slave territory. The struggle over Texas and the Mexican War quickly followed. Expansionist schemes, at least in part related to the slavery issue, also took place in the Far West. Without pause, then, the westward stream flowed over the entire Northwest and Southwest. Hunters and trappers were succeeded by farmers, and they in turn were followed by land speculators and town builders. In a short time the various phases of the westward movement had their recorders in fiction.

1. *The Kentucky Frontier*

During the early years of the Republic much attention centered on Kentucky. Daniel Boone's successive removals from North Carolina to Kentucky and then to the Missouri frontier synchronized with the course of manifest destiny. Boone was in imaginative literature the acknowledged prototype of Cooper's Leatherstocking, and the forerunner of similar romantic heroes in later fiction. Washington Irving, Cooper's chief rival in early American fiction, came in person by way of Kentucky to the Indian territory (Oklahoma) and recorded his experiences in *A Tour on the Prairies* (1832).

In that very year, Irving's friend, James K. Paulding, wrote a first novel of the Kentucky wilderness, *Westward Ho!* based on Timothy Flint's *Recollections of the Last Ten Years.* This novel, one of the best descriptions of frontier Kentucky, is a romantic account of a prodigal Virginian who with his family migrates shortly after the Revolution to Kentucky. On their journey, by way of Pittsburgh, and down the Ohio on a broadhorn, they are companioned by one of Boone's men, a grandiloquent frontiersman who speaks the racy idiom of the West. The Indian, Black Warrior, is rather wooden; but the

Negroes, who share the author's humorous comments on frontier orators, fanatic preachers, and political gossips, are better drawn. The principal episode is the daughter's love for an introspective young man whom she nurses through a period of religious insanity. Too much clinical discussion hampers the course of the narrative—a failure common to several others of Paulding's novels.

James Hall's *Harpe's Head* (1833) resembles Paulding's story only in outline and is a livelier, if less amusing, tale. In this picaresque romance, a late eighteenth century gang of ruffians, headed by Harpe, waylay the heiress Virginia Pendleton, who, with her cousin George Lee, is on her way from Virginia to an uncle in Kentucky. After several narrow escapes from the gang, and from roving bands of Indians, Virginia marries young Lyttleton Fennimore, who twice saves her life while on his way to General Wayne in Ohio. The author personally collected his frontier material, and introduced into the narrative, without satisfactorily blending romance and realism, such local elements as a barbecue, a deer hunt, a coon hunt, a tussle, and various frontier types at wayside taverns. For many years Hall's fairly veracious fiction was a source and model for later writers on the West.

Another Philadelphian, Robert Montgomery Bird, followed the picaresque pattern of Hall in his popular Kentucky romance, *Nick of the Woods, or The Jibbenainosay* (1837). Bird had the advantage of a dramatic sense, having won national recognition as a playwright. After reading McClung's *Western Adventure* and Marshall's *Kentucky*, he made three trips to the locale of his story. He differed with Cooper about the red men; like Simms, he pictured them as ferocious, and was equally convinced that they must make way for a superior race. According to the story, the atrocities of the Shawnees have so crazed the wandering Quaker Nick (the Jibbenainosay) that his implacable ways of revenge seem to the Indians the work of the devil incarnate. The love story, by contrast, is conventional: Edith Forrester, the heroine, falls into the hands of the Shawnees through the trickery of Richard Braxley, a shyster lawyer with designs on the girl's fortune. The frontiersmen, however, are portrayed realistically. Big Colonel Bruce, with his Salt River dialect, and Roaring Ralph, "the ring-tailed squealer" and captain of horse thieves, smack of the region as truly as Simon Kenton, Davy Crockett, or Mike Fink. George Rogers Clark and the Kentucky Volunteers are introduced at the end of the story to put the Indians to rout. This thrilling tale of adventure with a slight admixture of history anticipated the technique of the dime novel, such "thrillers," for example, as James Weir's *Lonz Powers, or The Regulators* (1850) and *Simon Kenton, or The Scout's Revenge* (1852).

When historical romance was revived many years later, James Lane Allen brought out the conflict between aristocratic Virginia and frontier cultures in the bluegrass region of Kentucky through a highly popular sentimental tale, *The Choir Invisible* (1897). Its jeweled prose depicted a Galahad in buckskin who was to be an "improvement" on Natty Bumppo. The story of the young schoolmaster and his thwarted love for Mrs. Falconer was more psychological, however, than historical.

More satisfying to modern taste is *The Great Meadow* (1930) by Elizabeth Madox Roberts. The plot is not new: Berk Jervis and his kinsfolk, accompanied by the resourceful frontiersman Evan Muir, travel from Virginia over the Wilderness Road to Harrod's Fort, Kentucky. Each season has its task, spinning wool in the summer and weaving linen during the winter months. But all is not placid. During an attack by the Shawnees the family is separated. Giving Berk up for lost, his wife Diony at length marries Evan; but to their surprise, Berk, after many hardships, returns. Diony, according to frontier custom, now chooses between them, taking Berk, as she admires his unconquerable spirit. Evan then withdraws to a life of solitude. But there is more to this story than plot; in full overtones the figure of Daniel Boone imposes itself on these people.

Thus Miss Roberts, with true historical sense, makes the reader feel the country and people generically. One secret of her illusion, her richly sensuous style, is the product of an interesting experiment. By taking the living speech of the Kentucky hills and laying strong emphasis on its archaisms and racy figurativeness, she solved the problem of reproducing authentic pioneer dialogue. She transcended the effect of literal realism with an infusion of folk poetry that is essentially a reverie illuminating the universal values of human nature. It is not overstating to say that *The Great Meadow* is one of the finest historical novels of our time.

Similar in background, and more thrilling as a story, is *The Long Hunt* (1930) by James Boyd. It is a western, but is so honestly imagined that it refutes the notion that a western must be shoddy. In this robust tale Murfree Rinnard, one of the Long Hunters, leaves North Carolina soon after the Revolution to blaze the way for settlers into the Indian country of Tennessee. There the love-crossed trapper finds himself among red men, squatters, speculators, and other restless elements of the frontier. For good measure the story includes scenes at backwoods inns, the siege of a fort, a bear fight, and a flatboat trip to Natchez and New Orleans. This novel, though it includes no historical figures, well describes the life of the times.

Closely related to the early history of the Kentucky-Tennessee frontier was the alleged conspiracy of Aaron Burr and others to separate this territory from the Union. Whether this design aimed ultimately at Louisiana or Mexico, or both, Burr's fall was as complete as Lucifer's. Apparently he planned to lead a filibustering expedition into the Spanish Southwest to annex that territory first, but was betrayed by James Wilkinson, his partner in the grandiose scheme. What actually took place is not known definitely, but fictional attempts to whitewash or to defame Burr's character have been numerous. Among more or less sensational early versions were *Burton, or The Sieges* (1838) by Joseph Holt Ingraham, *The Conspira-*

tor (1843) by Eliza Dupuy, *The Minister's Wooing* (1859) by Harriet Beecher Stowe, and *The Rivals* (1860) by Jeremiah Clemens.

Edward Everett Hale, after arousing the nation with his short story, "The Man Without a Country," purported to tell the story of the real Nolan in *Philip Nolan's Friends* (1877). It appears that Nolan was a contraband horse trader along the Texas-Louisiana border, in league with Burr's associate, James Wilkinson, who intrigued with the Spaniards in Louisiana.[2] The novel relates the horseback journey of Inez and Eunice Perry across Texas from New Orleans by way of Natchitoches to San Antonio. Nolan, who escorts them part of the way, is shot by Spanish troopers. The women return to New Orleans by the Gulf route, arriving safely, thanks to the kindness of a mysterious Englishman. The author, after exhaustive research, suggests that the British, with the connivance of the governor of Canada, had designs on Louisiana. He recalls, in this connection, the jealousies aroused when the territory passed from Spanish into French, and finally into American, hands. Hale regards Nolan as a victim of "Spanish honor" and pays tribute to him as "the man who gave us Texas." *Philip Nolan's Friends* is an urbane and authentic pioneer work on its subject.

At the turn of the century, Charles F. Pidgin revived fictional interest in the Burr episode with a popular novel, *Blennerhassett* (1901). He darkened the conduct of Blennerhassett, Burr's stooge on an island in the Ohio River, in order to rehabilitate Burr. He also vilified both Hamilton and Jefferson. Burr, he suggested, was a visionary, but one whose ideas of empire were carried out later by the government. In Mary Johnston's *Lewis Rand* (1908) a tobacco roller's son is intrigued by Burr's visions of Napoleonic conquest. Against a background of conflict between Federalists and Democrats, the author unfolds the story of this self-made lawyer, driven by

---

[2] *Tarnished Warrior* (1938), by James R. Jacobs, is a scholarly and entertaining biography of Wilkinson.

ambition till it masters him. Jefferson befriends him, but Rand ignores him in favor of Burr. Rand wins Jacqueline Churchill, niece of two staunch Federalists, from Ludwell Cary, but murders him later and in the end has to stand trial. Mainly, *Lewis Rand* is a picture of a feudal society on mimosa-scented plantations, with soft-voiced darkies singing in the moonlight, and an occasional conflict between neighbors and hotheaded sons. Its psychological approach to character, however, is superior to that in Miss Johnston's other works. It throbs with life.

A famous Tennessean who took the side of Burr in his trial for treason, and who, incidentally, was one of the best exemplars of the frontier spirit, was the redoubtable Andrew Jackson. Hero of the dramatic Battle of New Orleans, winner of the loyalty of Lafitte, and relentless enemy of Creeks and Seminoles, "Old Hickory" was an ideal subject for historical fiction. When Meredith Nicholson wrote *The Cavalier of Tennessee* (1928), he brought Burr and Lafitte into the story, but he focused attention on the turbulent life of Jackson. That gallant knight, not unlike one of Arthur's men, was sorely tried by Fortune. Not the least of his worries was the public attitude toward his romantic attachment to Rachel Robards before she could get her decree for divorce. But after the spectacular victory at New Orleans, Fortune smiled upon him, made him a national hero, and tossed the presidency into his lap. Jackson's frontier days, as well as his later life in Washington with his protégée Peggy Eaton, has been the subject of a lively novel, *The Gorgeous Hussy* (1934) by Samuel Hopkins Adams.

A more realistic account of the Old Southwest than Nicholson's appears in *Oh Promised Land* (1940) by James Howell Street. At the time of this story, about 1800, the area west of the Alleghenies was a ripe plum that might fall into anyone's hands. While the British to the north pursued a policy of watchful waiting, "spiced by intrigue," Tecumseh planned a confederation of the Indians. Then Napoleon sold Louisiana; the British and Tecumseh went down together; Jackson's buckaroos won the Battle of New Orleans; and the settlers took matters into their own hands, while Jackson rode rough-shod into Washington. This is a long, full-blooded story of romantic action, but the author does not overlook economic drives: he knows that pioneers had their eye on the main chance. Thus the "Dabney brats," Big Sam and his hellcat sister Honoria, play out their melodrama of love and revenge. The panoramic structure of the story suggests it may have been intended for the cinema; its frequent soliloquies and asides testify to careful research, however, and it is hard to lay down. In subsequent novels, Street carries the Dabney fortunes through the Civil War and beyond.

2. *The Northwest Territory*

The winning of the Northwest Territory, first from the Indians, then from the French, and finally from the English, has already been discussed in the chapter on the American Revolution. In the northwestward thrust of the American people, the pioneers trapped and hunted and fought Indians as they did in the Southwest, but they also established settlements. Land-hungry sons and daughters of the Puritans, York state men, and Pennsylvanians advanced through northern Ohio, Michigan, Illinois, and Wisconsin; from Virginia, North Carolina, and Kentucky poured a stream of families into southern Indiana, Illinois, and Missouri. It is amazing how rapidly these migrants subdued the wilderness.

The bee hunter and the trapper came in advance of civilization and roamed at will over the unexplored West. During the last decade of the eighteenth century, fur traders, indifferent to questions of political sovereignty, penetrated the Michigan wilderness. In *Wolves Against the Moon* (1940), Julia Altrocchi tells the dramatic story of Joseph Bailly, a contemporary of John Jacob Astor, though less prosperous than he and less suspect. After disappointment in love, Bailly goes on long fur-hunting expeditions to Mackinac, to the Little Calumet, to Detroit and St. Louis, and even so far south as Baton Rouge. While at Mackinac he marries a half-blood Ottawa girl and eventually settles in northern Indiana. This panoramic tale of tribal restlessness, of fur-trade rivalries, and of the westward surge of the settlers constitutes an interesting pioneering record of the transition period between the era of French domination and the development of commercial America.

The advance of the whites left the red men of the Great Lakes region only the prairies between the Illinois and the Wisconsin for hunting ground, and even these were being encroached upon by 1830. When in accordance with a treaty made in 1804 the Indians were to be moved west of the Mississippi, Black Hawk, leader of the Sac and Fox Indians, refused to comply. On the Sac Prairie in 1832 he took the last stand in the Northwest Territory in defense of the red man's lands. This episode furnished the subject of August Derleth's best-known novel, *Wind Over Wisconsin* (1938). Chalfonte Pierneau, friend of Black Hawk and hardheaded idealist, exemplifies the transition from fur trading to farming. He lives on a baronial land grant, with the friendly Sacs near by. When they leave and landseekers intrude upon his domain, he is finally persuaded to turn from buying peltries to growing wheat.

Derleth's *Bright Journey* (1939) deals with fur trading during the period 1812–43. The first of the two parts of the plot relates the boyhood of a historical character, Hercules Dousman, on Mackinac Island during the War of 1812; the second part depicts him as an employee of the American Fur Company at Prairie du Chien. Dousman is a Hentylike hero, but the novel is more accurate, less overwritten than its predecessor, and the Indians seem much more real than, for example, Cooper's. Derleth is a poet who loves the land and blends characters and landscapes into lyrical evocations of his locale.

The latest novelist to come to the defense of Black Hawk

and the once powerful Sac nation is Iola Fuller. In her first novel *The Loon Feather* (1940), Miss Fuller presented a fictional autobiography of Tecumseh's daughter, retailing in a style of lambent beauty that promised well for her future as a novelist, the Arcadian life of the Ojibways and their dealings with the Mackinac traders. In *The Shining Trail* (1943) this promise was fulfilled. Like Derleth, Miss Fuller completely identified the natives with their surroundings and showed how their peace was challenged by newcomers eager for wealth from the lead mines. When the exasperated Indians were finally driven to attack, they were hunted down like wild beasts. *The Shining Trail* relates this shameful episode with exceptional sensitiveness and understanding. Black Hawk lives, and these Sac Indians live, and no anthropological inquest is needed to induce nostalgia.

The most stubborn problem in the westward movement was that of transportation. When Merle Colby in *All Ye People* (1931) pictured the migration in 1810 of John Bray from Vermont to Ohio, he vividly recalled the rumbling of covered wagons, the shouts of bargemen, and the boisterous merriment in frontier inns. So strong, indeed, was the author's antiquarian sense, that his story of the itinerant preacher was almost submerged in the plethora of information on vehicles, food, legends, and the like. In *The New Road* (1933) Colby had history better in hand as he traced the development of an Ohio hamlet on the Maumee about 1820–40. This story of typical community building in the days of Monroe and the second Adams pictures speculators replacing Indian fighters, horse-thieving interlopers actively pursuing their business, and restless settlers moving west when the chinch bugs depleted the crops. The town builder stayed on.

Early migration westward moved along the Erie Canal, down the Ohio River, or over the Old Cumberland Road. One of the most vivid and accurate accounts of canalboat life on the Erie during its heyday is *Rome Haul* (1929) by Walter D.

Edmonds. This story of DeWitt Clinton's "ditch," with its roistering crews and its heterogeneous, teeming life, sprawls somewhat, but it conveys a good understanding of the "canawlers" and their lore. As the canalboats move from Albany to Rochester during the eighteen fifties, the reader experiences the feeling of a lusty young empire undergoing growing pains.

Canalboat life had been touched on by Herbert Quick in *Vandemark's Folly* (1922), in which the protagonist was for several years employed on the Erie Canal before setting out for Iowa. More recently, Samuel Hopkins Adams in *Canal Town* (1934) has pictured Palmyra, a wide-open town in western New York during the eighteen twenties, when "Clinton's Ditch" was its most ambitious undertaking. In the raw town flourish all the virtues and vices. Against this background Adams delineates the struggles of a young doctor who, despite the opposition of wealth, insists that cupping is futile and that filth may cause disease. *Canal Town* is a buoyant and vivid re-creation of a period of ferment and social change.

Conrad Richter's *The Trees* (1940), although it introduces no historical figures, is so well impregnated with the epic import of the pioneer's daily struggle for security that the reader feels the experiences of the Luckett family as his own. In the Ohio Valley at the close of the eighteenth century, the Lucketts find themselves in conflict not only with the forest primeval but with each other. The settler instinct of the wife clashes with the hunter instinct of the husband. She succumbs, but the daughter carries on, and, in the end, the husband hears his doom when the great hickories crash, marking the evolution of the pioneer from hunter to farmer. *The Fields* (1946) continues the story of the tilling, when towns are only beginning to appear, and when personal conflicts further reflect the conquest of the frontier. The author's lyric style takes its quality from the simple, primitive life in forest and field. Its idiom of the past is folk music, lovingly recorded. Quickened by humor and suspense, these quietly exciting and excellent novels wear lightly their author's extensive research on pioneer activities. Here is the living core of history.

The best-known early novelist of what Hamlin Garland was later to call the "Middle Border" was Edward Eggleston of Indiana. His well-known *Hoosier Schoolmaster* (1871) is a "culture-history" of the southern Indiana backwoods. In spite of its sentimentality it was sufficiently realistic to start a vogue for local color that for the first time made the nation aware of its enormous territory, its variety of racial stocks, idioms, and traditions. *The Mystery of Metropolisville* (1873) depicts a Minnesota hamlet during the land boom that ended in the panic of 1857. *The Circuit Rider* (1874), describing the adventures of a traveling evangelist at the beginning of the century, brings out the fact that Methodism was to the lawless frontier of Ohio and the Middle West what Puritanism was to New England. *The End of the World* (1872) deals with the Millerite hysteria in southern Ohio in the eighteen forties. *Roxy* (1878) pictures the colorful "Tippecanoe and Tyler" campaign and such folk customs as an infare, a barbecue, a hoedown, and a revival. *The Graysons* (1887) deals with young Abraham Lincoln in Illinois, the central scene being based on the young lawyer's securing an alleged murderer's acquittal because the moon could not have shone on the night of the murder as the prosecution had claimed. Eggleston's work has stereotyped characters, is not well organized, and tends to be didactic, but his pictures of frontier folk and social customs in four states are sound historical documents.

Eggleston tried to portray frontier life in the faithful, undoctrinaire spirit of a Dutch painter; Joseph Kirkland went a step beyond him toward naturalism. *Zury, the Meanest Man in Spring County* (1887) and its sequel, *The McVeys* (1888), show potentially splendid men in a harsh struggle with the natural environment. Zury Prouder, a fundamentally honest farmer, becomes, through usury and hard bargaining in the poverty-stricken region of southern Illinois, rich and politically powerful. But riches do not satisfy; his wedded life is child-less. He compromises a young New England schoolmistress, and she marries a suitor, McVey, to cover her sin. After the deaths of McVey and Zury's wife, Zury marries the former teacher, who is now preparing his political speeches for him. The sequel is concerned with the drab lives of Anne McVey's illegitimate twins, and includes an account of early railroading. Kirkland well knew farm life and its round of backbreaking toil. Indeed, he inspired Hamlin Garland to tell the truth about it in such books as *Main-Traveled Roads* and *A Son of the Middle Border*. Kirkland's farm stories contained valuable in-formation on pioneer customs and types, but he lacked the fus-ing powers of imagination to give his works coherence and last-ing vitality. Movement, in historical fiction, was to come later.

3. *The Louisiana Purchase*

One autumn day in 1803 in the exotic town of New Orleans a motley gathering of gaily uniformed French soldiers, Spaniards, French Creoles, frontiersmen in hunting shirts, tawny Indians, and ebony slaves watched while the Stars and Stripes replaced the ensign of France. This act signal-ized that the United States had doubled its territory. Jefferson had taken advantage of the fact that Napoleon, who had been able to force the weak Spanish government to cede the great tract called Louisiana back to France and who had planned a huge colonial empire west of the Mississippi, needed money. Napoleon feared, moreover, the United States' possible al-liance with Great Britain in an impending war and was will-ing to part with the vast territory for fifteen million dollars. The imagination of the people was immediately directed to the immense new frontier which stretched from the Mississippi to the Rockies, but some time elapsed before the area was treated in historical fiction.

New Orleans, the capital of this large domain, has always had for Americans the fascination of the exotic. The city has also had a practical significance. For products grown in the Ohio and Mississippi valleys, it was the indispensable port. Almost a century before it became American territory, the machinations of a Scottish banker, John Law, in attempting to control the finances of this area, had attracted a wild frenzy of speculation resulting in a bubble of inflation. Then the "bubble" had burst. This incident, with its glamour and its tragedy, was the theme of a highly romantic but hardly memorable novel, *The Mississippi Bubble* (1902), by Emerson Hough.

The later life of the province, including its transfer to American possession, has been most vividly pictured in *The Grandissimes* (1880) by George Washington Cable. The chief setting of the romance is New Orleans, but the action shifts at least by report to near-by plantation and bayou, to forest and swamp. Various races intermingle to lend atmosphere—French and Spanish, Creole and quadroon, Yankee and German, Indian aborigine and Negro slave. A highly involved plot and an elliptic style add to the confusion, but in the main the story follows the Montague-Capulet formula—in this case, a feud between the Grandissimes and the DeGrapions. Honoré Grandissime, banker and free man of color, is in love with Aurora, last of the DeGrapions. But his uncle, Agricola Fusilier, an unreconstructed Grandissime, antagonizes Honoré's quadroon half brother, and fatally stabs Aurora's husband before a reconciliation of the families can be effected. Other colorful figures are Frowenfeld, the shadowy Teuton apothecary who is in love with Aurora's daughter Clotilde; Bras-Coupé, an African king, whose haughty soul is crushed out in a dramatic episode; the King's widow, Palmyre Philosophe, the voodoo woman; and Clemence, the Negro cake seller. Over all hovers an atmosphere of suspicion, innuendo, and fear; all is locked in tradition; only Honoré appears to see what the transfer of territory really means to a proud race conquered for the nonce by aliens.

So well is this atmosphere realized that *The Grandissimes* ranks as an important historical novel.

Amid the unrest among the French and Spanish population of New Orleans, plots soon developed to overthrow the new American government. The hero of Edward C. Carpenter's *The Code of Victor Jallot* (1907) checked one such attempt. The romantic Jean Lafitte and his Baratarian pirates furnished an element of mystery for other writers of fiction, but except for his inclusion in minor episodes of Hervey Allen's *Anthony Adverse*, Laura Krey's *On the Long Tide*, and Odell and Willard Shepard's *Holdfast Gaines*, he seems to have been treated mainly by the writers of dime novels. His possible connection with General Wilkinson's schemes for territorial aggrandizement and with General Jackson's fight at New Orleans during the War of 1812 have already been considered.

4. *The Fight for Texas*

In many ways the most colorful events of the American frontier were the struggle for Texas independence in 1836 and the Mexican War ten years later; for in the opening of the great Southwest the charm of an older civilization was brought into sharp contrast with the vigor of new blood. These were far-reaching events, too, for through the settlement of Texas and its indirect developments, the United States came into more than 40 per cent of its present continental area. Romantic though the early novels about Texas were, they were usually based on records of real adventurers. Thus the author of *Mexico versus Texas* (1838)—probably Anthony Ganilh, using the pen name A. T. Myrthe—composed a romantic story of the Texas war for independence. Jeremiah Clemens used both his own adventures and the exploits of one Mabry Gray in his novels, *Bernard Lile* (1856) and *Mustang Gray* (1857). As a result, these books have a definite air of reality which makes them more readable than most of the novels of that period. Mustang Gray, after ruthless raids on Mexican ranches between the Nueces and the Río Grande, serves as a Ranger and commands the Mustang Grays. His Byronic gloom is the author's sop to literary convention; his exploits as border raider, smuggler, and killer of Mexicans are the reality. Life in that place was very much of a gamble. It is fitting, therefore, that *Bernard Lile* should begin with a game of poker, and that the principals should then cast their lot with Ben Milam, Davy Crockett, Bill Travis, and Jim Bowie at the Alamo. Lile escapes the assault by the Mexicans because Travis sends him on a mission to Houston. When he learns of the surrender, he goes on to Cuba and later to New York, and then returns to fight the Comanches. Still later, he joins the forces of General Taylor in their invasion of Mexico, on which expedition he is wounded and dies. The story moves along leisurely, and although the middle portion has too much history, the narrative rings true and still holds interest.

Other early novels of the Southwest had slight historical value. Captain Mayne Reid's subliterary "thrillers" helped form the concept of a wild West still held in the East and in Europe. A highly sentimental writer, Augusta Evans Wilson, wrote a love story with anti-Catholic bias, *Inez, A Tale of the Alamo* (1855). Amelia Barr's *Remember the Alamo!* (1888), though slightly more historical, was mainly about a Spanish-American family whose conflicting loyalties were resolved by opposing Santa Anna in the war for independence. Mary Watts's novel of the Middle Border, *Nathan Burke* (1910), touched on the Mexican War, but only in passing.

Not until the period of the Texas centennial were novels written which did justice to the dramatic history of the area. A forerunner was *Gitana* (1931) by that inveterate historical romancer, Robert W. Chambers. This story of love and war begins with General Taylor's operations at the outset of the Mexican struggle and ends with the Battle of Buena Vista. The

romance of the gypsy dancer is absurd, but the military movements are authentically presented. Pendleton Hogan in *The
Dark Comes Early* (1934) wrote a sounder novel, fuller historically, and poetic in style. Arabella Todd, the heroine, leaves
Boston in 1834 to visit her Aunt Vicky on a hacienda in Texas.
On the way her father dies, and her own search for marital
happiness is thrice darkened. But through dust and sunshine,
crop-gathering, and plotting and revolution, amid Spanish
grandees, Mexicans peons, Negro slaves, gamblers, and immigrants, she sees Texas develop into a republic and become a
member of the Union. The liveliest character in the novel is
the crusty aunt, who goes to Mexico to intercede with Santa
Anna for the imprisoned Stephen F. Austin.

In *The Road to San Jacinto* (1936), J. Frank Davis, long
a resident of San Antonio, skillfully brought out the conflict
between two civilizations. Making Mark Lyle, the secret agent
of General Houston, his hero, the author untangled the complicated web of Texas-Mexican politics which most squatters,
absorbed in their own affairs, glimpsed rather dimly. The plight
of the Mexicans is presented feelingly; the enigmatic Houston's case against Austin is made plausible; the massacre at San
Jacinto is realistic; and for full measure, in addition to un-
disciplined pioneers, renegades, and scoundrels, there is the
whole roster of Texas heroes. To cap all, Mark falls in love
with a Quakeress whose pacifism comes near undoing him as
a warrior. With this novel should be considered Anna Brand's
Thunder before Seven (1941), whose hero, a misogynist, loses
the one woman he eventually loves. In the five years the firebrand Blazeley Tyler is a member of Austin's colony, that irresponsible Brazoria storekeeper incites his neighbors with alternate devotion to Austin and to Houston—that is, when they
find that Andrew Jackson is unable to buy the territory outright. At length, the clashes with the Mexicans end with Houston's unexpected defeat of Santa Anna, which enables the
weary settlers to return at last to their deserted homes. The

story is rich in local custom and conversation, in humor and in tragedy; and the narrative, well mortised in the facts of history, drives steadily toward its climax at San Jacinto.

The shadow of the Alamo lies across Laura Krey's novel *On the Long Tide* (1940). The story begins conventionally with the hero's journey to South Texas. Jeffrey Fentress comes with his father, a cousin of Thomas Jefferson, from Virginia to Tennessee, where he helps General Jackson against the Creeks, and then goes on to New Orleans. Here Lafitte inspires him to join in the fight for Texas. After an abortive escapade with Long's buccaneers, Fentress becomes the intimate of Stephen F. Austin, whose colony of settlers finally tire of appeasing the Mexicans and take their stand against Santa Anna for independence. On the whole, political events in this novel are but slightly related to the personal fortunes of the fictional characters; Austin is well drawn, but Houston and Crockett seem shadowy, and other characters are somewhat undermotivated; yet the reader has a sense of participating in colorful events from which the strong tide of the nation swells.

In *Star of the Wilderness* (1941), by Karle Wilson Baker, a reckless young Ohioan, Paul McAlpine, is in 1829 persuaded by Dr. James Grant, his cousin, to leave his farm for a future with the doctor in the Southwest. Dr. Grant dreams of uniting the northern tier of Mexican states with the Union, but both men and troops are ambushed and killed near San Patricio. The story continues with Paul's son escaping from Goliad before the massacre, and concludes with Santa Anna's capture at San Jacinto. Mrs. Baker has well integrated military affairs in a framework of romance, giving her record the poetry and simplicity of a saga.

The point of view of Mexico during our war with that nation is the theme of Herbert Gorman's *The Wine of San Lorenzo* (1945). The protagonist is a young American, picked up during the massacre at the Alamo, and reared as Juan Diego in Santa Anna's establishment. As Juan grows up, he serves on

Santa Anna's staff and goes through the horrible battles of
Buena Vista and Chapultepec. He falls in love with the mysterious beauty Doña María and eventually wins her. Her father,
Don Isidro, is a wealthy ranch owner who distrusts the Bishop
of Puebla, believing that the Church, in order to preserve
wealth and prestige, is conniving with the grasping gringos for
a negotiated peace. When Juan is taken by the Americans under General Taylor, he meets his brother, but cannot accept
the brother's view. Not until Juan observes the chaos into
which Mexico has been plunged by her politicians, who use
Santa Anna as their pawn, is he ready to exchange blind patriotism for the "good neighbor" policy. *The Wine of San
Lorenzo* is a full-bodied and spirited tale that is at once good
history and good fiction. It is the best of the novels that treat
of the winning of Texas independence.

During the conflict with Mexico, imperialist senators saw
nothing disgraceful about sending blundering generals into the
unmapped frontiers to the west of Texas. Three or four novels
have recently been devoted to the bloodless capture of Santa
Fé. Hoffman Birney's *Eagle in the Sun* (1935) tells of an
American trader, John Chain, who in his journeys from Missouri to the Río Grande falls in love with a mysterious beauty
supposed to be a Mexican spy, but who furnishes General
Kearny with valuable information for the taking of Santa Fé.
Following the General's reverses in Chihuahua, the story concludes with the riot of the Indians in Taos. *Jornada* (1935), by
R. L. Duffus, relates the same episode with more imagination,
but less history. Anna Robeson Burr's *The Golden Quicksand*
(1936), while it has moments of vivid drama, is on the whole
conventional and slow moving. Stanley Vestal's *Revolt on the
Border* (1938) introduces into the account ragged but heroic
Missouri volunteers, gallant West Pointers, Spanish-American
types, mountain men, and traders, but the characters are hardly
alive, and the story moves slowly.

5. *The Far West*

Not all the visible benefits of "manifest destiny" were in the Southwest. Oregon and California also were attracting settlers. The publication of Lewis and Clark's journals, as well as Pike's account of his expeditions, aroused the adventurous and the land-hungry, who pushed over prairie, desert, and mountain to far places on the Pacific. While Stephen Austin was busy with projects in Texas, Jedediah Smith, a Yankee fur trader, without asking the permission of the Mexican governor or bothering about passports, had come after a long tramp with a party of trappers to San Gabriel Mission in southern California. He defiantly continued his explorations for a decade, cutting a way from California to Oregon, and apprising his fellow Americans of the virtues of the country.

In the Northwest, John Jacob Astor challenged the dominance of the Hudson's Bay Company by planting Fort Astoria near the mouth of the Columbia for his increasingly lucrative fur trade. Washington Irving was engaged to put the picturesque record in pleasing style, which he did in *Astoria* (1836). His account furnished the basis of Gilbert Gabriel's exciting narrative, *I, James Lewis* (1932). This almost incredible story recounts with honest naturalism a tangled skein of relations woven during the long voyage of the chief clerk on the *Tonquin*, Astor's boat, as he sails from New York around the Horn for the Columbia. He trades with the tricky Chinooks, and after a massacre, in final desperation he lures three hundred natives aboard and blows up the ship. Thus a spectacular chapter from actual life has been given relation to its background by the skillful use of fiction. The novel is the product of extensive research, skillfully subordinated to the artistic necessities of its theme.

Irving was not alone among early writers to show interest in the West. Fenimore Cooper laid the last of the Leatherstocking series among the Sioux and the Pawnees of the trans-Mississippi plains. In *The Prairie* (1827), Natty Bumppo, now an aged trapper and frontiersman, saves an emigrant train from an Indian raid, and after several escapades with the Sioux, a prairie fire, and a buffalo stampede, finds refuge for his last days with the troops of Captain Middleton, grandson of his old friend Duncan Heyward, and with the friendly Pawnees. In unfolding his plot, Cooper was drawn toward naturalism in depicting a renegade squatter, but quickly turned to the conventions of the genteel tradition, even subordinating his rather vital scout to the puppet hero and the helpless Inez. He himself had of course never been in the West and, as a matter of fact, wrote the story in a Paris boardinghouse. Naturally his book did not radiate the spirit of the region, although it depicted the prairie with poetic largeness, and concluded the Leatherstocking series on a note of spiritual elevation.

Timothy Flint found in Missouri enough scraps of information for *The Shoshonee Valley* (1830), the first novel about settlers in the Oregon territory, to supply a melodramatic background for his theories of primitivism. R. H. Dana, Jr., had actually made the voyage around the Horn and had spent a year and a half on the California coast before confiding his journal entries to the well-known personal narrative *Two Years Before the Mast* (1840). The great majority of westward migrants went by land, of course, and the classic account of this travel is Francis Parkman's *The Oregon Trail* (1847). Parkman, Harvard graduate and student of Indian life, went over the Trail in person to observe frontiersmen and Indians at first hand. Possessing the instinct of a good reporter, the knowledge of a botanist, and the imagination of a poet, he wrote succinctly and vitally of what he saw and heard. His account is not unbiased, but it has served novelists as a valuable comment on the life and times of those who took the great overland route to the West.

Few of the great stories of exploration are more stirring than that of the Lewis and Clark Expedition. No one knew how rich was the territory to be explored, nor how dangerous the task. President Jefferson had commissioned the party to trace the Missouri River to its source, to locate the headwaters of the Columbia, and to chart a water route to the Pacific. This they did, with the aid of Sacagawea, the Shoshone guide, covering the outward trip of four thousand miles in eighteen months, and turned in their report in 1806. Among the novelists who have retold these experiences are Eva E. Dye, Emerson Hough, Honoré Morrow, Ethel Hueston, Donald C. Peattie, and John Upton Terrell.

Mrs. Dye included in her account of the expedition, *The Conquest* (1902, 1922), the rush of settlers to the newly opened West, the subduing of the Indians, and even the rise of cities. A reasonable adherence to the records lends an air of verisimilitude to her narrative, but the style is overpoetic and discursive, and the story zigzags in a way to confuse the reader. In *McLoughlin and Old Oregon* (1900, 1936) she did belated justice to a factor of the Hudson's Bay Company but for whose tolerance Americans could not have taken the territory.

In *The Magnificent Adventure* (1916), Emerson Hough addressed himself to the diplomatic questions involved in delimiting the Oregon territory and to questions revolving about the annexation of Texas. He used a vast canvas to present the exploits of Captain Meriwether Lewis, and the fair Theodosia, daughter of Aaron Burr, who is to advance her father's dreams of Western empire by preventing Lewis' departure on the transcontinental expedition. Lewis is represented as very much in love with Theodosia, but true to Jefferson. The best portraits are those of the democratic President at the dinner during which Burr makes advances to the British and Spanish ministers, and of Sacajawea,[3] the Indian woman, who gains in winsomeness from the author's transcript. Except for the romance, the author adhered to the facts of history, although he stressed their picturesqueness.

[3] Variant spelling of *Sacagawea*.

In the eighteen forties insistent demands had been voiced by expansionist senators urging that the United States reannex Oregon by taking it from the British as far as parallel 54 degrees, 40 minutes. On this slogan James K. Polk was elected president in 1844. Hough, an intense nationalist, took delight in un-tangling the threads of the Oregon question in *Fifty-four Forty or Fight!* (1909). Pakenham, the English minister, Yturrie, the Mexican envoy, Van Zandt, the Texas representa-tive, and even the headstrong Polk are depicted as pawns in the hands of the Russian Baroness Von Ritz. Calhoun, on the other hand, is the man of tact. His secretary, Trist, persuades the Baroness to inveigle the lustful Pakenham into surrendering the territory as desired, but jealousies cause Trist to agree to the forty-ninth parallel as the northern boundary. Then, to spite Pakenham, the wife of the Mexican representative per-suades her husband and Van Zandt to agree to the annexation of Texas. The story was bound to captivate feminine as well as please masculine readers, and the book became widely popular.

Among the more recent stories of the Lewis and Clark Expedition, Ethel Hueston's *Star of the West* (1935) is full and accurate and pulsates with the spell of new frontiers. Every incident is based on the journals; background and conversa-tion are true to the period; but the story is less sweeping and heroic than the great exploration really merits. The paradoxi-cal nature of Lewis is well conceived; Clark, the redhead who could not spell, is more the pioneer than the backwoodsman; Sacagawea, who shared the hardships of the journey, helping with guides and horses, is Indian in all but her thought proc-esses. More suited to the author's powers of romance is the sequel, *The Man of the Storm* (1936), in which Mrs. Hueston introduces a member of the expedition, John Colter, who re-mains in the West to hunt and trap, and eventually discovers the Yellowstone. The central character, however, is his friend Tempete, and much of the action takes place in St. Louis while the town passes swiftly from Spanish to French and then to

American rule. As the author's interest is in the romance of Colter and the ward of Tempete, this historical backdrop is suggested, rather than re-created.

Donald C. Peattie's *Forward the Nation* (1942) is hardly a historical novel, rather a prettified account of the Lewis and Clark Expedition, a "lyric of its romantic and historical import." Tribute is paid to the two stouthearted captains, to the Indian "guide," Sacajawea, and to President Jefferson for his farseeing vision in acquiring the territory. Since the story ends when the party reaches the Great Divide, it omits some of the more stirring adventures, although there is considerable theatrical heightening.

John Upton Terrell's *Plume Rouge* (1943) centers attention on the McKenzie Expedition, after Lewis and Clark had made their famous journey, but before the Oregon Trail had taken form, and, for good measure, includes the story of John Colter. Terrell, writing as a modern realist, describes going overland from St. Louis by ascending the mountains and striking westward as not romantic, but tough. Hunger and thirst in hard winters and strange mountains were bad enough, but even more insistent and bothersome was woman trouble.

Tough is the way the pioneer keelboatmen found the journey to the headwaters of the Missouri, as Alfred B. Guthrie describes it in his remarkably vivid novel, *The Big Sky* (1947). There were those, however, in the late eighteen thirties who loved that Western country with its sweeping winds and endless sky, for it was a country where a man felt free. It called for robustness, and Guthrie's is a robust, masculine report. The protagonist is a semibarbarian, a Kentucky boy, who, after killing his vicious father, wanders to the mouth of the Missouri. Here he falls in with sordid, matter-of-fact boatmen and shares their toil and the hazards of the journey up the river, as well as the sexual hospitality of the Indians. His vicious temper costs him the Indian woman he loves; for the blindness of his child is owing to his own excesses rather than to a friend's hypocrisy.

The story is a skillfully planned and finished work, obviously the product of many years' gestation. It honestly imagines and re-creates the spirit of the beaver trappers in the time of Ashley, Fitzpatrick, Glass, and Bonneville, as they wander around the Yellowstone, follow the Snake, and stumble down the Columbia to the sea. It depicts, with stark frankness and little use of humorous mythmaking, the brutality and squalor of the region. Westerners are shown to have been frank materialists and ruffians, with a hatred for women and homes, but with a fierce fondness for sun and sky, and, alas, given all too soon to spoiling their paradise! Although none of the other characters is so clearly realized as the Kentuckian, the dialogue rings true, the action is unflagging, and the moods of the mountain country pervade the story. *The Big Sky* is a first-rate imaginative re-creation of its time and country.

Guthrie's second novel, *The Way West* (1949), takes a small emigrant train over the Oregon Trail a decade later, and, if anything, realizes that Western experience even better than *The Big Sky*. It is a heterogeneous party which Dick Summers, the older trapper in *The Big Sky*, now guides up the Platte to Laramie, along the Sweetwater to South Pass, and along the Snake through endless mountains to the Columbia. There are men of all faiths and occupations and men of no faith, troublesome McBees and cumbersome Byrds, and the dictatorial Tadlock, who must be replaced by the abler, more conciliatory Lije Evans if the party is ever to reach the goal of the two-thousand-mile trek. The author's love of this Western country informs and makes vivid its everyday life—in such details as handling thirst-crazed oxen, cooking over buffalo chips, matching wits against a war party of Sioux, and devising ways of keeping up morale amid endless bickering. The faithful re-creation of the idiom and the humanity of this "on-to-Oregon" company definitely puts the author among the front rank of present-day historical novelists.

The next four novels likewise pertain to the later migrations to Oregon. In Honoré Willsie Morrow's *We Must March* (1925) a small band of missionary-pioneers cross the seemingly impassable barrier of the Rockies by wagon, and, undeterred by hardships, hostile Indians, or even the long hand of the Hudson's Bay Company, carry Christianity and civilization into the new territory. The astounding Narcissa Whitman sways not only her impetuous husband Marcus, but also Sir George Simpson, the lordly governor of Rupert's Land. While governments are not sure how far their jurisdiction extends, missionaries and settlers lay claim to their land with the authority of church and plough. *We Must March* is packed with history, accurate in the main, although the Oblate Annals and Jesuit Reports cast doubt on the notion that Roman Catholics forwarded the destruction of Protestant missions. It appears that doped whiskey, given the Indians by rival traders, brought on the trouble which resulted in the massacre of the Whitmans. Despite a weak plot, this novel is the work of a born storyteller; its revitalization of old diaries and musty records constitutes a reasonably authentic chapter in the fiction of the Northwest.

Emerson Hough's *The Covered Wagon* (1922) traces the epic migration of a wagon train of two thousand men, women, and children on their five months' journey from Missouri to Oregon in 1848. Jesse Wingate is chosen to head the train, but as he is not a born leader, dissensions soon arise. When, midway across the continent, news is received of the discovery of gold in California, so many of the adventurous are attracted southward that only a few reach the intended destination. Although the love story is conventional, the graphic picture of daily events in the life of a community on the march offers recompense.

As if to offset the sentimentalism in some of the older stories of overland travel, Archie Binns wrote *The Land Is Bright* (1939) with a certain grim realism. In this pageant of simple people in the grip of fundamental human emotions, three

generations of Greenfields, Lanes, and Thomases leave Kanes-
ville, Illinois, for Oregon. Gideon Black, the young leader, has
been over the trail and knows its difficulties. McBride, the dog-
matic schoolteacher, has to be ordered out, and bides his time to
kill Black. All the hazards—death, cholera, thirst, dust, heat,
cold, war with roving Indians, river perils, deceit, and trickery
—are vividly recounted. Intense suffering and shocking cyni-
cism go hand in hand. Against the rivalry of McBride and Case
Ford, Gideon wins Nancy Greenfield, and leads that ingenue
from blithe adolescence to competent womanhood before he
is murdered by McBride. The author has the dramatist's gift of
persuading his readers to identify themselves with the characters; he communicates a deep feeling for the beauty of the
wilderness, and comes perhaps as near as anyone to suggesting
the vaster, more significant story inherent in the materials.

This observation applies with equal force to Binns' story
about Indian wars and farming in Washington Territory,
Mighty Mountain (1940). While men in California are forsak-
ing ships for the diggings, and thousands are falling by the wayside of the Oregon Trail, the Yankee protagonist of this story
settles down in the shadow of Mount Rainier. His uncle has
married a Nisqually Indian, and is on friendly terms with Chief
Leschi, the sensible leader of that gentle tribe. But when, in
1854, Governor Stevens hands the Indians an ironic Christmas
present in the form of the Medicine Creek Treaty, they realize
it means being pushed out, no matter how. Stark's Volunteers,
obliged to carry out orders, hardly know how or why they act
as they do. The result is tragedy. The author has kept his story
well in line with the events and so has brought to life the very
thoughts and movements of those times.

Up to the middle of the nineteenth century the Santa Fé
Trail to California was less known than the northern route to
Oregon. Pack trains at first passed over it before wagon trains
came in 1822. Kit Carson traveled it many times, and from

1843–44 guided Frémont's second expedition over it.[4] Carson's exploits, including his part in the conquest of California, have inspired many westerns. The discovery of gold in the Sacramento Valley in 1848 started the legend of a fabulous land, for which Bret Harte set the pattern in fiction. His only novel, *Gabriel Conroy* (1876), was, however, a medley of cannibalism, intrigue, and escape, an anticlimax for his earlier tales of the Argonauts. Mark Twain also fostered the extravagant legend of the West by his exuberant tale of the overland trip and the silver rush in *Roughing It* (1872).

For later novelists the real Eldorado has lain in the color and romance of Spanish California before the American invasion. Mary Austin's *Isidro* (1905) has the afterglow of an Indian summer. Its account of adventures with the Indians centers around the lost daughter of the commandant. The languorous charm of the hacienda, the subtle humor, and the excellent character development mark the novel.

Gertrude Atherton, too, has loved to picture the peaceful life of Spanish California before the mercenary gringos came. *The Californians* (1898), *The Valiant Runaways* (1898), and *Rezánov* (1906), overwrought and uneven as they are, continue Harte's pattern of sentimental melodrama. In *The Californians* the luxurious and cloistered life of a Spanish Jane Eyre is contrasted with the strenuous activities of the Americans. *The Valiant Runaways*, with its tale of incessant feuds, pictures the Spaniards in their decadence before the union. *Rezánov* is based on Russia's attempt to gain a footing in California in 1806. Interest is divided between a recital of diplomatic relations and a story of frustrated love: While Russia, Japan, and the American Trading Company are battling for their "rights," the love of the Russian envoy Rezanov for the

---

[4] Frémont was one of those nuisances, a soldier with glamour but without political sense. Irving Stone's *Immortal Wife* (1944), a biographical novel, shows him as seen by an adoring wife, concealing nothing, seeing everything.

daughter of the Spanish commandant is balked, and she hides her bleeding heart in a Dominican convent. Mrs. Atherton's panorama of California history, by introducing the main characters of one book as subsidiary in others, has built up a fairly convincing illusion of sustained reality despite her strident manner.

The transition from the Spanish regime to the American conquest of California was the subject of an earlier book, Helen Hunt Jackson's popular romance *Ramona* (1884). Señora Moreno, a haughty Spanish woman with an eligible son, Felipe, is alarmed over a possible union between her ward, the half-Indian, half-Scottish Ramona, and the full-blooded Indian Alessandro, who visits their ranch in southern California. The desperate couple elope and are obliged by the encroaching Americans to move from village to village until finally Alessandro becomes insane and is killed. Ramona's foster brother Felipe now takes her and her child to the old estate, but is forced by the avaricious Americans to sell the beloved ranch and move on to Mexico. The story is intended to fictionize the plight of the Indian, which it does by dressing its sermon in seductive garb, but the atmosphere of Spanish days in California is so vividly evoked that the book has been read quite as much for its picturesque scenes. A more realistic picture of the era is George Stewart's *East of the Giants* (1938), in which a New England girl who weds a Spanish rancher helps shape her community.

The most tragic episode in the migration to California was the fate of the Donner party in 1846. This group of three hundred persons, half adults, half children, started hopefully from Missouri on the long trek, but were misdirected, and, after horrible suffering from snow and hunger, most of them perished. Bret Harte used the cannibalism to which the party was driven as a shilling shocker in *Gabriel Conroy*. In more recent fiction, Hoffman Birney's *Grim Journey* (1934), John Weld's *Don't You Cry for Me* (1940), and Vardis Fisher's *The Moth-*

ers (1943) have dealt with the matter, each in its own way, adhering more or less to history.

The most comprehensive survey of California life from the gold rush to the present is found in Stewart Edward White's trilogy—*Gold* (1913), dealing with the days of forty-nine; *Gray Dawn* (1915), with the stirring period from 1851–56, when the vigilantes determined to bring about law and order; and *Rose Dawn* (1920), with the transition period of the eighteen eighties, when the great ranchos of the cattle era began to give place to small irrigated fruit farms. In the course of this series, the theme of California fiction, like that of other American fiction throughout those years, changes from one of picturesque romanticism to that of economic realism.

In his last trilogy of western novels White partly parallels this earlier series. *The Long Rifle* (1932), to be sure, goes back to the fur trappers and their contribution to the opening up of the West. It centers on the adventures of Andy Burnett, who inherited a long rifle from his grandfather's friend, Daniel Boone. During the rivalry of the fur companies he becomes a "mountain man" of the Rockies, is captured by the Blackfoot Indians, and is adopted into their tribe. This story is solely a romance of adventure, with no love theme, but it offers a great deal of information for the nature lover and the reader interested in the history of the westward movement. The sequel, *Ranchero* (1933), treats of Andy's settling down in southern California in the eighteen forties amid an atmosphere of political and personal enmities; and *Folded Hills* (1934) shows that prosperous ranchman, after fighting the Mexicans, enjoying the American occupation of the territory. A number of characters well known in the early history of the West appear in these pages. White's writing is swift and dramatic and historically convincing. It deserves a high place in western fiction.

Once the long trail to Oregon had been established, there sprang up at Salt Lake City a colony of Mormons. The migration of this colony forms one of the strangest chapters in our annals. This religious sect, the Latter-day Saints, had been founded in western New York by the Prophet Joseph Smith. After suffering persecutions in Missouri, Illinois, and Iowa, Smith's disciples, under his successor Brigham Young, made the two-thousand-mile trek to Utah, where they finally established a theocracy. The early travails (1823–44) of this band of believers were set forth in Lily Dongall's *The Mormon Prophet* (1899), a rather apologetic study of Joseph Smith and his brethren in the Middle West.

Recently the Missouri-Illinois period of Mormon history has been the subject of two better novels, both as it happens setting forth the woman's point of view on plural marriage. These are *And Never Yield* (1942), by Elinor Pryor, and *A Littler Lower than the Angels* (1942), by Virginia Sorensen. Miss Pryor's book, a buckskin-and-crinoline romance, is the story of Linsey Allen, who vows she will not join the Saints, but is swept off her balance by Joseph Smith's devoted follower Nathan Welles. Smith's doctrine of polygamy brings havoc to Linsey, but when Welles is murdered by an Illinois mob and she is offered escape from the community through the reappearance in her life of a frontier major, she is reconciled to her lot. Although the book is long and episodic, and the characters tend to prototypes of the author's ideals, the unforgettable scenes of violence and bigotry are ably dramatized.

Nevertheless, Mrs. Sorensen's picture of the domestic problems of polygamy during the sojourn at Nauvoo, Illinois, is the better of the two novels. Her story focuses on Simon Baker and his sensitive wife Mercy, who suffers the ignominy of having another wife in her home because her faith in Simon is greater than in Mormonism. The story is outspoken, poetic, and movingly human. It is in a heroic key; the author's passionate sympathy is with the Saints, who never flinch amid adversity or the assaults of their intolerant neighbors. Smith is presented as a magnetic person, though somewhat paradoxical in wanting to reconcile physical cravings and a religious spirit.

In this novel, Mormonism, despite its stern heritage and frontier hardships, appears a fresh, mystic cult expressing itself in a vital, equalitarian spirit.

Mrs. Sorensen's narrative ends with the trek of Smith's followers to Utah.[5] No adequate account of the migration itself appeared in fiction until Vardis Fisher wrote *Children of God* (1939), for although Harry Leon Wilson's *The Lions of the Lord* (1903) dealt with Brigham Young's trek and the Saints at Salt Lake City in 1847, it was in a rather sentimental, melodramatic fashion. Fisher's account is more satisfying because it is objective, straightforward, and thoroughly alive. The book, with frequent shifts in point of view, describes the entire dramatic history of the Mormons—their strange beginnings, their growth and persecutions, their heroic migration, and their possession at last of Canaan, the great socialistic experiment, and finally its crumbling under the opposition of press and government. The author's flair for coarseness and violence causes him to dramatize the fighting Mormons more adequately than the Mormon idea. Thus, Joseph Smith is portrayed as an austere, sanctimonious individual, endowed with an unusually vivid phantasy, while Brigham Young is all steel, an empire builder, taking his sick caravan across wintry plains to faraway Utah. Though *Children of God*, in its zest for the Saints, inclines to subordinate Mormon smugness to Gentile wiles, it is nevertheless a remarkably well-balanced, vital piece of historical fiction.

6. *The Slavery Issue*

If the whole westward movement culminated with the United States' becoming in 1846 a continental power,

[5] In one of her latest novels, *On This Star* (1946), Mrs. Sorensen tells a love story of Mormons in central Utah during the nineteen twenties. She shows with a great deal of insight why Mormonism has had a continued social vitality.

the question naturally arose who would control this power—the free-labor North and West, or the slave-labor South? According to Bernard DeVoto, whose *Year of Decision: 1846* (1943) integrated the various movements considered under the last heading, it was the willingness of Polk to sell out the Northwest at the forty-ninth parallel, at the same time that he was ready to fight for Texas, that widened the split between the West and the South, which in time doomed the Confederacy.

With the Western frontier in process of settlement, the slavery issue became the question of the hour. In the area of the Middle Border, economic interest dictated abolition, and found a hero in Abraham Lincoln. In the Old South the plantation aristocracy was on the defensive, and novels adverting to it were full of esteem for its gracious way of life. With something of premonition of its passing, writers as early as John P. Kennedy, in *Swallow Barn* (1832), and William A. Caruthers and John Esten Cooke in their romantic novels established the tradition of Southern aristocratic gentility, and Thomas Nelson Page and F. Hopkinson Smith came enough later to sentimentalize it. There is no middle class in this fiction, only nabobs with baronial halls, and flunkies. It has been the task of some twentieth century novelists to correct this romantic conception.

An early incident in the race conflict occurred in Virginia in 1810 when eleven hundred slaves on the plantation of Thomas Prosser planned to take the city of Richmond and were prevented only by an unprecedented rainstorm and the betrayal of the plan by two satisfied slaves. Arna Bontemps used this incident in *Black Thunder* (1936), and although the historical element in the novel is slight, the atmosphere is faithfully maintained, the dialogue is accurate, and the story has tragic dignity. A later episode of the race conflict was the subject of *Toucoutou* (1928) by Edward Larocque Tinker. In this tragedy of miscegenation in New Orleans during the eighteen fifties the daughter of an octoroon and a Creole planter is the central character. Although the story is weak in character portrayal, it is rich in picturesque detail and strange atmosphere, and includes such incidents as a yellow fever epidemic, slave uprisings, voodoo ceremonials, visits to the French Market, and the festival of Mardi Gras.

A recent novel of a Negro insurrection, Frances Gaither's *The Red Cock Crows* (1944), is laid in Mississippi in 1835. It shows, without moralizing, life among blacks and whites on a model cotton plantation during one "incredible week" of mounting horror, when the plot against the whites is suppressed at a fearful price to all. The story, fast-paced and rich in atmosphere, shows that slavery was an anachronism even during the period of its economic success.

The chief apologist for the plantation tradition among modern novelists is Stark Young. *Heaven Trees* (1926) is a tender and affectionate description of the lavish hospitality, the genial conversation, and the lighthearted romance on a Mississippi plantation during the period immediately before the War Between the States. In that spacious life the family is the unit, and kith and kin are constantly coming and going. Uncle George Clay, the easygoing owner, is surrounded by a ménage of women, including besides his efficient second wife and blithesome daughter, an analytical New England cousin and a Miss Mary, who orders everybody around. The darkies are, of course, a happy and contented lot. This full and easy life had been extolled from Cooke to Page. *Heaven Trees*, then, was the swan song of feudalism in the Old South tradition.

A more realistic account of ante-bellum days is *Lamb in His Bosom* (1933) by Caroline Miller. It is a picture of pioneer life in Georgia from 1810, when Lonzo Smith brings Cean Carver as a bride to those piney woods, until the time when Cean, white-haired, welcomes back her second husband from the War Between the States. An atavistic nostalgia inspires this leisurely novel of the soil and its simple folk. Little of external moment occurs, but so sensitive is the narrative to the traits of frontier life—its warmth of manner and the accent of its living speech—and so shrewd are the comment and humor, that this indigenous parish register is as richly redolent of the past as *The Great Meadow.*

The mature art with which *Lamb in His Bosom* calls forth the prewar South suggests Willa Cather's *Sapphira and the Slave Girl* (1940), a lyrically poignant evocation of the Virginia hill country and its social conflicts during the eighteen fifties. In this quiet study of character and situation, Miss Cather concentrates on an invalid wife who married beneath her and vents her jealousy on a beautiful mulatto girl whom the husband eventually assists in fleeing to Canada. Sapphira really belongs to the eighteenth century, but the husband and the slave anticipate the bourgeois future. Around them, seen through the pathos of distance and perished beauty, are the wrecks of a slave-owning society. Miss Cather's conversation piece achieves its fine effect in one-third the number of pages required in most historical fiction. Other novels about the antebellum South carry the record well into the bloody conflict and will be considered in the next chapter.

In the pre–Civil War North the two focal points of interest for later novelists have been Abe Lincoln in Illinois and "bleeding Kansas." Although agitators for abolition were few throughout the North, feeling on the subject was strong in Illinois. There Lovejoy, after suffering the loss of three presses, was shot to death while attempting to protect the fourth. In the East there were those who compared that mob with the patriot Fathers who made up the Boston Tea Party. In Katherine H. Brown's prize-winning story *The Father* (1928) an overardent abolitionist is forced out of New England to new beginnings in Illinois. There his fiery editorials attract the attention of young Lincoln, who becomes his friend and co-agitator. His chief partisan, however, is his daughter, whose romance is a part of the story. This novel moves rather slowly, but gives a fairly vivid picture of a pioneer family during a troubled period.

The Lincoln myth was inextricably interwoven with the story of pioneering. The great man's humble origins, his struggles for a livelihood, and his reverses and successes synchronized perfectly with the various movements on the frontier. Lincoln is shown as a young lawyer in Eggleston's *The Graysons* and in a few chapters of Kirkland's *The McVeys,* but in the novels thus far considered he appears as a rather vague, elusive figure, not the protagonist. In Winston Churchill's *The Crisis* (1901) he is shown developing from a rough Western frontiersman with a Southern background into a saintly martyr as the years take their toll. *The Valley of the Shadows* (1909), by Francis Grierson, reveals how the people on the Illinois prairies are stirred to rise against slavery by the mystic genius of this man. In *The Southerner* (1913), Thomas Dixon, Jr., vindicated Lincoln for the South and chivalry by contrasting his plans for reconstruction with those of others. Maria T. Daviess erected a pious memorial to the romance of Thomas Lincoln and the self-reliant Nancy Hanks, which she called *Matrix* (1920). Abraham Lincoln's own tragic romance is the subject of Bernie Babcock's *The Soul of Ann Rutledge* (1919). Irving Bacheller in *A Man for the Ages* (1919) pictured the rail splitter, storekeeper, and incipient politician as a Yankee sage in the New Salem community, and in *Father Abraham* (1925) as more homely, less sage, but always dominating the action. Carl Sandburg's dramatized biography of the "prairie years" and the "war years" is of course monumental.

Recent fiction about Lincoln has dealt with his origins and his early life. In Harold Sinclair's *American Years* (1938), Lincoln himself is not convincingly realized, but the life of an Illinois town, with its hardihood and its brutality, its humor of barbershop, hog-caller, revivalist, and plugshot is well brought out. Bruce Lancaster's *For Us the Living* (1940) effectively re-creates Lincoln's early life and environment in

Indiana and Illinois up to the time he enters the legislature. Ben Ames Williams' *House Divided* (1947) brings out the misgivings of Southern aristocratic relatives of Lincoln in regard to his birth and humble origins.

Meanwhile what was becoming of the slavery question? After a series of compromises which left both factions unsatisfied, the issues of the irrepressible conflict were transferred from the forum to the field. The Mexican War had been a precipitant; the Kansas struggle over squatter sovereignty was the last flare-up before the cannon boomed. The proslavery Missourians determined to conquer Kansas for bondage, while the Northern abolitionists, equally resolved to seize it for freedom, stirred the country by bloody deeds and equally bloody reprisals. The climax came in 1859, when John Brown, after a stormy career in Kansas, tried to start a slave rebellion by making a raid on Harpers Ferry for which he was hanged.

Margaret Lynn's *Free Soil* (1920) is a story of Kansas during the turbulent fifties. John and Ellen Truman give up their New England home and make the difficult journey to Kansas, where they soon have an active part in the struggle to make it a free state. There are differences, however, even among the free-soilers, some advocating violence and others favoring peaceful methods. John Brown lends a somberness to the story which is relieved somewhat by the romance of Phoebe and Lewis Hardie and by the author's very evident love for the prairies. The many characters in this book are really alive; fiction and history are well blended.

In *God's Angry Man* (1932), by Leonard Ehrlich, not only Brown and his clan, but the whole abolition movement comes to life. Regarded by some as a martyr, by others as a criminal who got his just deserts on the gallows, Brown of Osawatomie here appears as a man of Old Testament stature and fiber, the fantastic leader of a forlorn hope, the slayer of innocent men, yet desperately sincere, and pathetic at the last. Abjuring political wars among nations, he was willing to do violence for what he considered social justice. The author, in transferring his subject from the key of Oswald Garrison Villard's biography to that of fiction, has used the method of a symphonic poem, beginning with the trouble in Kansas which made Brown an outlaw, then offering a cutback, followed by a lovely andante when as a boy he saved the crops from frost; the book concludes with the death march to Brown's execution. All the motives of the story are focalized in Brown: the conquest of the soil, the struggle between North and South, the pitiful dream of social justice. It is a powerful novel that sweeps the reader along with its dramatic force.

A more recent novel which seeks to bring the whole anti-slavery movement into historical perspective is *The Drums of Morning* (1942) by Philip Van Doren Stern. Jonathan Bradford, whose father was martyred with Lovejoy, is well informed on the subject of slavery. As a protégé of Theodore Parker, he makes an extensive tour of the South in 1852 to see what slavery is really like. He notes the economic wastefulness of the system, gets mixed up with a wayward Southern beauty, fights a duel in her behalf, and, after freeing a small group of slaves, is branded and nearly loses his life. Next he establishes a station on the Underground Railroad, meets the famous John Brown, who is recruiting in the neighborhood, is in Charleston when Fort Sumter is fired upon, and is captured and consigned to Andersonville prison. Cut off as he has been from news of the struggle, he comes at last to see in truer perspective Lincoln, whom he execrated, and the newer issues that grew out of the war. The author possesses a historian's knowledge of the period, but has rightly been first concerned with telling a good story. He not only makes his historical characters and their period live but links their struggle with the larger struggle for human freedom.

Novels of the westward movement have on the whole been as satisfactory as those of any other period in our history.

It would be difficult to match from another period such works, to name only the most outstanding, as *The Great Meadow, The Long Hunt, The Trees, The Grandissimes, The Big Sky, Lamb in His Bosom,* and *God's Angry Man.* The frontier is in the writers' blood, and they have generally written with penetrating insight; there has been little danger of overwriting because the events themselves were gigantic. The relative lateness of the appeal of this material has also acted in its favor; fictional technique has developed to a point where the account must be convincing. Certainly the general average of achievement in these novels is high. If no work of fiction has been quite commensurate with the materials, the fact may be ascribed on the one hand to the genteel tradition which at first cramped the style of novelists treating this movement, and, on the other, to the physical-adventure tradition, the two-gun tradition, which emphasizes incident, but ignores character. Until the melodrama of the pulps and the cinema is transcended, it will be difficult to present the winning of the West in literature of real merit.

IV. The Civil War
and Reconstruction

THE CIVIL WAR was our War of the Roses, so complex and dark were its motives and long-drawn-out hatreds. Essentially it was a conflict between the agrarian South and the increasingly industrial North. Slavery, it now appears, was a political issue largely in the sense that it was an anachronism. The institution was costly and cumbersome, and would have been abandoned if political agitators had not put the South on the defensive. Certainly as provocative as the slavery issue, and more fundamental, were the unsettled questions of states' rights versus federal power, and the right of secession. It has been said that no struggle is so intense as fratricidal war, and in that respect the Civil War was no exception. For decades novelists were unable to write calmly, if at all, on the subject. Not until the nineteen thirties, after the publication of *John Brown's Body* by Stephen Vincent Benét, had feeling quieted down enough for a wide, relatively impartial, retrospective interest in the war.

Late in 1860, after the election of Abraham Lincoln to the presidency, the Southern states, with South Carolina leading the way, began to secede. News of the firing on Fort Sumter the following April spread throughout the nation like an electric shock. All who had been dallying with peacemaking now ceased their efforts and took sides with or against the Union. Virginia, Arkansas, North Carolina, and Tennessee joined the Confederacy; later the others followed. The border

states—Missouri, Kentucky, and Maryland—were held official-
ly in the Union, but furnished tens of thousands of soldiers to
the Confederacy, and were subjected to guerrilla warfare of
the intensest kind.

As the war advanced, dramatic situations developed chiefly around two centers, Richmond in the East and the Mississippi River in the West. There were of course skirmishes elsewhere; most notable of these were the Battle of Atlanta and
the two major conflicts about Chattanooga. The first important battle in the East occurred at Manassas Creek along Bull
Run, in which Beauregard of the Confederacy defeated Mc-
Dowell. John Esten Cooke, Mary Johnston, and Upton Sinclair have made use of this battle in their fiction. In the West,
Grant and Farragut took control of the Mississippi in 1863, and
the battles of Fort Henry, Fort Donelson, and Shiloh, and the
siege of Vicksburg marked this part of the conflict. *The Long
Roll* by Johnston and *Kincaid's Battery* by Cable have dealt
with the warfare on the Mississippi. No important fiction has
treated Farragut's victory at New Orleans, nor has the naval
duel between the *Merrimac* and the *Monitor* in the East in 1862
attracted the attention of anyone except Mary Johnston.

The Peninsular campaign, and particularly the Battle of
Chancellorsville the next year, have been favorites of Southern
novelists, for it was in that battle that Stonewall Jackson lost
his life. Cooke's *Surry of Eagle's Nest* and Dixon's *The Southerner* treated it, and it furnished the climax of *The Long Roll;*
Stephen Crane's *The Red Badge of Courage* is supposed to
have been laid at Chancellorsville. After the drawn fight with
McClellan at Antietam, Lee determined to invade Pennsylvania, and was not stopped until the three-day Battle of Gettysburg, the most dramatic conflict of the war. The Battle of
Antietam is described in Boyd's *Marching On*, and the Battle
of Gettysburg has been most fully treated in Kantor's *Long
Remember*. The day before Lee began his retreat to Virginia,
Pemberton surrendered at Vicksburg. This surrender has been

described by Garland in *Trail-Makers of the Middle Border*, in Cable's *Kincaid's Battery*, and in Mary Johnston's *Cease Firing*. In the fight over Tennessee the Battle of Chickamauga —thanks to General Thomas, a Virginian who stood by the Union—failed to become a rout. Charles King's *The Rock of Chickamauga* and Townsend Brady's *The Southerners* have memorialized this event.

By the beginning of 1864 the South had its back to the wall. The blockade of Southern ports was a cordon which few vessels could pierce. Factories were running out of materials, and railroads falling into decay. Offensives were undertaken spasmodically, like Morgan's cavalry raids into Ohio, Early's dashes against Sheridan down the Shenandoah Valley, and Hood's desperate rush on Nashville, but they were unavailing. In fiction, Cooke dealt with Sheridan in *Hilt to Hilt*. The unexpectedly successful career of Grant as a soldier was depicted by Garland in *Trail-Makers of the Middle Border*. When in 1864 Grant was made commander of the combined Northern armies, he at once crossed the Rapidan and entered a region of tangled underbrush near Chancellorsville known as the Wilderness. The battles here and at near-by Spottsylvania Courthouse were almost as hard-fought as the one at Gettysburg, and ended in a bloody repulse to Grant, but that did not stop him. Cooke, Brady, and Weir Mitchell have all dealt with these battles.

The war as a whole now rapidly came to a close. Grant, with heavy losses of his own, gradually drove the Confederate Army back until he entered Richmond in April, 1865. In the meantime, Sherman had advanced to Atlanta on his way to the sea to cut the Confederacy in two. Although Sherman was blamed for great devastation, much of the destruction was actually wrought by marauders who followed his army. Novelists like Mary Johnston in *Cease Firing* and Margaret Mitchell in *Gone With the Wind* have pictured this devastation in lurid colors. The morale of the Confederate Army was completely broken after a few other engagements in which Sheridan defeated Early, and Thomas annihilated Hood's army. Ellen Glasgow's *The Battle-Ground*, Hervey Allen's *Action at Aquila*, and Clifford Dowdey's *Bugles Blow No More* have treated the campaign around Richmond. On the ninth of April, 1865, Lee met Grant at a farmhouse near Appomattox and surrendered. The Northern commander requested only that the Southern soldiers return to their homes to take up the work of reconstruction. The pathos of the surrender of the ragged soldiers has appealed to some novelists, while the magnanimity of Grant has attracted others. Few writers who have treated the whole course of the war have omitted this incident.

1. *Novels of the Civil War*

Soon after the close of the conflict, memoirs appeared based on army experience. John Esten Cooke's *Surry of Eagle's Nest* (1866), written in the First-Families-of-Virginia tradition, was the first of these to be widely read. It began with the raid on Harpers Ferry, included the Battle of Manassas, and ended with the death of Jackson at Chancellorsville. *Mohun* (1869) took the account through "the last days of Lee and his Paladins" around Richmond. Cooke was a romanticist who idealized his leader and exalted chivalry and war. Other writers wrote of the period in terms of civilian life. *Miss Ravenel's Conversion from Secession to Loyalty* (1867), by John W. De Forest, showed the effects of the war on one New Orleans family. This book's leading characters, its analysis of the feelings of the time, and above all, its realism, remarkable for its period and best shown in the storming of Port Hudson, all startlingly anticipate *Gone With the Wind*, though the point of view is that of the North. *Miss Ravenel's Conversion* is thoroughly informed about the attitudes of both sides, the official delays, the effect of army maneuvers on noncombatants, and the actual feelings of men in battle. It is the one novel of the decade that is still readable.[1]

Throughout the seventies the blighting effect of Reconstruction left its mark on fiction. Tourgée's incendiary novels, for example, pertained mainly to what Claude Bowers has called "the tragic era." But by the eighties the election of Cleveland assured the South that the war was over. A sufficient period of time had passed to enable writers to view it in calmer temper and with some perspective. A sentimentalist like E. P. Roe, in such works as *His Somber Rivals* (1883) and *An Original Belle* (1885), however, saw in the battles of Manassas and Gettysburg mainly a means of keeping the hero's passion in suspense until his ultimate reward in conjugal bliss. Roe had a dependable formula of rewarding his middle-class hero with love and money and his renunciation with the crown of religious bliss in a way that proved widely acceptable. Captain Charles King was only slightly less successful with another pattern in such romances as *Between the Lines* (1889), *The General's Double* (1898), and *The Rock of Chickamauga* (1907). The repeated use of marriage between a Northern hero and a Southern heroine prefigured in the national mood the reconciliation of the former antagonists. But King's military novels, like the romances of George Cary Eggleston, Cyrus Townsend Brady, and others, were too hackneyed and sentimental to survive.

Signs of better understanding between the sections were at hand. Soon after the war, *Scribner's Monthly* sent Edward King throughout the South for a series of articles to cultivate a friendly interest in the late foe. In 1883 the *Century Magazine* published a series of contributions by generals on both sides recounting their war experiences. The North, engrossed in business prosperity, had every reason to look back with satisfaction on its exercise of patriotism; and the South, without quite

[1] DeForest, a Union line officer, gives the bases of this novel in *A Volunteer's Adventures* (1946).

knowing how, was beginning to accept Appomattox as the work of Providence rather than of Yankee villainy.

In fiction, more realistic standards were being advanced by Howells and James. An adherent of the realistic school was Dr. S. Weir Mitchell, an army surgeon during the Civil War, afterward an internationally famous neurologist. His novels, *In War Time* (1884) and *Roland Blake* (1886), were the first to employ the new psychology in works of fiction about the war. *In War Time* is a case study of the effect of civil strife on civilians, notably on a sensitive physician. The only battle which is described is the Battle of Gettysburg, and it is reported indirectly in a hospital in Philadelphia. *Roland Blake*, on the other hand, deals with General Grant's movements near Richmond. It portrays the effect of the war on Blake, a Union officer, and on Richard Darnell, a Southern spy, who with the aid of his neurotic sister hopes to obtain the Wynne fortune. The Battle of Spottsylvania Courthouse is described in detail, but is used only so far as it affects the fortunes of the hero, and not for its own sake. Many years later, Mitchell returned to the war in *Westways* (1913), showing its effect on a divided family, the Penhallows, living in a small Pennsylvania town. The wife is of Southern birth and sympathies and the husband and nephew are for the Union. There are glimpses of Lincoln and Stanton when the father visits in Washington, and later there is a vivid picture of Gettysburg, where he fought. The nephew is with Grant, first in the West, and later in the campaign around Richmond. The suffering borne by the women in wartime is brought out when the elder Penhallow is taken home to his wife, wounded in body and broken in mind.

By the eighteen nineties the new naturalism was vying with the romantic attitude in picturing the war. Young Stephen Crane, with no more military experience than his lively imagination could cull from *Battles and Leaders of the Civil War* and from Tolstoy, told so graphically how a raw recruit feels

in battle that *The Red Badge of Courage* (1895) must be regarded as the first artistic approach to the war. It pictures no
historical figure or event, except that Chancellorsville is its
setting, but its sense of the helplessness and meaninglessness of
the common soldier, maneuvered by superiors and circumstance, is a brilliant achievement in impressionism.

On the march to battle, Henry Fleming forgets his en-
thusiastic enlistment, and wonders why a merciless government
has compelled him to participate in this terrible conflict. As he
notices the mangled bodies on the way, his fear increases and,
when he approaches the actual fighting, turns almost to frenzy.
Finally, during the battle he throws down his rifle and runs.
Then he falls in with a group of wounded soldiers and becomes
ashamed of himself, until a man hits him and, drawing blood,
gives him the red badge of courage. Next morning when the
battle is resumed, he leads the charge. Thus at the same time
that the book destroys the concept of chivalric romances, it
realizes an experience which is valuable in its own right. Its
illusion of authentic experience in battle has made it a minor
classic of the war.

The victory for realism was not, however, to be won so
quickly. With the revival of interest in historical romance in
the late nineties, the cloak-and-sword romance was to have its
heyday. Most writers turned to the Revolution, or looked to
the Colonial era, for their inspiration. Some even preferred
the time "when knighthood was in flower." Among those who
used the Civil War was Irving Bacheller, popular for his romantic pictures of American life. In *Eben Holden* (1900) he
used as setting his own northern New York at the beginning
of the war. Eben, a blunt but kindly hired man of the Brower
family, rears an orphan, William, who grows up to become a
reporter on Horace Greeley's *Tribune*. When the war begins,
William joins a regiment, and after he is wounded in the fight
at Bull Run, returns to marry Hope Brower. The war is used
only to bring out the character of William, the narrator, though

there are glimpses of Greeley and his eccentricities and of Lincoln as the conventional man of sorrows.

A well-planned and reasonably accurate trilogy on the Civil War is Honoré Willsie Morrow's *The Great Captain*. The first book, *Forever Free* (1927), begins with Lincoln's inauguration in 1861 and concludes with the signing of the Emancipation Proclamation two years later. Except for a hardly credible subplot, built around a beautiful Southern spy in the guise of Mrs. Lincoln's social mentor, the period is successfully reconstructed. Lincoln's tense struggle in deciding whether to emancipate is particularly well dramatized. In the next novel, *With Malice Toward None* (1928), the last two years of Lincoln's administration are depicted, the years when Lincoln wrestled with Charles Sumner and Thad Stevens over plans for reconstruction. Lincoln is presented as a developing personality, human, but hardly as subtle as he actually was, and Mrs. Lincoln is shown as a loyal, lovable wife. Life in Washington is vividly detailed. In the author's attempt to humanize the era, everything is placed in the foreground, and complex forces of the period are somewhat oversimplified. In *The Last Full Measure* (1930), in which the narrative oscillates between Lincoln's plans for reconstruction and Booth's conspiracy to assassinate the President, there is an authentic, simple portrait of the kindly, shrewd, harassed statesman. Lincoln's domestic life and his tribulations with office seekers are presented in these novels in a slightly labored style and with some sentimentality, but with a sense also of drama and with a great deal of reality.

The best portrayal of Abraham Lincoln in a novel of the Civil War appears in *The Crisis* (1901) by Winston Churchill. This novel humanizes Lincoln, and offers a panorama of the war as a whole. St. Louis, on the border between North and South, is the well-chosen center of the romance. Stephen Brice has just come here from the East to study law, but finds himself in conflict with the strong secessionist feeling. He develops an admiration for the rising young lawyer in Illinois, and hears one of his famous debates with Douglas. When the war begins, Stephen joins a regiment under Sherman's command, while his sweetheart's father, Colonel Carvel, and the cousin to whom she is engaged, Clarence Colfax, join the Confederates. At length, when Virginia goes to Washington to ask the President to pardon Clarence, who has been captured by Federal troops, Lincoln's sympathy, surmounting his gaucheries, brings Virginia and Stephen together. The story closes with the death of the great martyr.

Aside from its memorable portrait of Lincoln, this novel displays a comprehensive grasp of the underlying causes of the war and the operation of these factors in the ensuing struggle. It brings out, for example, how the border state of Missouri was full of unrest but was saved for the Union by the large German element in St. Louis. The battles of Gettysburg and Vicksburg are given by report. The pictures of Grant and Sherman appear natural, and although all the characters are somewhat romanticized, there is a quality of moral earnestness about them and their conflicts which has made the book, despite slight defects, a general favorite.

By contrast, the novels of George W. Cable, *The Cavalier* (1901) and *Kincaid's Battery* (1908), are melodramatic and old-fashioned. In *The Cavalier*, Cable draws upon some of his own experiences in the army of General Joseph E. Johnston. He uses the skirmishes of guerrilla fighting as a backdrop for the absurd movements of one Coralie Rothvelt, a Confederate spy whose husband is a Federal sympathizer. The most dramatic scenes are a raid upon the dance at Gilman's plantation and the deathbed scene of the Yankee captain when he asks the reluctant Coralie to sing "The Star Spangled Banner" for him. *Kincaid's Battery* is a better novel. It deals with the Federal occupation of New Orleans, the attack before Vicksburg, and the naval battle in Mobile Bay. The Confederate battery which does much of the defensive fighting in these places is owned largely by Ann Callender, Kincaid's sweetheart. Their *bête noire* is a wily Creole, Flora Valcour, who stops at nothing to thwart them. After they are taken prisoner at Vicksburg and returned to New Orleans, they escape to aid the Confederate forces near Mobile. The description of this battle, showing the *Tennessee* in the moment of defeat returning to fight Farragut's entire fleet, is excellent.

Ellen Glasgow's *The Battle-Ground* (1902) is the first realistic treatment of the war from the Southern point of view. Miss Glasgow's strongly ironical turn of mind doubtless saved her from the sentimentalism of her contemporaries. On the Virginia plantation of his grandfather, Dan Mountjoy is attracted to the vivacious Betty Ambler. She has been expected to marry Champe Lightfoot, but early gives her admiration to Dan's independence and courage. Dan has the misfortune to be expelled from college, and, after being disinherited by his grandfather, wanders aimlessly until the war begins. In the first Battle of Manassas, Dan is wounded, and by the close of the war he becomes reconciled with his grandfather. Meanwhile, Betty, the first of Miss Glasgow's series of resourceful heroines, has looked after her own land as well as the Lightfoot plantation. The events of the war are given impressionistic, rather than detailed historical, interpretation, and center largely on the life of noncombatants. The terrible summer days, when McClellan sweeps toward Richmond from the Chickahominy, follow each other with the indirection and delay of real life. The suffering troops are well described, and the Negroes are portrayed with humor and understanding. The chief historical figure, Jefferson Davis, is pictured in the Confederate White House, which is filled with representatives from the South, and with Richmond belles. The novel, by breaking with the sentimental and "fire-eating" tradition, helped remove the principal traces of resentment against the North.

Upton Sinclair, like Ellen Glasgow a Southern rebel

against Southern tradition, tried in *Manassas* (1904) "to make
the War itself a living, breathing reality." He succeeded. The
greater part of the work, however, describes social and political conditions during the decade which preceded the war: the
enforcement of the Fugitive Slave Law, the operation of the
Underground Railroad, and the raids of John Brown. Allen
Montague, a Southern youth, after experiencing prosperity on
a Mississippi plantation, goes to Boston to college. There he
overcomes his aversion to abolitionists. Shortly afterward, on
a visit home, he witnesses such cruelty to slaves that he returns
to the East and enlists in a Northern regiment, which is mobbed
in passing through Baltimore. In the fierce Battle of Manassas,
Montague is badly wounded. The author described the ani-
mosities of the time with the trained eye of a reporter, and he
made the excitement and confusion of the hand-to-hand combat near Bull Run intensely real. Several implausible features,
however, mar the book. Everyone appears a coward or a
weakling. The protagonist is whisked from place to place to
enable the author to give a candid-camera picture of the firebrand William Yancey, the freed slave Frederick Douglass, the
refined President Davis, and the uncouth President Lincoln.
"Dixie" is sung several years before it was written.

John Fox, Jr., and Randall Parrish described the guerrilla
warfare in Kentucky and Virginia in the sentimental tradition. Fox's best seller, *The Little Shepherd of Kingdom Come*
(1903), has for its principal historical character General John
H. Morgan, but owes its popularity to the thesis that no matter
how bitter partisan warfare may be, the love of a devoted
maiden may shine clearly in the gloom. Parrish's Civil War
novels use the hackneyed theme of the divided allegiance of
lovers. *My Lady of the North* (1904) depicts a Southern captain winning a Northern woman, while deserters from both
armies plunder the Shenandoah Valley; in *My Lady of the
South* (1909), for compensation, one of Rosecrans' men is rewarded with the love of a Southern girl. Cyrus Townsend

Brady's *The Patriots* (1906) has interesting pictures of Lee,
Stuart, and Grant, but its plot is too facile and overdrawn to
merit further discussion.

Most novelists wisely concentrated on a small portion of
the conflict, or focused on one historical figure. Mary Johnston, however, in her two novels took the entire war for her
theme. In *The Long Roll* (1911) she covered the period from
its beginning to the death of Stonewall Jackson in the Battle
of Chancellorsville, and in the sequel, *Cease Firing* (1912), the
period from Vicksburg to the close of the war. In the former,
the hero is Stonewall Jackson, and the South is winning; in the
latter, Lee is the central figure, battling against terrific odds.
The two volumes thus form a continuous story. In the beginning, the Virginia boys start lightheartedly to a war that must
soon be over; but Manassas disillusions them. Jackson's men
at first consider him a cold disciplinarian and threaten to
mutiny, but after they see how indomitable he is in battle, they
come to revere him. In the fictional plot, Richard Cleave is
tricked into an ambush by his jealous rival Maury Stafford,
and as a result Cleave is court-martialed and dismissed. He re-
enlists, however, under an assumed name and vindicates himself as an artillerist. Stafford, after being finally rejected by
Judith Cary, is captured, and Cleave is offered a new trial by
Jackson only the day before the General is shot accidentally
by his own men.

The second book opens with the army under Generals
Johnston and Pemberton during the siege of Vicksburg. Edwin Cary, Judith's brother, is injured in an offensive against
Farragut and, while recovering, falls in love with Desiree Gal-
liard, who follows him through later campaigns until both are
killed. The author describes in heroic terms Pickett's memorable charge at Gettysburg, and then the fortunes of Lee, Longstreet, and Stuart in the East. She thinks that Johnston's replace-
ment by Hood during Sherman's famous march hastened Confederate defeat. In Richmond as in the West, women are shown

busy as nurses, noncombatants watch anxiously, prisons are overcrowded, food is scarce, and homes are pillaged. The story concludes with a note on the futility of war.

No novel of the Civil War exhibits more careful research; in fact, at times the wealth of historical detail clogs the action of the story. The author owed her fine knowledge of strategy and tactics, and her intimate sidelights on the leaders to her father, Major Johnston, an actual participant in the struggle. General Lee is pictured as an unostentatious gentleman, a natural leader; General Sherman is heartily disliked; Stonewall Jackson is heroized, but not without qualification. If the heroic note in these novels is sounded a little too often for modern taste, that fact should not be allowed to obscure a real achievement in following the record and in understanding the struggle. Miss Johnston attributes the ultimate defeat of the Confederacy to the inability of an agrarian society to equip a large army and to the lack of a valid currency.

Hamlin Garland's *Trail-Makers of the Middle Border* (1926) likewise was based on his father's experiences in the war, but as seen from the Northern side. Richard Graham, after farming in Wisconsin, meets an unsuccessful business man at Galena, Illinois, one Ulysses S. Grant. Grant applies for a commission and gradually advances to the generalship of all the Union forces. Graham himself enters the conflict as a pathfinder for the army before Vicksburg. Garland describes at some length the siege and surrender of the city. He shows the Union forces stealthily approaching the stronghold, and the Confederates under Pemberton attempting to thwart their movements by various skirmishes. After weeks of waiting, the Confederates surrender, rather than starve. Graham goes home on furlough, and his martial adventures are over. This is the least satisfactory of Garland's historical fictions, but it presents one of the most intimate pictures of Grant in all literature.

After Garland's book, detailing the campaign of a private, it became increasingly fashionable for novelists to describe the fortunes of the ordinary soldier, the "forgotten man" of the war. James Boyd, a Pennsylvanian of Southern extraction, had himself served in such a capacity in World War I, and now depicted the lot of the common soldier during the Rebellion. In *Marching On* (1927) the hero, James Fraser, is a small-farmer descendant of the North Carolina Frasers who, in Boyd's earlier novel, *Drums*, fought during the Revolution. James is in love with Stewart Prevost, daughter of a proud planter, but finds it impossible to bridge the social gulf; besides, there are aristocratic rivals. When the father objects to the hard-working James's courting his daughter, the boy goes away to work in the railway shops. Then the war draws him into its vortex, and he is off with the Cape Fear Rifles. He marches endlessly with heavy equipment over bad roads, faces battle with the trepidation of Crane's raw recruit in *The Red Badge of Courage,* but acquits himself well both at Antietam and at Chancellorsville; then, during the last two years of the war, he stagnates in a Federal prison. In the end he returns to the broken South and marries Colonel Prevost's daughter.

It is an old-fashioned plot, with swords clashing, hearts fluttering, houses burning, and men dying by scores, while the hero bears a charmed life. But there is a freshness in the telling, for the author reinterprets the happenings in the light of realistic historians. Disillusion there is, but no rancor, and no heroics. The conflict between the sections is regarded as the rich man's war but the poor man's fight. The defeat of the South dissipated the glamour of tradition. It emancipated the blacks, but it also gave the poor whites a better status. In style, the author, like his hero, is short in poetic expression and psychological analysis, yet the incidents are full of color, with an admixture of the sordid and ugly. *Marching On* is a humanly convincing story. It is hard to forget James's first meeting with the planter's daughter while he is piling rails on the great estate, or the fiddlers' contest in the old schoolhouse, the long marches and the endless days in prison, and the happy homecoming, even though it is interwoven with the collapse of an era. For, while the South was defeated, romance was not defeated.

Evelyn Scott's *The Wave* (1929) marked a new advance in the technique of historical fiction. Instead of introducing a human protagonist, the author declared, "War itself is the Hero of the book, for this propulsion of the individual by a power that is not accountable to reason is very obviously like the action of a wave." War, as here described, is a mass movement, with some seventy scenes flickering by as on a screen. From time to time appear excerpts from letters and newspapers, army reports, or short, stream-of-consciousness narratives, instead of scenes. North and South, upland and swamp and battlefield, prim New England villages and Mississippi flatlands, Sumter, Bull Run, home and camp and hospital, soldier and civilian, black and white, Richmond bread riots, draft strikes in New York, Grant in the Wilderness, Meade, Sheridan, Lincoln's assassination, war songs, ladies' costumes, plantation melodies —all are carried along on the surge of the author's creative power and are given the titanic unity of a great wave. This terrible inundation sweeps away the securities that have been built, the ties that have developed, and leaves, after shame and glory, only the debris for survival. At the same time, in a dozen scenes of sacrifice and longing and valor there appears a profound affirmation of the value and dignity of all living. It is not one man's war, nor one family's, but everyone's, from Lincoln down to Ginny peddling the extras of Lee's surrender. The narrative is too disintegrated to sustain interest continuously. So many crises, packed with visual and auditory metaphor, blunt the impression of the reader and obscure any continuous sense of the great national cataclysm. On the other hand, it is a remarkable achievement for the author to have projected herself into the personalities of so wide an array of characters with so much vitality. What formlessness the fragments exhibit appears, to some extent at least, inherent in the meaningless horror of civil strife itself.

Outside the Deep South of plantations and manor houses was a large middle class, about whose position in the conflict readers were at last getting information. T. S. Stribling's *The Forge* (1931) is a study of the effect of the Rebellion on such a family of yeomen, the Vaidens, in northern Alabama. Jimmy Vaiden, commonly known as Ol' Pap, is a Hard-Shell Baptist. Once a blacksmith, he is now a slaveholder with a house that is half fort, a gin, a forge, two sets of children—three if you count Gracie, the young quadroon—but without any of the niceties of the aristocratic Lacefields on the neighboring barony. In the course of the war he loses his slaves and his cotton gin when he falls into debt to the storekeeper, and his son is forced to become the Lacefield's overseer. On a lower level are the trader BeShears and the quadroon Gracie, who connects the world of the whites and that of the blacks, a pathetic symbol of an enfranchised Negro as she wanders back from her carpetbagger lover.

Stribling studies his people from the objective point of view of a sociologist, and with a sense of ironic humor lacking in predecessors who wrote of race relations. He notes the surface friendship, but does not overlook the basic hostility between the two races. There is a good description of the Battle of Shiloh, but in the main the book is a social commentary rather than a drama, one in which the author of a later generation pushes the pawns with sardonic gusto. The sequel, *The Store*, Pulitzer prize winner in 1932, continues the story of the Vaidens, with the middle-aged former colonel and Klan leader settling down into a shiftless store owner. The lynching of his octoroon son marks the close of one era and the beginning of a new, as one crusader sees it.

In striking contrast to the baseness of this society is the rich and colorful Old Charleston aristocracy in Dubose Heyward's *Peter Ashley* (1932). Ashley is a young Charleston idealist, an Oxonian inclined to speculation rather than to action. He disbelieves in war and thinks slavery is bound to go, but he capitulates to social respect, forthwith leaves his conscience and the lovely Damaris behind, and with other gentlemen rides off to war. In attempting to recapture the mood of the Old South just prior to the war, the author uses historical references sparingly, but shows with full effect the gradual sunderance from the North.

As in Allen Tate's Virginia novel, *The Fathers* (1938), the mores of the planters are the hero of this novel. The story opens with the excited anticipations of youth, qualified by the apprehension of their elders lest they may never know the gracious, leisurely life of their fathers. This is the South which regarded slavery a beneficent institution and whose cotton monopoly was to force the world to its feet. The story rambles from race week and love of the turf to an excellently described duel, to a slave auction debased by traders, to the St. Cecelia Ball, to political discussions. The poets Simms, Hayne, and Timrod drift in and out of the narrative. The climax of the piece is the attack on Fort Sumter when all Charleston watches the flames through the darkness. *Peter Ashley* is a romantic story, which becomes poignantly ironic when the hero, in order to win Damaris, a maiden fashioned after Simms's ideal of Greek democracy, concludes to accept that society's nostalgic values in spite of his own inner promptings to rebel against them.

Another story in which a young man questions the wisdom of entering the conflict, but finally goes to war, is Mac-Kinlay Kantor's *Long Remember* (1934). When Daniel Bale returns to his native Gettysburg, with a sense of shame for having killed some Indians in the West, he resolves to be neutral in the battle that is about to break around him. But after he mingles with the villagers, the war virus gets into his blood and throws him into compromising relations with Irene Fanning, the wife of a former friend who is wounded fighting on the Union side. The observer's personal drama merges with and heightens the effect of the battle when Daniel forces his way through the lines to lie to Tyler Fanning for Irene's sake. The tragic spectacle of Gettysburg becomes comprehensible less as a turning point in history than as a place where human beings were torn to bits blindly doing the bidding of an elemental force. Kantor reports with thoroughness and accuracy the terrific personal combat of three days when Meade faced Lee on Missionary Ridge and Pickett made his famous charge. Graphic as is the picture of war, even more vivid is the account of the rash things it makes people do. The picture never quite focuses, yet it reproduces the pulsating past as truly as *So Red the Rose* or *Gone With the Wind*—and more devastatingly. Undoubtedly the literature of World War I helped the author to balance the mood and style of his book, to give the reader at one and the same time an understanding of the horror and the inevitability of war.

In a second novel by Kantor, *Arouse and Beware* (1936), the war is an ever sinister background for a more personal, anecdotal tale. The story is a picaresque yarn about three fugitives, two of them Yankee soldiers making their way from Belle Island prison, Richmond, toward the Union lines across the Rapidan. They are joined by a Confederate officer's mistress who has just stabbed him and come away. At first the wretched and feeble men, struggling through the war-scarred desolation, disregard the woman; but in time both covet her, and in the end they are separated by their passions. Psychologically and emotionally the story is much slighter than *Long Remember*, but in depicting the terror of flight it graphically captures the atmosphere of the period.

It has been said, and in a sense it is true, that the South was beaten in the war because it did not know the outside world. Its gracious slave culture was provincial, and that provincialism was in a measure its undoing. In *So Red the Rose* (1934), Stark Young, a scion of the planter aristocracy, contributes his memorial wreath to a cherished tradition and a generous way of life now gone. The book evokes the Old South of culture and ease. The war is presented, except for a glimpse of Jefferson Davis and one of General Sherman, chiefly as it affects two wealthy cotton-planting families near Natchez, Mississippi—the Bedfords and the McGehees. The deaths of loved ones, the destruction of homes and property, the presence of Federal troops—all tragedies and changes leave their indelible marks on the characters. Sallie Bedford, whose husband dies of wounds received at Vicksburg, and Agnes McGehee, whose son Edward is killed in the Battle of Shiloh, bend to fate's blow with fortitude and strength. A pleasant way of life has been doomed. As Hugh McGehee points out, after his fields have been devastated, "There was still goodness that comes of harmony" in the old leisurely living "where interest, pressure, and competition have not got in the way." Although torn by love for the Old South, yet he is conscious of the approaching changes and the necessity for many of them. Thus the author, while cherishing the passing order, sees that it must give way to the new.

Gone With the Wind (1936), by Margaret Mitchell, is not a picture of idle, gallant, romantic Southern life. The people are hard-working provincials, with enough middle-class genteelness to prevent their ready adaptation to the new order of things. After Sherman destroys Atlanta, Scarlett O'Hara, daughter of the Irish immigrant owner of Tara plantation, is uprooted, as were all Southern ladies; but being possessed of peasant cunning as well as beauty, she resolves to use her power over men to regain financial security for the old estate. The price she has to pay is fearful, for it causes her to lose all that Tara stood for, including the one man she could really love.

As the war is about to break out, Scarlett, in a fit of pique marries Charlie Hamilton to spite Ashley Wilkes, who she learns plans to marry Charlie's genteel sister Melanie. In the course of the war Charlie dies in camp, Scarlett's son is born, and she leaves Tara for Atlanta to stay with her Aunt Pitty-Pat and Melanie. Here she scandalizes conservative society by discarding mourning, flirting outrageously at balls, and driving alone. During the fall of the city to Sherman's invaders, Scarlett uses Rhett Butler, the blockade-runner, to make her escape to Tara with Melanie and her newborn baby, and a slave girl.

Tragedy greets her at every turn, as she labors to overcome the handicaps of Reconstruction. She marries for money, supervises a sawmill, loses her husband, marries Rhett for spite as well as out of dire need, and is left by him just as she realizes that she truly loves him, the practical man, and not Ashley, the traditionalist. Like Becky Sharp, this girl with the green eyes rises bravely to whatever the occasion demands, whether it be to kill a thieving Yankee, to marry for money, to associate with scalawags, or to lie and cheat; for Scarlett has vowed that come what may to the old gentility, she will never go hungry again.

The warp and woof of the story—the fine house with its retainers and its indulgent master, the Wilkes's barbecue, the young men riding off to war, the bazaar, the sack of Atlanta, the ragged Confederates, and the night riders and the black days of Reconstruction—are all seen from the woman's angle. Genteel Southern women rely on their social system and training to guide them in crises. Melanie is unbending toward all Yankees; the maiden aunt never realizes that the ancient props have been knocked out. Scarlett's resourcefulness is the order of the new day. In 1936 that much could be admitted, but it was a hard saying in the South.

In order to minimize sentimentalism, the author made Scarlett's story ironic and thereby made her seem emotionally not quite adequate. At the same time, her delineation of the tenderness and courage of the traditionalists, Melanie and Ashley, appears less authentic than the brutality of Rhett and Scarlett, the nonconformists, even though Rhett is a stagy composite. The story, for all its length and overembellishment, moves swiftly, with all sails set in the best tradition of historical fiction. *Gone With the Wind* offers no profound reading of life, but the balance between the historical and the psychological forces is nicely kept. It is above all an entertaining story.

The setting of Caroline Gordon's *None Shall Look Back* (1937) is the Allard plantation in the Cumberland Valley of the border states of Kentucky and Tennessee. Above plot and background looms the figure of Major General Nathan B. Forrest, of the Confederate cavalry. He enters the novel late, after the charming life of Kentucky at the outbreak of the war has been depicted, but he dominates the action nonetheless. He does so partly through the impression he makes on the hero, Rives Allard, his cousin and scout, and partly through the awe and trust he inspires in Southerners high and low by his vigorous organizing and quarreling. When others surrender at Fort Donelson, he gets his men out. Then he captures Murfreesboro, makes his famous raids, fights the Battle of Chickamauga, and has his quarrel with his martinet commander Bragg. Forrest appears as an ill-disciplined, dominating person, a natural man using natural means, who rose from poor-white poverty to wealth and to sectional leadership with the slogan, "Git thar fustest with the mostest." At the end of the story, Rives, the fictional hero, dies in battle, leaving the heroine Lucy's life empty and ruined, while Forrest, the real hero, still battles on. The swallowing up of private lives by the war gives the reader a sense of tragic desolation. The character drawing is not very convincing, however, and the battle scenes dependent on it lack dramatic power and passion. The novel is less spectacular than *Gone With the Wind,* and less verbose, yet in the plantation scenes is more quietly effective.

The collapse of the Confederacy, rather than anyone's private fortune, is the theme of Clifford Dowdey's *Bugles Blow No More* (1937). As pivot for this panoramic narrative, the author relates what happened in Richmond from the time of the hysteria of Secession Night to the terrible awakening at Appomattox four years later. The feeling of hatred appears worse in the beleaguered capital than in the army. So devoted are those Virginians to the Cause, that when the Yankees come near, some commit suicide rather than live under Yankee rule.

On the other hand, *Bugles Blow No More* is as partisan against Jefferson Davis as against the Yankees. The author, by using one city for his setting, is enabled to weave together in a single pattern the military, political, and social history of the war. Wild rumors, false hopes, jealousies, greed, bread riots, looting, and confusion are all a part of the city's daily routine and are presented vividly. The historical impedimenta threaten to submerge the love story, but the outline remains clear. Mildred Wade's love for the commoner Brose Kirby, like that of many others, is nurtured and humbled by the war. As in *Marching On*, Mildred gives up a member of her own patrician class, Dennis Leatherburg, for Brose, a clerk in her father's warehouse. Such a breaking down of conventional barriers offered writers a dramatic opportunity which few of them have overlooked. Too, this novel brings out forcefully the new way in which individual experience is made to yield to social significance. When Brose returns from the campaigns a tired, broken man, Mildred realizes that war kills those who go on living as well as those who die, and "she must summon up the courage by which she would endure through all her living days." The novel thus ranges itself with the modern fiction that deglamorizes war.

Virginia—the Shenandoah Valley—has been the setting of two recent novels of the Civil War which differ considerably in treatment. *Action at Aquila* (1938) by Hervey Allen, author of the popular novel *Anthony Adverse*, uses the journey motif for the story of a man who hates soldiery, yet when the test comes, gives a good account of himself in battle. This man, Colonel Franklin, is ordered by General Sheridan in 1864 to put the torch to the Valley. His ride from Philadelphia to Virginia brings out the Union attitudes toward the war, ranging from noncombatant fierceness to resignation in death, discovers characters as diverse as Buchanan and Sheridan, bares the brutality of guerrilla warfare, and finally takes him into the fight itself. Once back in the Valley, Franklin is in a dilemma because of a former infatuation that still smolders, but he manages to take care of Mrs. Crittenden, even though her high house lies in ashes. This "memoir" has sentiment and a bit of the grand manner, but it is stirring and essentially fair to both sides. The action is itself only a small cavalry brush; what mainly concerns the author is that with the war something precious in American life has died. But, "If Lee and his gallant rebels succeeded," he says prophetically, "there would be wars, endless Gettysburgs, raids, burnings, implacable anger and growing hatred, reprisals for generations to come."

The other novel, *Lone Star Preacher* (1941), by Lieutenant Colonel John W. Thomason, Jr., links Virginia and Texas during the Civil War. Elder Swan, a fire-eating Methodist preacher and captain of infantry in Hood's brigade, here displays his hell-defying courage with the Army of Northern Virginia. He had originally gone to Texas from Virginia, after quarreling with a rich uncle. In Texas he had married the prettiest girl, and attained considerable substance and power. Then disregarding Sam Houston's advice, he goes fighting. West of the Dismal Swamp he sets an ambush and bags sixty Federals; he fights at Gettysburg and at Chickamauga, at the Wilderness, Spottsylvania, and Cold Harbor. In all of these conflicts, with the exception of Gettysburg, this Andrew Jackson extrovert with his roughhewn Texas fighters holds the field. The eight unified short stories about this "Hurricane of God" are hardly subtle or complex, but they are stirring and clear, rich in salty talk, and offer spirited vignettes of army life.

Philip Van Doren Stern's novel, *The Drums of Morning* (1942), is again referred to here (although it was discussed as an abolition novel in Chapter III) because it marks a return of Northern writers to the theme of the Civil War. At the outbreak of hostilities, Jonathan Bedford is in the Charleston jail, conjecturing how the battle is going. After several years he escapes, but is soon caught and consigned to the notorious Andersonville prison in Georgia. In that hellhole he learns to his disgust the part which greed, compromises, and politics play in war, but appears unable to do anything about the corruption he sees. It is not easy to admire this bloodless hero, nor to get excited over the three women in his life, who are on the whole rather stereotyped. Even the historical figures lack vitality. The novel is well documented, however, and has color and movement; it takes a passionate stand for human freedom.

An unbiased attitude toward both armies appears in *The History of Rome Hanks* (1944) by Joseph S. Pennell. Rome's grandson, Lee Harrington, a neurotic modern, learns about his illustrious ancestor's part in the Civil War from Thomas Wagnall, over a jug of cheap whiskey. This sometime surgeon of the 117th Iowa tells him about such major engagements of the war as the Battle of Shiloh and Pickett's desperate charge at Gettysburg, about the filth and smell of battlefields, about debonair Jeb Stuart and plodding General Grant, and about many "kindred matters," such as love on a Mississippi plantation and villainy in Washington. In other words, he learns about America as well as about the members of his family who bore arms for the Confederacy: about Zouaves, hillbillies, aristocrats, scoundrels, preachers, doctors, Indians, Yanks, Rebs, good women, harlots, heroes, and cowards—enough to fill half a dozen novels.

This story of the underside of the war is chaotic and kaleidoscopic and overwritten in the manner of Thomas Wolfe. It is unnecessarily vulgar and gruesome, rarely inspired, but never dull. It reverses the time-honored formula in which the Blue and the Gray fought gallantly for a glorious cause. In this novel, nobody knows what the fighting is for, and all die ingloriously. The technique of matching a story of the past with one of the present in depicting the meaninglessness of war marks *Rome Hanks* as one of the newer experiments with historical material.

House Divided (1947), by Ben Ames Williams, avoids the meretricious eroticism of its predecessor, and exceeds even *Gone With the Wind* in factual information; but despite its clear, and on the whole, just summary of four years of warfare, it is lacking in one respect—it gives little sense of the *esprit de corps* which held the Confederacy together. This neglect is owing largely to the technical demands made by the grafting of a family saga on a narrative of war. As the Currain family are numerous, the many minor figures require a constant shift of focus. In the main, *House Divided* is a narrative of this planter family's decline in fortunes during the prewar period of agitation, when they stand between hotheads and abolitionists; their change for the better during a brief period of Southern victories, when Longstreet is the outstanding leader and Gettysburg the climactic event; and their final ruin and disaster. Because the clan ramifies widely, it reaches into the various levels of Southern society, including the reckless and the corrupt. In one way or another it is involved with many of the notables of the time, its most notorious connections being with the clouded ancestry of the Northern President, the ogre responsible for the bloody combat.

House Divided, though related from the point of view of a Virginia aristocrat, is fairly free from the usual clichés about the Old South, except at the end. The documentation is impressive, though of course the plot is the principal thing. The fiction seems somewhat contrived, however; the characters lack motivation and do not fully come alive. The history, too, emerges somewhat dimly through the haze of mismanagement, draft-dodging, profiteering, and delusions of grandeur. So far as a thesis appears, it is Trav Currain's growing conviction of the integrity of the common man, who, despite his belief that this was a planter's war, and his knowledge of the graft and corruption, yet fought loyally for the Confederacy from Manassas to Appomattox. On the whole, *House Divided*, although it lacks the flinty humor of *Action at Aquila* and the nostalgia of *Long Remember*, is the work of a good storyteller, though by no means a stylist.

This survey of the novels about the Civil War does not take into account the fact that for half a century the most artistic expression of the war in fiction was in the form of short stories. It seems to have been easier to give a mosaic of short individual scenes rather than to attempt to see the war as a whole in relation to American life. Artistically, it is easy to find fault with the naïveté of design exhibited by some early Civil War romances. The picture of leisurely days before the war, the chivalry and arrogance breaking into flame against the abolitionists, the heartbreaking sacrifice which went into the lost cause, and the destruction and hate which swept over the land with Sherman's advance to the sea—all were set in a convenient, comprehensive mold. Since in retrospect the struggle seemed short, a panoramic method was sometimes used, according to which the hero of those braveries happily chanced to be at Fort Sumter for the bombardment, participated in the first battle of Manassas and the battles of Antietam and Chancellorsville and then necessarily went west for Vicksburg. In addition to all these adventures, he had informative letters from Gettysburg, found leisure to detect Copperhead activities in Ohio, contrived to be with Sherman at Atlanta and with Grant at the Wilderness and wound up as an aide at Appomattox when someone thoughtfully sent him theater tickets for the appropriate evening in Washington. It was entertainment pure and it was entertainment simple.

In more recent novels about the Civil War the writing has become much more sophisticated. Realism has forced writers to be more convincing in motivating character and incident, and more accurate in the use of history. Evelyn Scott, by applying the method of the cinema, secured a plausible variation of the panoramic method. MacKinlay Kantor used a single battle as a focal point about which the war swirled; Clifford Dowdey used a city; others a family or a single character. None of these methods is entirely satisfactory, for all result in partial misrepresentation. But there are compensations in vividness.

Also in recent novels the atmosphere is homelier. Where once the central figure was the general on horseback, lately he has been the common soldier. War is now conceived of as a mass phenomenon affecting the spirit of a whole people—for the worse, not for the better.

2. *Novels of the Reconstruction*

Following the Civil War, Congress divided the South into military districts and sent in Federal troops as an army of occupation. Southern whites were compelled to give the Negroes, most of whom were illiterate, equal rights and to allow them the privilege of the ballot. To assure that this would be done, Negro voters and poor whites, together with carpetbaggers from the North, were to set up new state governments throughout the South. Some good was achieved in building roads and improving education, but on the whole, government was corrupt and wasteful. Southerners, mulcted of their property by former slaves and carpetbaggers, struck back through the Ku Klux Klan, and race relations fell into a rhythm of violence from which they have not altogether emerged. Economically, too, the South has hardly yet recovered from the setback of radical policy. The period of Reconstruction proper occupied all told a dozen years, from the close of the war in 1865, to 1877, when shortly after the inauguration of President Hayes the Federal troops were recalled.

Out of the confused and unsettled conditions in the South and the aggressive growth of the North, emerged a literature of local color which helped to understand and to reconcile the antagonistic sections. But there was much to overcome. The end of the war found the South if anything more unified than before. Agrarian interests, as opposed to those of the manufacturing centers in the North, stimulated self-consciousness. Ruin and poverty developed in Southern fiction a feeling of nostalgia for the lost cause. Northern writers, on the other hand, maintained that an outmoded caste system had retarded industrial progress in the South; that this area wanted to re-enslave the Negro; and that carpetbag activities were prompted by a feeling of good will. Writers from both areas hoped that education would in time solve all problems.

The most prolific novelist to deal with Reconstruction was an Ohioan, Albion W. Tourgée. After serving as an officer in the Union Army, Tourgée went to North Carolina as a carpet-bagger and served as judge, editor, and pension agent during a turbulent period. He had a deep sympathy for the South, but his ideas were radical. In *Toinette* (1874), republished as *A Royal Gentleman*, he dealt with the love of an octoroon for her former master, but that melodramatic story was more con-cerned with the Southern attitude toward miscegenation than with actual events of Reconstruction. *A Fool's Errand* (1879), his best-known book, recounts the foolishness of carpetbagging when pleas for investigation and for militia fall upon deaf ears in the national capital and when Southerners resent missionary endeavors. Colonel Servosse's reform movements are too pre-cipitous. But for the love of the Colonel's daughter for a South-ern gentleman, amicable relations between the opposing fac-tions could not be effected. The plot of this novel is negligible, the style is turgid, and the digressions in the form of passionate speeches for the radical cause seem endless. Had Tourgée looked forward to reconciliation instead of backward to sec-tional opposition, he might have produced a permanently im-portant work, but it should have been put in dramatic form.

Tourgée held that Negroes were kept down by head-strong Southerners; he barely suggested the intelligent idea that only by extensive education could the racial situation be improved. In *Bricks Without Straw* (1880), Tourgée formu-lated his idea more completely. He created a plot around the efforts of a young Yankee schoolteacher, Mollie Ainslie, to aid the Negro community of Red Wing, North Carolina.

While Mollie is nursing a planter's dying son—and falling in love with the planter—the Klan destroys the Negro community and leaves it without its "straw" for economic and social development. Mollie returns to the North, but, when differences are reconciled, comes back to her planter, and the two resume their work in behalf of the Negro. Although Tourgée wrote many more books, these three absorbed his burning enthusiasm, and the later works attained little success.

George W. Cable, who had served for a time in the Confederate Army, was concerned in *John March, Southerner* (1894) with the problem of creating a new South, tolerant, intelligent, strongly unified in state governments, and with good educational facilities. The story shows the evolution of March's character from his boyhood in the state of Dixie to the time when his father's business associates and enemies—in particular the former Confederate Major Garnet, whose daughter he loves—plot to defraud him of land titles. Northern adventurers lead him into schemes involving corruption and, after robbing him, leave him in the lurch. In time, March is able to carry out his father's will by establishing a co-operative Negro settlement on his estate; his relations with Barbara Garnet also meet with success. Cable's depicting the former Confederate as villain was in striking contrast to the worshipful attitude of the South toward its heroes, but was not surprising, since after Cable had published the reformatory papers, *The Silent South* (1885), he had taken up his abode in the North. *John March* was rewritten to make over a tract, but the issues still smother the characters.

By 1909, Walter Hines Page, a distinguished North Carolinian, crusaded against a provincial caste system, antiquated educational facilities, and overrespect for tradition, in *The Southerner, an Autobiography of Nicholas Worth*.[2] Worth's

[2] *The Southerner* (1913), by Thomas Dixon, Jr., illustrates the theme of reconciliation between South and North, emphasizing Lincoln's Southern characteristics. The heroine loves Lincoln and is loved by brothers on opposite sides of the conflict.

efforts at reconstruction are constantly misconstrued and thwarted by politicians and by heroizing women. Nevertheless, he and Professor Billy secure state funds for educating Negroes and poor whites in agriculture and cotton crafts and sanitation and hygiene. Although the frank presentation of Reconstruction problems had once incurred resentment among Southerners, Page's novel raised no outcry.

So far had Reconstruction advanced by the eighteen eighties that novels with a neutral attitude could appear. John W. DeForest in *The Bloody Chasm* (1881) made a direct effort to write a novel of reconciliation. In this novel the chasm between North and South is to be bridged by the will of a wealthy Northerner which brings together his nephew and his niece. The nephew is dissuaded from marrying a poor Irish girl with a beautiful voice; and the niece in South Carolina, who is proud but poverty-stricken, has a husband and a home. Necessity proves a hard taskmaster, but Virginia Beaufort at length learns to love her husband in Paris, where South Carolina and the war mean nothing. For his part, her husband has to learn that underlying Southern braggadocio and vindictiveness there is a real pathos, one well illustrated by the life of that poverty-stricken aristocrat, Aunt Dumont. As one of the first realists, DeForest pictured in detail the scenes of near starvation, and delineated well the Negroes Aunt Chloe and Uncle Phil. Several coincidences and melodramatic scenes mar the smooth action of the story, but the character drawing, particularly of the women, is excellent.

In Maurice Thompson's novel of sectional contrasts, *His Second Campaign* (1883), a poor but lovely Georgia girl, too young to share her family's prejudice against the Yankee, falls in love with a worthy young Northern lawyer. But when it is discovered that he burned the family plantation while with Sherman on his march to the sea, an insuperable barrier arises. In time, the family is compelled to recognize the energy and intelligence of the hero, and in a most romantic scene Rosalie accepts Julian.

Mary Noailles Murfree enlisted sympathy for the devastated South in her novel, *Where the Battle Was Fought* (1884), deprecating the duels and the high-flown oratory. In one of the two plots of her story she delineates an unreconstructed Southern gentleman; in the other, she shows how the designs of a carpetbagger on a girl's lands are frustrated; but the Reconstruction atmosphere is conveyed mainly through reflection, with Southerners beginning to question the validity of some of the institutions they fought for.

In the hard-worked theme of intersectional marriage, whether used by Southern or Northern novelist, there was a decided preference for a Northern hero over a defeated Cavalier as the favored suitor. On the other hand, while a Southern girl visiting in the North might admire the aggressiveness of that section, usually the romantic scenes could be best placed among the soft winds of the South. In Constance Fenimore Woolson's *East Angels* (1886), a New England schoolteacher marries a Southern planter and strives to become a Southern woman, but without real success. So does Margaret Harold, who at seventeen marries the charming but selfish Lansing. When he leaves her shortly after for a Frenchwoman, Margaret blames herself for their inharmonious union, and remains true, despite the importunities of the affluent and cultivated Evert Winthrop. When her husband finally returns to her as an invalid, the renunciative Margaret devotes herself to nursing him.

Not until thirty years after the close of the war did Southern novelists express their true sentiments concerning the attractive old days in their beloved Southland and their real attitude toward the cruel treatment experienced during Reconstruction. Northern as well as Southern critics commented favorably upon the first novel with this attitude, *Red Rock* (1898), by Thomas Nelson Page.

This novel owes its excellence to the fact that its impressions are conveyed with restraint; its sentimentalism is of course characteristic of the age. It describes the effect of political, economic, and social changes upon the lives of two old Virginia planter families, the Grays and the Carys. Returning after the war to their overrun estates, Jacquelin Gray and Steve Allen soon take their stand against the cruelties and frauds being perpetrated by the newcomers. Steve leads the Ku Klux Klan, and Gray the old-guard aristocrats; they encounter deep antagonism from Jonadab Leech, carpetbagger, and his secret henchman, Hiram Still, former overseer of the Gray plantation. The elaborate schemes of Leech to secure the Negro and poor white vote in the county afford the author opportunity to display excellent use of dialect.

As the story advances, smoldering resentment bursts into flame when a Negro attempts to attack Ruth Welch, daughter of a Northern promoter. Ku Klux members now take over the county government, while Leech cowers under the protection of the Federal troops he summons; Steve is put in jail, but is rescued in an exciting scene. Propaganda and lawsuits favor the rascals, but the tide turns when Dr. Cary, an old-time Whig who had turned Secessionist, and Ruth's father work together to persuade their Northern friends in Congress to heed their pleas for reform in the state Reconstruction administration. The secondary plot of the love story is sentimental, but the marriage of Jacquelin to Dr. Cary's daughter Blair, and of Steve to Ruth Welch, brings to a happy culmination a novel largely concerned with tragedy.

Joel Chandler Harris, genial Southern humorist, did much by his writings to foster an understanding between the two sections. In *Gabriel Tolliver* (1902), the story of a Georgia lad who reaches manhood during Reconstruction and falls in love with a Northern woman spy, the author laughs alike at "fire-eating colonels" and "pestiferous reformers." The false arrest of the hero for the murder of the carpetbagger Hotchkiss and the clever rescue of Gabriel by his friends make up the most exciting episodes of the story. The unraveling of several love affairs offers opportunity for the display of local color. The author's masterful characterization appears in Billy Sanders, county philosopher and wit, whose subtle activities are most effective against the Yankees. In this way Harris softens his recital of the real cruelties inflicted upon the South.

The antagonism against the North was most sensationally exploited by Thomas Dixon, Jr., in *The Leopard's Spots* (1902), *The Clansman* (1905), and *The Traitor* (1907). Dixon was a Baptist minister whose emotional outlook was colored by some of the worst experiences during the Reconstruction era. *The Leopard's Spots*, with its description of a Negro legislature, its pillaging and lynching, attempted to show the fearful results of educating the Negro above his station. *The Clansman* traced the rise of the Ku Klux Klan in South Carolina until the overthrow of carpetbag rule. Thaddeus Stevens, the most rigorous promoter of Reconstruction measures, is fictionized under the ironic name of Stoneman. When his son narrowly escapes execution by Federal troops for the murder of a Negro, the terrified politician begins to work for kinder measures. *The Traitor* described the dissolving of the Klan in North Carolina by order of General Forrest, but as the author had exhausted both his indignation and his material, this work formed an anti-climax to the series.

The attitude of the New South toward the aristocratic tradition was first expressed in fiction in the novels of Ellen Glasgow. The South she depicted was a land of tenant farmers, small merchants, and poor whites alongside colonial mansions on the one hand and happy darkies on the other. Favoring the self-made man, the author turned the irony of her wit with affectionate derision on the pretensions of caste. The hero of *The Voice of the People* (1900), Nicholas Burr, is the son of a Virginia tenant farmer during the years immediately after the Civil War. His rise in politics is limned against the background of shifting economic and social standards. While his sweet-heart, Eugenia Battle, marries within her own patrician class, he rises to the governorship, and is well on the road to the Senate when he is accidentally shot while pacifying a mob bent on lynching a Negro. The novel makes clear that if the South is to play a part in national affairs, it must favor men of the independence, initiative, and vision of Nicholas Burr.

The Deliverance (1904) pictures a similar struggle with the caste system. The aristocratic Blakes have been defrauded of their large estate, in a perfectly legal manner, by the villainous overseer, Fletcher. Young Christopher Blake, cheated out of his inheritance, denied an education, and forced to toil in the tobacco fields, tries to preserve for his blind mother the illusion that she is still mistress of the estate. Complications arise, for just as he has struck back at Fletcher by leading the overseer's favorite grandson Will into dissipation, Christopher falls in love with Will's sister Maria, and is more than horrified when Will, in a drunken frenzy, murders his own grandfather. Blake assumes responsibility for the deed and serves several years in the penitentiary before Will's confession enables Blake and Maria to marry. Together they await a new order in which all men shall be delivered forever from the spirit of caste. In this respect *The Deliverance* differs radically from Page's *Red Rock*, despite a slight resemblance in plot. The overseer's theft of the plantation interests Miss Glasgow much less than the consequences of that act upon the two families. Page would never have had an overseer's granddaughter marry a scion of the F. F. V.

In faraway Texas the problems of Reconstruction were apparently as serious as in the Old South. Two novelists, John W. Thomason, Jr., in *Gone to Texas* (1938), and Laura Krey, in *And Tell of Time* (1938), have used Texas as background during the decades of Yankee military control after the war. Thomason fell back on the traditional plot of a Northern man in love with a Southern girl. As neither of the lovers is strongly characterized, reader interest is sustained by a vigorous style, aided no little by the author's superb pen-and-ink drawings. Edward Cantrell, young Yankee army officer, comes to Texas soon after the war to reside at Fort Carmen on the Río Grande. Not long after his arrival in this romantic new country he falls in love with Brandon Hawkes, but becomes involved in trouble with her fierce uncle, Major Hawkes, and her hotheaded cousin Rance. Matters are further complicated by the brother's secret participation in smuggling arms, with the assistance of the rebellious Mexicans across the border. In time, Cantrell rescues Rance from the Mexicans and wins the lady. The atmosphere of the period is conveyed by the arrogant attitude of the Texans toward the bluecoats, the rascality of the carpetbag government, and the activities of the Freedmen's Bureau. Difficulties with Negroes were less serious, however, than with soldiers of fortune who made the state their rendezvous.

Ever since the popular reception of *Gone With the Wind,* Yankee-baiting has thrived in Confederate historical fiction, and it is not surprising that Mrs. Krey, one of the planter descendants, who calls Stark Young her master, should make pointed, though restrained, remarks on the subject in her book, *And Tell of Time.* In the novel, Cavin Darcy, a former Confederate soldier, and his cousin-bride from Georgia begin life together on a Brazos River cotton plantation and pass through the trials of postwar corruption and brutality. Northern officials ravage the countryside, grafting wherever possible, and making demagogic promises to the Negroes. The Darcys rear nine children, all but two of whom are the orphans of relatives and friends. Essentially a family chronicle, the book is dynamic in its defense of a decadent feudalism. The members of the Ku Klux Klan are likened to Arthurian knights, no man appears worthy of any woman, Negroes must be kept in their place, and the best social system is one in which planters are on top. In all of this, the emphasis, as the title suggests, is on man's insignificance in the face of time. The story would have been improved if it had been less congested and if its points had been more often made through dramatic incident instead of through exposition.

Francis Griswold's *A Sea Island Lady* (1939) reverts in plot to the earliest type of Reconstruction novels, the coming of a Yankee schoolma'am to the Old South, her marrying a Southern gentleman, and, despite revilings, making a home for him in the best tradition of both sections. The book is unusual in its extension, despite its limited locale, through half a century of Reconstruction. When Emily goes to Beaufort, South Carolina, as the wife of the Reverend Aaron Moffett, agent of the Freedmen's Bureau, her husband becomes one of the vilest carpetbaggers in a land prostrated under military rule. After he is shot, Emily remains to marry Stephen Fenwick, embittered sea-island planter, rears his children, survives his dissipation, as well as a hurricane and a fire, and as a gracious hostess earns the right to be a Southern lady. The story is long, because time here as in other recent historical fiction is a major factor in the drama, but as the author is a first-rate storyteller who writes of his region with beauty and fidelity, the reader hardly minds, particularly since the temptation to people the novel with stock types has been gallantly resisted.

An answer to the melodramatic novel of Reconstruction is Howard Fast's *Freedom Road* (1944). Ever the champion of the proletariat, Fast here transposes the heroes and the villains, replacing the time-honored picture of overweening carpetbaggers with one in which Negroes fresh from the cotton fields and poor whites work out an experiment in co-operation. Gideon Jackson, an unusual Negro, former soldier in the Union Army, on his return to Carwell plantation, South Carolina, is troubled when he finds that he is free and can vote. Elected by the group at Carwell as a delegate to the constitutional convention, Jackson, who must learn to write, is weighed down by his obligations, but has a new perspective. Feeling that simple people may work out their destiny together, he tries to meet incompetence and corruption, but receives only sneers and disdain from the defeated landholders. The constitutional convention, realizing that poor whites and blacks are being betrayed by a planter group, works out a communal plan for the purchase and division of Carwell estate. School and church are established, and town meetings are instituted. A practical democracy begins to function. In Congress seven years later, Jackson is stunned when, the author avers, the Republicans sell the Reconstruction by withdrawing troops from the South in exchange for the election of Hayes. Now the cynical planter Stephen Holms has his revenge. The Klan rides and Carwell is destroyed. *Freedom Road*, although told with restrained passion, is admittedly partisan. The Negroes are exceptional, and the story misses the tragedy implicit in the abrupt change for both white men and Negroes. But though it is somewhat overdone, it recognizes the basic economic problem, and the total effect is moving and inspiring.

The Civil War was in a sense our Trojan War, and any novel about it and Reconstruction has the advantage that the conflict is still alive in the consciousness of the American people. Time has mitigated much of the sectional bitterness, though some ill feeling still continues. Some insist that Southerners are unduly sentimental about that period and tend to romanticize the Old South. Many of the nostalgic novels that have appeared since *Gone With the Wind* have been written by Southern women, naturally, since the defeat of the Southern way of life has been a severe blow to women. As to romanticizing the charms of that mode of living, it may be argued that the period was romantic per se,[3] and if novelists had written in contrast to the spirit of that time, the result would have been not far

---

[3] "If I dealt with romance," says Ellen Glasgow in *The Battle-Ground* (Old Dominion ed., New York, 1929), *ix*, "it was because one cannot approach the Confederacy without touching the very heart of romantic tradition. . . . For Virginia, the Civil War was the expiring gesture of chivalry."

from worthless. The sacrifices and the hazards of the war were borne mostly by the South.

On the other hand, one may consider the words of no less a Southerner than Jonathan Daniels when he says: "For all its tragedy and loss, the South was never so deeply stricken as it believed that it was." The legend of the war, he continues, "became the somnambulent alibi for every fault of the section and for every deficiency of its people." But by 1870 "the South produced the biggest cotton crop, and got the most money it had ever received from cotton for it. . . . Tenant farming, which preserved most of the advantages of slavery and few of its obligations, had been instituted. . . . The War was cruel, but the War gave gallantry a chance where good sense in the economic and social order had been too much wanting." The problems of Reconstruction are still with us, and it may be presumed that the best novels on the period as a whole are yet to come.

V. National Expansion

THE PERIOD from the Reconstruction after the Civil War to World War I had many interests, but essentially it was an era of national expansion. The term often applied to this period—"the Gilded Age"—although it characterizes the boom time and the attendant speculation, is inadequate to describe the complex interests of the times. In the main it was an era of pioneering. The problem was how to possess, organize, and develop the huge territory beyond the Mississippi. Congress tried to distribute the domain equitably among those who needed assistance by passing the Homestead Act. Railroads were flung across the continent, and settlers, taking advantage of the Homestead Act, flocked to the Middle West, and some went on to the Pacific. Towns and cities sprang up where Indians and buffalo had roamed a short time before. To clear the way for acquisition, the Indians had to be subjugated, even if promises to them were broken. Once or twice there was a flare-up, as in the Custer massacre and in the Apache uprising in the Southwest, but the opening of Oklahoma in 1889 announced that the conquest of the aborigines had at length been accomplished. According to Frederick J. Turner's notable essay, "The Significance of the Frontier in American History," the year 1890, with free lands gone, marked the close of the frontier. Then came the growth of cities and the rapid industrialization of the country. Vast profits were made during this period, and an orgy of speculation and corrupt politics was in turn swiftly succeeded by strikes and panics. The machine displaced traditional rural economy, and there arose a new urban philosophy. The sense of nationalism became intensified after the Centennial in 1876. By 1898 the Blue and the Gray served side by side in the war with Spain, and newly acquired power gave the nation a stake in world order.

Although pioneering is the most distinctive motif of American life, it should be observed that most novels on this subject appeared when no more free lands were available, and when Europe, which the nation had looked to, began to crumble. Later, during the depression of the nineteen thirties, the city bread lines brought about retreat to the farm. Some writers wrote a defense of the frontier—its courage, rough humor, and life of action—which they addressed, perhaps unconsciously, to city dwellers. Others saw in it symptoms of decay, and issued tracts of agrarian protest. At first the experience was couched in conventional forms to suit a conventional public. Later, the arbitrary limitations of a plot were waived in favor of a direct paraphrase of that experience, with introspection working out its own artistic form. The dramatic element was never far to seek: when the weather was not the villain, then the cattleman or the banker or the railroad or the settler's own rugged individualism was.

1. *The Midwestern Frontier*

In a country lacking a strong literary tradition, writers of the soil have had to create for themselves appropriate techniques and standards of expression. This truth applies with peculiar force to Hamlin Garland's *A Son of the Middle Border* (1917), the first psychological synthesis of personal and general conditions in the western half of the Mississippi Valley. Using his own family and the McClintocks as chief actors in the drama of frontier experience, Garland was able to give this work more flavor and a more convincing sense of form than he gave his so-called novels. Like a poem it reflects the beauty and the coyness of that nature who relinquishes her

192

fruits only grudgingly. Here are experienced the toil early and late in heat and cold, the stench of sweat, the relaxation in dance and story and song—in short, all the hardships, ironies, and excitements of pioneer life. For, rough as it was, this life had a margin. As the father had ventured from one western frontier to another, so the son "pioneered" when he risked his hoarded dollars to back-trail to that Eastern culture which the struggle on the plains had crowded out of his life. His parents, harried by droughts and blizzards, by insect pests and the battle with the soil, never gave up the spirit of intrepidity, even when after half a century amid that withering life they back-tracked from the parched Dakota farm to the home in Wisconsin which they had left so long before. It is this spirit of endeavor and endurance which has constituted us a people, a vigorous America, which, as Whitman prophesied, might develop great personalities. By catching not only the material facts, but the spirit of the time, the place, and the people, Garland's memorial to a frontier generation is a genuine contribution to our social history. If there is a defect in the work, it is his obstinate romanticism. But by and large, *A Son of the Middle Border* is not only a worthy record; it is a singular achievement.

Much of the hard work of pioneering in the North was done by immigrants. It is fitting, therefore, that some of the best novels should show foreign racial stocks in the process of adapting themselves to American ways. In the novels of Willa Cather, *O Pioneers!* (1913) and *My Ántonia* (1918), the vision and strength of character in girls of pioneer immigrant families triumphs over the hardships of subduing the untamed prairies. In *O Pioneers!* when the old Swedish father of Alexandra Bergson dies, worn out by the battle with crops, weather, and mortgages, she assumes responsibility for the farm, since her mother and brothers are incompetent to do so. She has confidence in the future, and by dint of hard work is rewarded at forty by material prosperity. But her life has been empty ever since Carl Linstrum left to be an engraver. In the end, with Carl's return, she has hope for emotional fulfillment on the farm. Of minor interest is the shooting of her young brother when he is found with Maria Shabata by Maria's hot-tempered husband.

Miss Cather has protested, in "The Novel Deméublé," against overplotting in novels, and is consistent in making her book a series of gaunt scenes relating states of mind to the conquest of the prairie. These scenes are heightened by genre pictures of Alexandra riding on horseback among the colorful Bohemians and Czechs, visiting the mentally unbalanced Russian, and attending weddings and funerals. Out of the abundance of sensory images—the smell of hayfields, the whir of ducks' wings, the songs of meadowlarks, and the blue depths of sky—there emerges a sharp sense of the land and all it stands for.

In *My Ántonia* a courageous Bohemian girl, sensitive and sturdy, achieves self-realization in happy motherhood on the farm. After her father commits suicide, Ántonia Shimerda works as a day laborer on Nebraska farms and as a hired girl in town. She loves dancing, and in her search for joy is betrayed by a railway conductor; she returns to the farm and settles down with a commonplace husband. Rather than longing for escape and social advancement, she becomes the happy mother of a large family. The book, a relaxed form of memoir, offers another quiet, detailed picture of daily life on the farm, with its round of plowing and reaping and feeding stock in winter, and its few social outlets. The author's style reflects the distinction of an artist whose imagination has been thoroughly imbued with the life of her plain and democratic people.

In *A Lost Lady* (1923), Miss Cather sets the heroic age of Western railroad building against the tarnished period of petty acquisition which followed it. The Forrester home in Sweet Water is known for charm and hospitality by all important railroad officials who traveled between Omaha and

Denver. Bluff, chivalrous Captain Forrester, one of the dreamers that settled the Old West, sacrifices his wealth to the depositors of a defunct Denver bank. Marian, his young wife, has a quiet but compelling charm. Then one day the boy admirer who tells her tale has his ideal of her shattered by her unworthy passion for the shyster lawyer Ivy Peters, who has "never dared anything, never risked anything." Accepting life on any terms, this modern Cytherea degenerates after the Captain's death into a libertine; she remains for the narrator only "a bright impersonal memory" of a spacious and noble way of life now dead. In suggesting the decay of the social and ethical life of this small Western town, Miss Cather breaks off where Sinclair Lewis begins. There is a wistful beauty in this short novel, as there is in all of her work, in particular the one next discussed; for in the grandeur of Old Captain Forrester there is already implicit the poetic concept of Archbishop Latour.

In *Death Comes for the Archbishop* (1927), Willa Cather has recaptured the colorful atmosphere of the old Southwest when in the third quarter of the century it was civilized by missionaries of the Catholic Church. In this vast area of desert and stunted junipers, of towering mesas and turquois sky, two French priests lay out their diocese. Father Latour, the fastidious vicar apostolic, who after patient labors becomes archbishop of Santa Fé, and his warmhearted vicar, Father Vaillant, whose activities take him to Denver during the gold rush, often go back in fond memory to their youth in faraway Clermont in Auvergne, but submit their spirits to the appeal of a land not yet committed to human purposes. On the many journeys throughout his diocese the Bishop reawakens the faith in isolated communities, struggles with the decadent Mexican clergy, accommodates his religion to the paganism of the Indians, plants orchards and schools, and founds the Romanesque Cathedral of Santa Fé.

This story of maintaining the faith on the raw edges of civilization is a fabric woven of many-colored strands. Recollections of seminary days and the mystic splendor of Rome mingle with images of bold, flashing-eyed Spaniards, Mexicans pushing across the deserts on muleback from the south, the Navajo chief Eusebio, and the scout Kit Carson. Memorable also are the guide Jacinto, who takes the Bishop through a blizzard to an ancient cave of superstition; and Martínez, the patriarch of Taos, among his herds and women. Central in interest is a winning and human portrait of the real Bishop Lamy, only slightly colored by tradition. With a rhythmic prose singularly appropriate to its subject and with a loving understanding of theme and setting, the author softens the outlines of this epic until it becomes an elegy of rare spiritual beauty. There is in *Death Comes for the Archbishop* no definite history, no climax, no suspense; yet out of its cadenced prose is distilled the essence of a picturesque part of the American past.

Willa Cather, it has been observed, pictured the immigrant on the frontier without our traditional condescension to foreigners. Now it is in order to consider what they had to say for themselves. Scandinavian writers like Johan Bojer, O. E. Rölvaag, and Sophus Winther doubtless owed more to Hamsun's *Growth of the Soil* (1920) than to Willa Cather, both in their technique and in their picturing life as essentially naïve and tragic. Bojer's *The Emigrants* (1924), written in Norwegian, is a penetrating study of the hyphenate pioneer. It relates the story of Erik Foss's land-hungry and impoverished colony of Norwegians who came in 1881 to take up sections of land in the Red River Valley of North Dakota. With a deeply penetrative feeling for the values of his material, Bojer describes the organic conflict with drought, frost, poverty, and isolation—a conflict which concludes happily, however, with the settlers at the end of half a century in possession of every civilized value, including an endowed university.

The finest novel of immigrant life, O. E. Rölvaag's *Giants in the Earth* (1927), is half adventure story and half a penetrating treatise on pioneer psychology. It is an epic of Western man in his struggle with inhuman destiny. To Per Hansa the Dakota prairie means life, an exhilarating struggle, and freedom; while to Beret, his introspective wife, it brings loneliness, terror, and despair. This conflict troubles Per Hansa, yet he hopes in time Beret will feel toward the frontier as he does. But nothing can change her; her chief comfort, her religion, becomes an obsession which brings about the final tragedy. Every detail lends sharpness to the daily triumphs and frustrations of rugged existence which give the story artistic unity. In such descriptions as the swarm of locusts, the blizzard, and the lone man battling with destiny, the book rises to great dramatic power. Its veracity, its straightforward simplicity and vigor, illustrated in the excitement over a hen coop or the wheat coming up, make most frontier novels beside it seem cheap. It was written originally in Norwegian, but the temper is that of America at its most American. Per Hansa's unwillingness "to follow an old path while there was still unexplored land left around him" incarnates the spirit of the West, as opposed to the East—its forthright excitement over *achieving* the amenities of life rather than merely possessing them.

Peder Victorious (1929) continues the story through the second generation of adjustment, when youth drifts away from the original idiom. In Peder, son of Per Hansa and Beret, the process of Americanization goes forward, involving politics, as South Dakota emerges from territorial status. Through all these experiences the mother endures agony, but mutual love suffices to reconcile her at length to the new conditions. *Their Father's God* (1931) completes the story when Beret's son, Peder Holm, marries an Irish Catholic girl, Susie Doheny, and a quarrel results over their children's religious affiliation. After many vicissitudes they separate, as much because of temperamental incompatibility as religious intolerance. The primitive Puritanism of these Norwegian settlers invests their story with a depressing atmosphere; yet despite the tragic element the story has a lift, because it exhibits a strong and steady faith in the human spirit. If the last two novels of Rölvaag are less interesting than the first, it may be because the author's talent was less given to domestic drama than to the sweep of the saga, but it is at least partly due to the fact that the town-building second generation appears to have less poignant personal problems than those individualists who first drove their rickety covered wagons through the pathless prairies.

Another trilogy of immigrant pioneer life is the Danish-American saga of Sophus K. Winther. In the first book, *Take All to Nebraska* (1936), the author sets the key of his grim family chronicle. On a tenant farm, barely eking out an existence, what with battling an alien soil and an unscrupulous landlord and moneylenders, in addition to learning a new language and being sneered at as an "ignorant foreigner," Peter Grimsen sustains himself and his silent Meta by the thought of eventual return to Denmark; but his sons, estranged by overwork and privation, will not return. All painfully become Americans. The author feels this experience so deeply that its unforced pathos marks the book off from merely "recollected" novels and puts it in a class by itself.

In the sequel, *Mortgage Your Heart* (1937), the worst hardships are over. The book is largely an account of Hans Grimsen's adolescence and the resultant conflicts with his father. The father finds it particularly difficult to surmount the barrier of foreign customs and ideals. He thinks his American neighbors idlers, and from a sense of thrift keeps his sons in the field when they should be in school. Hans finally breaks with the farm and goes off to college, at the same time losing his sweetheart and his religion. Finding his former copybook maxims inadequate, he becomes a rootless hero; his kin on the farm have one advantage—they have at least their hold on the land. In the final volume, *This Passion Never Dies* (1938), the struggle with the land continues. Peter dies when the land is sold under mortgage, but Meta is not discouraged. Hans, the symbol of liberation, is now needed on the land, where he battles with the difficulties besetting his work and with the problems of domestic harmony. Thanks to a number of coincidences, he succeeds, but the conclusion is hardly convincing. In common with many trilogies, the last book forms an unintentional anticlimax to the series.

A more conventional concept of the frontier than that presented in these immigrant novels appears in the work of two women, Bess Streeter Aldrich and Rose Wilder Lane. Aldrich's *A Lantern in Her Hand* (1928) relates with quiet force the long, full life of Abbie Deal, who in the sixties as a young wife journeys from a log cabin in Iowa to the Nebraska prairies. Here she brings her large family through the ordeal of poverty and the self-denials of frontier existence. There may be hokum in this and Mrs. Aldrich's other pioneer tales, but it cannot be denied that she makes pioneer hardships real and the accomplishments heroic.

Mrs. Lane's *Let the Hurricane Roar* (1933) and *Free Land* (1938) are accusing chapters in the history of American land ruined by greedy exploitation. The first is a brief pioneer idyll, in which a young couple on the Dakota plains in the eighteen seventies take in their stride such hardships as the grasshopper pest, starvation, and loneliness. It is a moving tale, because the author writes with simplicity, sincerity, and gentle detachment, but it was tailored to magazine demands, and is not as impressive as more definitely localized and better individualized stories. *Free Land* relates the desperate struggle of a young couple with blizzards, cyclones, heat and hunger, and illness and poverty on a Dakota homestead in the eighteen eighties. As a restatement of a frustrated new world's beginning, this simple story is more absorbing than its predecessor, though the taint of frustration impairs what glow the chronicle might possess.

An earlier novel of pioneer Iowa steered a middle course between the heroic and the dreadful-life-on-the-farm schools of fiction. The author, Herbert Quick, in *Vandemark's Folly* (1922) had given the social history of the first Iowa pioneers

—their conflicts with claim jumpers, horse thieves, and blizzards. In *The Hawkeye* (1923) he pictures life during the third quarter of the century in the same region, and in *The Invisible Woman* (1941), during the era of railroads and politics; but the local material in these is not so well integrated with the story. In *The Hawkeye*, Fremont McConkey's mother works hard to secure an education for her children—a sacrifice which Fremont rewards, first, by becoming a country editor and, later, by serving as an innocent accomplice in corrupt local government, though for a period his defiance of a mob makes him somewhat of a local hero. The story is rich in local lore, humor, and pathos, as nesters replace cattlemen, farming becomes diversified, and the Grange is organized. In depicting the eternal conflict between town and country, the author expresses a deep love of the land.

Nebraska Coast (1939), by Clyde Davis, is a swift-moving pageant of Western transportation, in which pack horse, wagoner, riverman, and brakeman contribute their part when in 1861 the Macdougalls move from York state by way of the Erie Canal to Nebraska Territory to grow up with the country. All the furnishings of the western novel are here—bars and sporting houses, Indians and gunplay, and a hand-hewn code of values that is usually underplayed in good American fiction. The tensions are all physical and produce a pageant, rather than a drama of intense wills in conflict with each other and with circumstance.

In Horace Kramer's *Marginal Land* (1939) the theme is the war between the cattlemen and the wheat growers in South Dakota. A young man, after a barren period in Chicago, inherits a wheat farm and with his city-bred wife endures all the afflictions of pioneer living, but wins a measure of success when he finds that wheat cannot be grown and turns to livestock. When his wife returns to Chicago, he weds a girl inured to hardship. The story is enlivened by rural characters, saloon brawls, and festivals, and appears to be based on firsthand experience.

For the small settler the winning of the West meant winning it not only from the Indians, but from the land barons and even from the government. Mari Sandoz told of these matters in *Old Jules* (1935), a biographical novel about her remarkable father's war with the cattlemen of the sand hills of western Nebraska. Tired of pretty stories of the frontier, she then wrote a powerful, realistic novel, *Slogum House* (1937), laid in the same territory at the turn of the century. Slogum House is a bawdyhouse, operated by a ruthless woman, who, after a shotgun marriage, vowed she would outprosper her genteel sisters-in-law in Ohio. Gulla Slogum's insatiable hunger for land drives her daughters to prostitution and her sons to cattle rustling and murder. By foreclosing mortgages and resorting to bribery and theft, she becomes wealthy, for no crime is too low or too vicious to attain her ends, although she finds no satisfaction in the results of her crooked policies. This somber and brutal story, in contrast to stories about brave pioneer women, also tells much about early ranching and vigilante activity, while it makes an incredible monster credible and unforgettable. It is a fine piece of reporting. Scenes like the dusty little courtroom where the trials are held, the parlor where officialdom is entertained, and the crow's nest where fugitives lurk, stick in the reader's mind like burs in a saddle blanket.

The Able McLaughlins (1923), a Pulitzer prize winner by Margaret Wilson, is a more sedate story of a Scottish community in Iowa during the sixties. Wully McLaughlin, the inarticulate, impulsive hero, has returned from Grant's army to find his sweetheart Christie McNair pregnant with the child of Peter Keith, the scapegrace of the community. After threatening Peter, Wully marries Christie and accepts the paternity of her child. When Peter later returns, Wully hunts him with a shotgun, and then forgives him in a surprisingly convincing conclusion. The plot is slight and conventional and the transition between incidents is not always smooth. The author's chief concern is with the human qualities of her rather dour

Scots—their struggle with nature and disease, their feelings of right and wrong. The background is not slighted but is properly subordinated to the simple, deftly drawn characters, in particular that indomitable woman, Mrs. McLaughlin, who would prefer to see any of her thirteen children dead rather than sinful. Otherwise the story is almost too dispassionate to evoke sympathy. There is just enough suspense to make the reader feel he is being entertained by a tale well told.

In chronicling life on the farm, some writers approximate the genealogical novel. *The Grandmothers* (1927), by Glenway Wescott, is such a stately elegy of an aristocratic Wisconsin family. As young Alwyn Tower, trying to understand himself, turns the pages of the family album, he develops a story out of each picture, from the period of the eighteen forties to his own day. It is a representative procession of Americans, some brave and some cowardly, all disappointed. There is grandaunt Nancy, whose husband smelled of cattle; Uncle Leander, who quarreled with his brother in a Civil War camp and never saw him more; Grandfather Tower, who is unable to convey to the younger generation the perils and labor of the past—these, and many more sensitive, passionate Towers and Duffs, conditioned by the farm, the Bible, the Mayflower Compact, and faith in the future. In this Proustian remembrance of things past the spirit of Anglo-Saxon Protestantism has moved westward and settled the Mississippi Valley. Like the *Spoon River Anthology*, though broader and less cynical, *The Grandmothers* is a record of the failures of interrelated lives, too fine or too perverted for success, and of their dispersion and despondency. Loyalty to clan is the only preservative. The framework of the book is mechanical, but the work is rooted deep in American soil, and the author's fresh imagery readily brings it alive.

The Limestone Tree (1931), by Joseph Hergesheimer, is another sweeping family chronicle, an epic-drama of several generations in Kentucky. It is in reality a collection of stories, given unity by the hereditary traits of the Sash-Abel clan. It pictures successively, and with skillfully varying art, the Kentucky of the Wilderness Road, the Kentucky of the racing estates of the eighteen forties, the period of the Civil War—in which the house was divided against itself—, Reconstruction, and events more recent. According to Hergesheimer, these bluegrass Lancelots and their camellia women think with their hearts; they are actually a compound of superstition, illiteracy, and mountain courage. Ill luck comes to them always from the south. Some are killed in duels, one runs away and is never heard of again, and none seems able to come to grips with a situation. The last, a Paris worldling, on hearing his grandfather reminisce, decides to return to the soil of his forebears, for to him Kentucky appears the last frontier of the sturdy North against the languorous, dangerous South. *The Limestone Tree* is a novel of pastoral beauty as well as rich historical lore. It differs from earlier romantic novels of deep passion by pitting in the modern manner personal integrity against a remorseless fate.

In some respects *The Limestone Tree* suggests *The Farm* (1933), by Louis Bromfield, "the story of four generations of an American family" in Ohio, from 1815 to 1915. *The Farm* describes a way of living that has largely gone out of fashion, a sturdy provincialism that cherished integrity and true idealism. When Colonel MacDougal came to Ohio he brought with him this gracious eighteenth century manner of life. With him came a New England peddler, symbol of the exploitative industrial order which manages in time to usurp the farm. Falling prices make farming unprofitable, the children move to town, and alien races take over. This is not a tract in the literature of agrarian protest, however; it touches lightly on the symptoms of decay. *The Farm* is rather a medium for an interpretation of the trend of American development: it includes religion, slavery, and politics; it is symbolic of the American people, with Utopia realized, then destroyed, but with the hope expressed that integrity and idealism will reappear. Although the narrative is disjointed and uneven, it is lucid, honest, and pungent. There is no outstanding character in the score of full-length portraits, but many of the scenes have the richness and charm of a Currier and Ives print.

The Limestone Tree and *The Farm* have something in common with the hunt for the mythical raintree, the theme of Ross Lockridge's novel of an America lost and found, *Raintree County* (1947). Set in the legendary framework of an Indiana community, and using the events of a single day, July 4, 1892, this Joycean dream-drama encompasses, in some fifty flash backs, the range of the American spirit since 1844. At the patriotic exercises of the town, the central character, John Wickliff Shaughnessy, middle-aged schoolmaster, pagan, and poet, meets three boyhood companions, now respectively a senator, a financier, and a wayward professor, with whom, in recalling his own past he develops, symbolically, an interpretation of the course of American life. Growing with America, Shaughnessy as a boy enjoys school picnics, attends revival meetings, listens to Fourth of July speeches, and watches the wagons heading for the Oregon Trail; as a young man he marches with Sherman in the "holy war" that was to weld the bands of union around the South and insure freedom for all; and later, as a father and citizen, having lived through the hatreds of the Gilded Age, he looks with the optimism of the nineties to good years ahead. "America," says the author, "is an innocent myth that makes us glad and hopeful each time we read it in the book of our own life." And he adds, "It is the same myth each time with multiple meanings." In offering these "multiple meanings," the work is a gigantic Whitmanesque poem of man and God, an elaborately ingenious compendium of myth, archeology, nympholepsy, historical lore, lyricism, ribaldry, Platonic dialogue, gusto, vision, and symbolism all compact. If the symbolism is at times murky, and the prolixity of the narrative exasperating, this comprehensive work also has robustness and exuberance. As a novel of the American past it is a striking and significant new experiment.

Another family album, Harold Sinclair's *The Years of Growth* (1940), records the growing pains of a prairie town from 1861 to 1893. It is an Illinois town, which in the author's *American Years* heard Lincoln and Douglas argue their case, and now witnesses the return of its men from the war, and sees the expansion of railroads and the influx of "foreigners." With the increase in wealth, there come frenzied speculation and political corruption as the town develops its hierarchy of leading families. *Years of Illusion* (1941), depicting a bank failure, a police court, and a generally low cultural level, was an inevitable sequel. What happened here happened throughout the Mississippi Valley from 1900 to 1914. If there are few dramatic highlights in *Years of Growth* and *Years of Illusion*, there are many and varied character sketches, drawn with humor and flavor in a panorama that naturally emphasizes economic and sociological aspects.

The Townsman (1945), by John Sedges, is the story of a dynamic town builder in Kansas. As clerk, farmer, carpenter, and teacher, this English immigrant, Jonathan Goodcliffe, struggles with his prairie community as it grows into a town. He advocates wooden walks, plants quick-growing cottonwoods for shade, and fights to keep Median from becoming a cattle town. He prefers a sober, quietly growing community to one cursed by quick prosperity. A blizzard and a prairie fire and scenes in tavern and town meeting provide atmosphere, but the heart of the novel is the plodding man who quietly dominates the community. *The Townsman* marks a turn away from the sensational element to those industrious citizens who, like Jonathan Goodcliffe, leave a permanent mark on a town's history.

Closely related to the novels of town life are novels which deal with the city. In such novels the growth of a metropolis is usually traced through the chronicles of a family. Booth Tark-

ington's *The Magnificent Ambersons* (1918), for example, delineates the experiences of an Indianapolis family whose sudden
wealth and gradual deterioration were characteristic of many
families in the Middle West during the eighteen seventies and
later. Edith Wharton's *The Age of Innocence* (1920) is a mas-
terly reconstruction of the "black walnut" era in New York's
social history. Janet Fairbank's *The Smiths* (1925), in following the fortunes of a typical magnate and his capable wife,
notes the development of Chicago into a metropolis, as Kathleen Norris' chronicle of the Crabtrees, *Certain People of Importance* (1922), tells of the rise of San Francisco. Edna Ferber's *Saratoga Trunk* (1941) combines life in New Orleans
and life in Saratoga in the heyday of the eighteen eighties,
dramatizing incidentally the brutal swindling by the "robber
barons." Boston and New Orleans have had their chroniclers,
and undoubtedly Cleveland, Detroit, Seattle, and Los Angeles
will have a future place in historical fiction.

Hand in hand with the growth of the cities has gone the
phenomenal development of industry. Great financial barons
like Andrew Carnegie, John D. Rockefeller, Edward H. Harri-
man, James J. Hill, and J. Pierpont Morgan became "titans of
big business." Railroads were subsidized, steel became a gigantic industry, and the farmer and smaller firms were strangled
by Wall Street. In *The Financier* (1912) and *The Titan* (1914)
Theodore Dreiser used business enterprise and its dubious
methods for a historical novel based on the career of Charles T.
Yerkes, traction magnate of Philadelphia and Chicago. As
Frank Cowperwood, this conscienceless financier and rake
rises until his plans to become the richest man in America come
to a sudden halt with his imprisonment for embezzling public
funds. Shortly after his release, the Chicago Fire of 1871 and
the failure of Jay Cooke, two years later, precipitate a panic
which permits him to make a second fortune almost overnight.
Cowperwood's business activities are paralleled by his philan-
derings, and help bring about his defeats, though the author

points no moral here. Cowperwood believes thoroughly in the law of survival, according to which the battle goes to the strong and the ruthless. In *The Titan* he stalks money and women even more assiduously. After buying up Chicago's street railways and reducing the system to chaos, he unloads it upon his old New York friends and decamps to London. *The Stoic* (1946), last of the trilogy, depicts his efforts to control the underground transportation system of London, efforts that are thwarted by his death. These novels are our most realistic account of American business—its flotsam and jetsam—during and after the Gilded Age. Dreiser's last novel, *The Bulwark* (1946), is a study of a Quaker banker in Philadelphia, who keeps the faith in the losing struggle between moribund religion and materialism.

2. *The Far West*

During a quarter-century of writing about the West, novelists have come full circle from romance through realism and back again. Westerns have glamorized rough-riding supermen, or exhibited land sharks and railroad profiteers luring sentimentalized pioneers into wastelands. Ned Buntline and Buffalo Bill, and more recently Hal Evarts, Gene Cunningham, Dane Coolidge, Harry Drago, and Ernest Haycox have given us in lavish profusion the conflicts between cattle rustlers and nesters and bad men. But the classic of the cowboy, despite its heavy lavendering, is Owen Wister's *The Virginian* (1902). It is true that compared with the sweating cowhands of Andy Adams and Gene Rhodes, Wister's gentleman from Virginia smells little of cows, but the code of the cowpuncher is authentically realized; and when the cowboy wins the prim schoolma'am from Vermont, the reader is given good measure. Thus, this tale of cattle-punching in Wyoming during the seventies and eighties is much more than a local tale;

it presents the conflict of East and West. So absorbingly is it told that it has become the chief range book known to the public. Everyone knows such colloquialisms as "familiarity is not equality" and the celebrated injunction, "When you call me that, *smile!*"

Walter Van Tilberg Clark's cowboy story, *The Ox-bow Incident* (1940), is a marked improvement on *The Virginian* both in style and in psychological insight. Laid in Nevada in 1885, it relates how the people of Bridger's Gulch organized a posse to punish a band of cattle rustlers who took several hundred head of cattle and murdered a local cattle rider. As in most lynchings, the evidence is garbled, but each participant is tensely realized, from the sadistic Tetley to Davis, the saint *manqué*. The conversations in the bar, the talk and incident at the poker table, the men reflecting on the trail—few willing to do what they are about to do, but herded into the certainty of doing it— these things are given without overstatement, rather with the implication that only a facet of each life here comes into play. Human beings under stress could act thus in any time or place. *The Ox-bow Incident* is a detailed and competent study of the imperfect nature of human justice.

The massacre of Custer and his men in 1876 by Chief Sitting Bull of the Sioux in the Big Horn country marked the last important opposition of the Indians in the Far West. Custer was a natural fool for chivalry and melodramatics, who regarded soldiers as simply machines to catapult him perhaps into the White House. In order to recapture his slapdash reputation, he recklessly sacrificed his troops on the Little Big Horn. To date no worthy novel has treated the subject. In 1913 Edwin L. Sabin wrote a facile romance for boys, *On the Plains with Custer;* then followed Courtney Cooper's *Last Frontier* (1924), a graphic but machine-made performance, and Frederic Van de Water's *Thunder Shield* (1933), perhaps the best of the lot, an account of Custer and the Dakota Indians. Harry Drago's *Montana Road* (1935), like Zane Grey's earlier *The*

U. P. Trail (1918), employed the grandiloquent staging and literary machinery of the movie thriller to bring together Custer, the Dakota Indians, and a railroad tycoon. One of the scenes in Cornelia Meigs's *Railroad West* (1937) depicts Custer's fight against the hostile Sioux; another, the labors of Bishop Whipple in Christianizing the frontier. Her story shows how the Northern Pacific thrust westward against all manner of difficulties—weather, land-grabbers, Indians, and mountains. Surely all these achievements should have a more worthy literary record.

An aftermath of the Custer massacre, so far as the army's relations with the Indians were concerned, was the subject of *The Last Frontier* (1941) by Howard Fast. This novel related the terrible flight in 1878 of some three hundred Cheyenne Indians from the reservation in Oklahoma, where they were starving, to their former hunting grounds in Montana. The cause of their plight was not the weak Agent Miles or the rigid militarist Colonel Mizner, but graft in Washington. For four months on horseback, these Indians—men, women, and children—dodged the army when they could, and fought it when they had to. In all, if the author's figures can be trusted, twelve thousand troops were sent after them before one band was cornered, when they split up in the Black Hills, and was shot down. With the temperature thirty below zero, many froze to death. Finally, Secretary Carl Schurz ordered Generals Crook and Sherman to let the remaining Cheyennes stay where they were. The subject, one of the most disgraceful in our long history of shameful dealings with the Indians, was perfectly adapted to the talents of the sensitive, crusading author. He made the most of it by showing how their struggle to survive impressed itself on the other characters.

There has been no well-written romance of a mining camp. Bret Harte's short stories, with their melodrama, and Mark Twain's *Roughing It* (1872), with its exaggeration, are about all that we have, though Mary Halleck Foote wedded a trite romance to substantial background when she described a feud between rival mining camps in *The Led-Horse Claim* (1911). More recently, Vardis Fisher has given an ironic twist to a fictionized account of Virginia City in *City of Illusion* (1941). This work is a recital of the remarkable discovery of the Comstock lode, of the resulting boom which raised Eilley Orrum to the position of "queen of the Comstock," and of the swift decay of Virginia City into a ghost town. It is a sardonic commentary on the vanity of human wishes.

The later fortunes of the Mormons have been the subject of *The Giant Joshua* (1941) by Maurine Whipple. The book is less a story of Mormon leadership than was Vardis Fisher's *Children of God;* rather is it concerned with the simple folk who struggle to build a life upon the rigorous tenets of the Mormon doctrine. Two moving themes run parallel throughout this book: one, the story of the valiant Dixie Mission, a Mormon outpost on the Utah desert; the other, that of the hardships and earnest efforts of a Mormon girl, the third wife of her forty-year-old guardian, to adjust her life on that frontier. The author has written of her country and people with sympathy and without bias; what irony is to be found between the lines is a comment upon natural human foibles rather than upon doctrine. The novel lacks the dramatic power of Fisher's work, including as it does considerable historical detail that is irrelevant, but it is sensitive and otherwise discriminating.

Some headway of late is being made on the part of realism in rescuing the West from the Beadle tradition. H. L. Davis' *Honey in the Horn* (1935) is a folk tale devoted to debunking the pioneers of twentieth century Oregon as a set of stupid rowdies whose only desire was to "get rich quick" by spoiling the country or each other. Clay Calvert, the shady as well as somewhat shadowy hero, after being mixed up in a jail delivery and associating with herders, half-bloods, and hop-pickers, wins Luce, the itinerant horse trader's daughter. The plot is picaresque: Clay wanders aimlessly in and out of Shoestring

Valley with an Indian boy who scarcely qualifies as a loyal Sancho. The real interest of the narrative lies in the variety of characters encountered in this lusty, restless civilization and in the homely comments the author makes in his unconventional Western drawl.

3. *The Southwest*

In the Southwest, two interesting episodes in economic and social history have been the subject of historical fiction. The first of these was the cattle drives from Texas into Kansas and Wyoming soon after the Civil War. The other was the rush of homesteaders in 1889 into what is present-day Oklahoma. The romance of the cattle drives has been treated by Emerson Hough in *North of 36* (1923). In that story, Taisie Lockhart, daughter of a murdered Texas rancher, finds herself, because of the activities of rustlers, with a depleted stock of cattle. She badly needs money, and as there is no market at hand, determines, with the aid of loyal cowboys, on the drive over the Chisholm Trail to the Kansas market. A conventional romance develops, but the pilgrimage itself is realistically described.

A less romantic treatment of the subject was Ross Taylor's *Brazos* (1938). During the Civil War the Federal soldiery stole the Boltons' Kentucky thoroughbreds, and renegades made off with their cattle. Now, at the age of sixteen, Brazos Bolton, having foregone schooling, drives cattle to Dodge City and incidentally has a liberal education in saloons, women, and thieves. He is thrown into jail for a period of four years, after which he grows up with the country as the boss of a railroad gang. *Brazos* is an adventure story, and in part a success story, which moves in the idiom of the period. It is not a great historical novel, but a homely and honest one.

How Puritanism and profit finally overtook the mores of

the old Wild West during a land boom is related in Edwin Lanham's *The Wind Blew West* (1934). This full-blooded novel depicts the complications that arise in a West Texas town in the seventies when settlers arrive who have been lured by a too-expectant group of railroad promoters. Amon Hall, a Prohibition lawyer, is the hero of this lusty tale. He builds up Rutherford, and he ruins it when he can not compromise, though in the end he saves his own soul. Excellent side shows are offered by an adventurous Frenchman Vidal and a windy Colonel Soward. The *feel* of the prairie landscape and the spirit of the adolescent town are in this book.

The other subject of outstanding interest in the Southwest, the settlement of Oklahoma, is treated with glamour in Edna Ferber's *Cimarron* (1930). Beginning with the famous "run" which opened the territory to homesteaders, the author takes her readers through the raw days of mushroom growth, and up to the time when oil was struck and a real boom was on. For her hero she created a picturesque superman, Yancey Cravat, gunman, dreamer, and wife-deserter. His consort, Sabra, at first seems languid, but in the end proves more heroic than her husband. When he is too quixotic to run their newspaper, she builds it up, and after his death enters the political arena on her own account. The book is a gorgeous pioneer fantasy of seekers for treasure in the unbroken West. But the material is not well fused. The characters are seen only from the outside and are often buried under the plethora of details. Although it may be good cinema for the bad men to take pot shots as they do, they hardly observe the code. Apart from the Galahad hero and the stage Indians, and the overuse of coincidence, the book has some of the elements of an American rhapsody. It is a chromo with some inaccuracies, such as the anachronism of Yancey's crusade to break up the reservations, but it offers a more memorable picture than the Oklahoma novels of John Oskison, Courtney Cooper, and others.

4. *The War with Spain*

The only war between 1865 and 1915 in which the nation engaged with a foreign power, the Spanish-American War in 1898, was perhaps too much of the nature of a melodrama to elicit valid and serious fictional treatment. A few novels about it are in the style of boys' books and have already disappeared. Joseph Hergesheimer's *The Bright Shawl* (1922) is a glamorous romance of Cuba before the American invasion. Hermann Hagedorn's *The Rough Riders* (1927) has taken for its theme one of the more romantic aspects of the one-sided conflict with Spain. While paying a tribute to Theodore Roosevelt and his motley aggregation of cowboys, college men, and miners who fought on San Juan Hill, the author supplies candid details of mismanagement in Washington and of the disorder and waste which characterized our entrance into the struggle. His work is a tract against unpreparedness, showing what happens to soldiers when well-meaning superiors are incompetent. About half a dozen figures are individualized, and a thin thread of love runs through the story, which on the whole is colorful, humorous, and interesting.

Other topics in the period of national expansion will no doubt be treated by historical novelists as they arouse interest and come into perspective, for it must be remembered that this era, being the most recent, has also been the least fully exploited in historical fiction. Generalizations about it, even on small points and over a limited period of time, are risky. Many of the novels, particularly among the large number reserved for briefer mention, have small historical or aesthetic value, tending as they do to stock types, situations, emotions, and rhetoric. But as yet our most effective presentation of the period is offered not by history but by fiction. Such treatment is marked by a wide range of human types, striking incidents, and an intimate knowledge of underlying conditions. *Death Comes for the Archbishop, Giants in the Earth,* and in many respects *Raintree County,* are great novels by any standards.

Conclusion

Historical novels, it is now evident, have interpreted many phases of the national history. On their broad canvas have been displayed the contests with the aborigines for the possession of a continent, the conflict with the mother country for independence, the onward push to Western frontiers, the strife between North and South, and the final occupation of all the land. No other literary form, so far as the majority of readers are concerned, has more acceptably expressed the nation's origins, its development, its ideals, and its meaning. In this genre have appeared the major works of Fenimore Cooper, Nathaniel Hawthorne, John Pendleton Kennedy, William Gilmore Simms, Stephen Crane, S. Weir Mitchell, Winston Churchill, Mary Johnston, James Boyd, Kenneth Roberts, Walter Edmonds, Le Grand Cannon, Burke Boyce, Willa Cather, Hervey Allen, and a host of others. Surely this type of novel deserves more than the passing mention it has received from the critics and historians.

It is not to be denied, of course, that many historical novels have been aesthetically deficient. The early experimenters were amateurs at writing novels and exhibited little sense of the organic relation between materials and form. They wrote in great haste. Their work was melodramatically plotted, drastically edifying, and much less carefully documented than that of today. However, writers were not far removed from their materials and did not err so much in their concepts as might be supposed. Some of them included too much history; they made the mistake of trying to reconstruct an entire era instead of some salient feature of it. Even yet most historical novels sprawl unnecessarily because their authors have not troubled to select and to achieve perspective. There might well be a little more technical adventuresomeness, a little more selectivity in what has come to be an overlengthy pattern. Many writers have been more successful with their fiction than with the handling of history; others, the reverse; some have written with too exuberant an imagination and have let their sense of drama interfere with historical fact. In several instances, contemporary events have shaped to some extent the interpretation of the past, and probably always will. In recent years much of American history has been rewritten as a drama of conflicting economic interests, a point of view which may be stressed less in a future age.

In style and method the novels have followed the conventions of contemporary usage. The genteel tradition affected the historical novel adversely, as it affected other forms of literary art; but novels presenting the past withstood the softening influence better than did the tales of contemporary domestic life. Because a sense of nostalgia is inseparable from the genre, it has been necessary to find some device to avoid excess of sentiment. The use of irony has proved to be an effective antidote for sentimentalism. On the other hand, historical fiction has been generally preserved from the vagaries of some recent experiments in literary art. When the influence of Freud impelled novelists to concern themselves with the inner life, it was the activism of the historical novel that furnished a means of escape from the delusion of the subjective. And when the trials and tribulations of proletarian fiction flagged, the historical novel offered a full-blooded world of adventure as a welcome alternative.

Normally a conventional and romantic genre, the historical novel has lately emerged considerably chastened in its romantic tendencies and has followed the tenets of realism in psychology and in social awareness. By embracing the realistic method, it has made great gains over the theatrical costuming, the faulty motivation, the elaborate description, the overplotting, and the clumsy, archaic diction which prevailed so recently as the turn of the century. Readers, thanks to modern technology, are swifter in their perceptions than formerly and comprehend a far greater number of things. These things the writer of fiction must take into account. Character must now be convincing and should be only secondarily related to greater events. The day for heroics is past. Storybook villains and demigods are no longer believed in. Legendary giants were men like ourselves, and their times no better than our own. There has been a loss, also, for realists are generally weak in conveying the total attitude of a period. They try hard to make up in psychological interest for the glamour which they avoid, but they seldom synthesize the special spiritual atmosphere of a movement or an era. They may be more accurate in details than their predecessors, but they are not therefore always better storytellers.

There have been compensations, however, particularly in the feeling for scene. Novelists, knowing their local history, have intuitively ferreted out certain aspects of national expansion before historians could hazard a generalization. Historians tell what men did, novelists what they thought and were. Thus the two arts complement each other in trying to account for the intangible motivations of life. Who can say that history did not take place as conceived by the historical imagination? By making history real to its readers, by showing what historical events meant to the common citizen who was caught in the current of swiftly moving events, historical fiction has greatly vivified and enriched our sense of the past. In doing this, it has developed a healthy skepticism in regard to the record. The modern temper in historical fiction is marked by a definitely revisionist attitude, not only concerning men like Benedict Arnold, John Paul Jones, George Rogers Clark, and Tom Paine, but concerning the bungling and the chicanery of men in high office as well. The inclusion of vice, profanity, and frustration, although it has been overemphasized of late, has added something like the fillip of horror in the old Gothic romances.

Whether the realistic historical novel has greatness remains to be seen. Most recent novelists have been more successful in their use of history than in their drawing of character. To some extent the blame for this state of affairs rests upon well-known periodicals of wide circulation in which many of the novels first appeared in serial form. These periodicals have encouraged, unconsciously perhaps, the use of more or less stereotyped characters. The art and popular appeal of the cinema are also in part to blame. Both media deserve credit for bringing reasonably authentic Americana before many people, and blame for the limitations of pattern imposed on novels tailored to fit the demand. It may be too early to see what possibilities lie within fictional experiments with the past. In any case, whether the historical novels as now conceived have in them the seeds of greatness or impermanence, those that make a serious effort to probe human relationships cannot be ignored by the social historian. They contribute to a living culture and thereby aid us in our endeavor to transform the present and illuminate the future.

After all, this is taking a very modest view of the situation. A few novelists have mastered the art of writing true historical fiction. They have told an important story superbly, they have handled their documentary material lightly and intelligently, they have characterized perceptively, and they have conveyed the atmosphere of the period they undertook to describe. In short, they have written good novels.

Appendix:
Additional Historical Novels

THIS LIST, while reasonably full, is selective. It does not undertake to include juvenile or dime novels dealing with the American past, although a few such items are included for certain reasons.

CHAPTER I. *Colonial America*

1822 [Neal, John]. *Logan, A Family Chronicle.* Yellow Creek massacre, 1774. Defense of a friendly and eloquent Indian leader at the time of Lord Dunmore's War.

1824 Anon. *The Witch of New England: A Romance.* Late seventeenth century.

1825 Anon. *The Christian Indian; or, Times of the First Settlers.* Defense of Indians in Massachusetts against Europeans.

[Furman, Garrit]. *Redfield: A Long-Island Tale, of the Seventeenth Century.*

Anon. *Salem Witchcraft; or the Adventures of Parson Handy, from Punkapog Pond.* Second edition with corrections.

1827 [Brainard, John G. C.]. *Fort Braddock Letters; or, A Tale of the French and Indian Wars in America.*

[Cheney, Harriet V.]. *The Rivals of Acadia.* D'Aulney and La Tour conflict during Winthrop's administration, 1643.

Judah, S. B. H. *The Buccaneers.* Captain Kidd in New York, 1689. Stodgy.

1830 [Cooper, J. Fenimore]. *The Water Witch.* Piracy on the high seas about 1710–20.

1831 [Bacon, Delia]. "The Regicides," in *Tales of the Puritans.* Romantic story of Whalley, Dixwell, and Goffe in Connecticut, based on Stiles.

1832 [Richardson, Major John]. *Wacousta, or The Prophecy.*
Pontiac's Conspiracy at Detroit, 1763–65. Falsifies a great
deal.

1835 Anon. *Blackbeard.* Philadelphia and neighboring colonies in
1732. Pirating by Captain Teach.

1838 [Ransom, J. B.]. *Osceola; or, Fact and Fiction. A Tale of the
Seminole War.* Florida.

1839 [Dawes, Rufus]. *Nix's Mate.* Revolt of Massachusetts Bay
Colony against royal oppression and Harvard pedantry.

[Motley, John Lothrop]. *Morton's Hope.* Mingles pictures
of romantic German student life with episodes of the
French and Indian Wars and the Revolution.

1840 [Lee, Eliza B.]. *Delusion; or, The Witch of New England.*
Salem in 1692.

1841 Williams, Catherine R. *The Neutral French.* Well-docu-
mented account of Acadians exiled by British in 1755.
Revolution. France.

1842 Anon. *The Salem Belle: A Tale of 1692.* Witchcraft. Cotton
Mather a secondary figure.

1844 Anon. *Old Fort Duquesne: A Tale of the Early Toils, Struggles and Adventures of the First Settlers at the Forks of
the Ohio, 1754.* Indians in western Pennsylvania. Washington and Braddock's defeat.

1845 Carpenter, William H. *Claiborne the Rebel: A Romance of
Maryland, under the Proprietary.*

Herbert, Henry W. *Ruth Whalley; or, The Fair Puritan.*
Granddaughter of regicide among the Indians of Massachusetts.

1846 Ingraham, Joseph H. *Leisler.* Rebellion against Catholics in
New York, 1689. Paper back.

Murray, W. W. *Isadore.* Indian fighting around Lake Wine-
pessauke, New Hampshire, 1721–22. Paper back.

1853 Bennett, Emerson. *The Fair Rebel.* Bacon's Rebellion, 1676.
By a partisan. Paper back.

Brace, John P. *The Fawn of the Pale Faces.* Hartford settlement's fight with the Indians, 1650.

Peploe, Annie Molyneux (Mrs. J. B. Webb). *The Pilgrims
of New England.* Indian wars. Juvenile.

1854 Banvard, Rev. Joseph. *Priscilla.* Strife between Puritans and Baptists from Baptist point of view. Trouble with Indians.

1856 Anon. *Edith; or, The Quaker's Daughter: A Tale of Puritan Times.*

1859 Thackeray, William Makepeace. *The Virginians.* Washington and colonial Virginia. Family divided by Revolution. Sequel to *Henry Esmond,* by a Victorian novelist.

1868 Cooke, John Esten. *Fairfax, or The Master of Greenway Court.* Young Washington and Lord Fairfax, rivals for Cannie Powell. 1748 Indian raid and reprisal. Close imitation of *The Last of the Mohicans.*

1879 Beach, Rebecca. *The Puritan and the Quaker.* Conciliatory.

1881 Austin, Jane G. *A Nameless Nobleman.* Plymouth a half-century after the Pilgrims. Woven from family traditions.

1886 Barr, Amelia E. *The Bow of Orange Ribbon.* Dutch maid's love for English sweetheart.

1889 Catherwood, Mary H. *The Romance of Dollard.* French and Hurons repulse Iroquois invading New France, 1660.

1890 Austin, Jane G. *Standish of Standish.* Plymouth colony. Alden and Priscilla. Juvenile.

    Bynner, Edwin L. *The Begum's Daughter.* Child of East Indian mother and Dutch physician in New York, 1689–90. Leisler's Rebellion, displacement of Catholic governor.

1891 Austin, Jane G. *Betty Alden.* Sequel to *Standish of Standish.* Bradford, Winslow, Sir Christopher Gardiner. Rigidly verified.

    Bowyer, James T. *The Witch of Jamestown.* Colonial Virginia. By an English writer.

1895 Abbott, Charles C. *A Colonial Wooing.* On New Jersey Quakers. Unsympathetic.

1896 Goodwin, Maud Wilder. *White Aprons.* Bacon's Rebellion in behalf of democratic ideals, 1676, and Court of Charles II.

    Parker, Sir Gilbert. *The Seats of the Mighty.* Memoirs of Captain Robert Moray on events from 1755–60, including the Battle of Quebec.

    Stimson, Frederic J. *King Noanett.* Ingram's rebellion in Virginia and later campaign in Massachusetts against South

Natick Indians. Third quarter of seventeenth century. Written by a lawyer.

1897 Child, Frank S. *A Colonial Witch*. Fanatical Puritans in Connecticut. Rich in social background, but conventional in plot.

1898 Murfree, Mary Noailles. *The Story of Old Fort Loudon*. Well-informed but poorly unified story of massacre by Cherokees in 1760.

1899 Altsheler, Joseph. *A Soldier of Manhattan*. One of many juveniles by this author. Ticonderoga and Quebec during French and Indian Wars.

1899 Rayner, Emma. *In Castle and Colony*. Swedish and Dutch rivalry along the Delaware, about 1650.

1901 Dix, Beulah M. *The Making of Christopher Ferringham*. Quakers in Massachusetts.

1902 French, Allen. *The Colonials*. Indians of the West and evacuation of Boston. History studied minutely.

Hotchkiss, Chauncey. *The Strength of the Weak*. Braddock and Sir William Johnson, with adventures of French and Indian Wars.

Stockton, Frank. *Kate Bonnet*. Daughter of eighteenth century pirate.

1903 Murfree, Mary Noailles. *A Spectre of Power*. Romance of French and Indian Wars near present Muscle Shoals, Tennessee.

1905 Parrish, Randall. *A Sword of the Old Frontier*. Fort Chartres and Pontiac Rebellion. Conventional.

1906 Murfree, Mary Noailles. *The Amulet*. Fort Prince George in 1763; sequel to *The Story of Old Fort Loudon*.

1911 McCook, Henry C. *Quaker Ben*. Pennsylvania in 1737.

1913 Seaman, Augusta. *Mamselle of the Wilderness*. La Salle and Mississippi River pioneers.

1917 Buchan, John. *Salute to Adventurers*. Good story of adventure in colonial Virginia, about 1690. By premier of Canada.

1920 Gregg, F. M. *Founding a Nation*. Mayflower Pilgrims versus Puritans.

1922 Johnston, Mary. *1492*. Romantic account of voyages of Columbus.

1924——. *The Slave Ship*. Slave trade in Virginia, 1661–80.

1925 Sublette, Clifford M. *The Scarlet Cockerel*. French Huguenots, Spaniards, and Indians in Carolina. Competent.

1926 Benét, Stephen Vincent. *Spanish Bayonet*. Pre-Revolutionary Florida. New York banker's son investigates divided
household on indigo plantation and returns with indentured laborer. Picturesque.

Sublette, Clifford M. *The Bright Face of Danger*. Rough-and-
tumble story of Virginia during Bacon's Rebellion.

1927 Crownfield, Gertrude. *Alison Blair*. Emigrant to America
finds refuge with Sir William Johnson in New York
province.

Havard, Aline. *Regicide's Children*. The Vanes at Hartford, 1689.

Pendexter, Hugh. *The Red Road*. Colorful, graphic romance
at time of Braddock's defeat.

1928 McFarland, Raymond. *The Sea Panther*. Lively story of sea
rovers and capture of Louisburg.

1929 Grimstead, Durward. *Elva*. Spread of Salem witchcraft
hysteria.

1931 Johnston, Mary. *Hunting Shirt*. Indian life in Virginia,
1775–80.

1932 Lovelace, Maud. *Charming Sally*. Love of a Quaker for an
actress in Philadelphia, 1752.

1935 Coryell, H. V. *Indian Brother*. Captivity in Maine and Jesuit
activity against the Crown, 1713f.

Snedeker, Mrs. Caroline. *Uncharted Ways*. Mary Dyer from
Yorkshire escapes hanging as a Quaker in Massachusetts.

1936 Coatsworth, E. J. *Sword of the Wilderness*. Fighting between French and Indians in Maine and Canada, 1689.
Juvenile.

1937 Lion, Hortense. *Mill Stream*. Conflict, 1790–1814, between
home industries and shipbuilders for foreign trade.

1938 Pawle, Kathleen. *Mural for a Later Day*. Founding of New
Sweden on the Delaware by Swedes and Finns.

1939 Dowdey, Clifford. *Gamble's Hundred*. Rise of planters over
Virginia small farmers, 1700–30. Popular.

Hughes, Rupert. *Stately Timber*. Fight for freedom in Boston, Virginia, Barbados, about 1650. Heavily documented and detailed.

Jennings, John E. *Next to Valour*. Rogers' Rangers at Champlain, Ticonderoga, Quebec. Characterization superficial and plot vapid, but detailed and authoritative.

Lofts, Nora. *Blossom Like the Rose*. New England stubborn religionists versus Indian savages, 1680.

Pound, Arthur. *Hawk of Detroit*. Cadillac and conflicting interests with government monopolies.

Schumann, Mary. *Strife Before Dawn*. Fort Pitt menaced by Pontiac and British. Girty, Clark, Logan. Dunmore's War.

1940 Erskine, John. *Give Me Liberty*. Patrick Henry and pre-Revolutionary politics. Protagonist an admirer of Henry.

Hammand, Esther. *Road to Endor*. Overcrowded novel of London, Barbados, and Salem during witchcraft period.

Seifert, Shirley. *Rivers Out of Eden*. French adventurer's journey up the Mississippi from New Orleans to St. Anne, 1763.

Sessler, Jacob J. *Saints and Tomahawks*. Moravian settlements in Pennsylvania, 1736–60.

1941 Allis, Marguerite. *Not Without Peril*. Jemima Sartwell's Indian captivity; pioneer hardships, folkways of early Vermont. Lively and veracious.

Gordon, Caroline. *Green Centuries*. Pre-Revolutionary frontier life in Tennessee and Kentucky. Boone, Henderson, Robertson, Sevier. Sensitive.

Lytle, Andrew N. *At the Moon's Inn*. Disjointed narrative of De Soto's travels in Florida.

Pinckney, Josephine. *Hilton Head*. English surgeon in South Carolina and Barbados during seventeenth century.

Sass, Herbert R. *Emperor Brims*. Uprising of Creeks in South Carolina in 1715. Background better than characterization or plot.

1942 Cabell, James Branch. *First Gentleman of America*. A prince of Ajacan (Virginia) accompanies Spaniards to Florida and to Spain. A comedy of conquest.

Jennings, John E. *Gentleman Ranker*. Swashbuckling romance. Braddock's defeat and Indian depredations in the Shenandoah Valley. Earthy.

Schachner, Nathan. *The King's Passenger*. Deported aristocrat comes to America and aids Bacon's Rebellion. Exciting.

Schofield, William G. *Ashes in the Wilderness*. Roger Williams and King Philip's War. Based on colonial diary.

Scruggs, Philip. *Man Cannot Tell*. Indentured servant helps Bacon's Rebellion against Berkeley and privilege. Sound economics, geography. Absorbing.

Singmaster, Elsie. *A High Wind Rising*. Conrad Weiser in Pennsylvania befriends Indians favorable to English against French, 1728–55.

Updegraff, Florence. *Traveler's Candle*. Rhode Island Quaker. Juvenile.

1943 Kenyon, Theda. *Golden Feather*. Overplotted romance of Cavalier England and Indian wilderness.

Marshall, Edison. *Great Smith*. Picaresque story of Virginia colony.

Miers, Earl. *Valley in Arms*. Conflicts with Pequots in Connecticut. Juvenile.

1944 Judah, Charles B. *Tom Bone*. Swift-paced novel of slave trading. Tom involved in Bacon's Rebellion.

1945 Marsh, George. *Ask No Quarter*. Colonial Rhode Island. Good nautical information.

Miller, Helen T. *Dark Sails*. Despite Spanish threats, Oglethorpe tries to settle the island of St. Simons, Georgia.

1946 Burt, Katherine N. *Close Pursuit*. Feminine account of romance in Williamsburg. William Fyfe, Tom Jefferson, Pat Henry.

Cochran, Hamilton. *Silver Shoals*. Cotton Mather in Massachusetts and treasure hunting with Captain William Phips off the Bahamas. Begins and ends in England.

Cooper, Kent. *Anna Zenger*. Credible defense of early advocate of freedom of the press.

Dodge, Constance W. *In Adam's Fall*. Salem witchcraft hysteria humanized.

Frey, Ruby F. *Red Morning*. Ohio Territory in seventeen fifties. Washington, Braddock, Franklin, Dinwiddie. Repetitive, but credibly human.

Grant, Dorothy. *Night of Decision*. Engrossing melodrama of New York under Catholic Governor Thomas Dongan, 1683–90, with Leisler's revolt.

Hersch, Virginia. *The Seven Cities of Gold*. Coronado's second expedition (from Mexico to Kansas). Colorful; overcrowded with history.

Page, Elizabeth. *Wilderness Adventure*. Garrulous detective travelogue. Abducted Virginia girl; New Orleans jails; England, 1742.

Phillips, Alexandra. *Forever Possess*. Wordy history of patroons and Leisler's Rebellion, 1689 and nineties.

1947 Stouman, Knud. *With Cradle and Clock*. Yellow fever, New York, and piracy, 1702.

White, Helen C. *Dust on the King's Highway*. The effort, 1771–81, to establish an inland route from Sonora to California missions.

1948 Costain, Thomas B. *High Towers*. French colonial aspirations in America: Sieur d'Iberville's explorations of the Mississippi and Sieur de Bienville's founding of New Orleans. Melodramatic.

Van de Water, Frederic. *Reluctant Rebel*. Green Mountain Boys under Ethan Allen against Yorkites and British. Earthy humor. Its sequel. *Catch a Falling Star* (1948), takes up the years 1780–81.

1949 Barker, Shirley. *Peace, My Daughters*. Vivid account of Salem witchcraft. Poetic style.

Hamilton, Harry. *Thunder in the Wilderness*. Colorful novel of Frenchmen and Indians in the Mississippi Valley during the seventeen sixties.

McCall, Marie. *The Evening Wolves*. Realistic picture of witchcraft terror in Boston.

Stover, Herbert. *Song of the Susquehanna*. Pennsylvania during the French and Indian Wars. Boquet, Morris, Cresap, Weiser, and Bartram.

CHAPTER II. *The American Revolution and Its Aftermath*

1797 [Mann, Herman]. *The Female Review.* Deborah Sampson's service disguised as a Continental soldier.

1816 Woodworth, Samuel. *The Champions of Freedom.* Melodrama. War of 1812, Revolution. Lawrence, Decatur, Harrison, Tecumseh, Jackson; Washington's spirit.

1823 [Neal, John]. *Seventy-Six.* Lively tale of the Revolution.

1825 Gazer, Giles, Esq., *pseud. Frederick de Algeroy.* Kidnaping story lightly connected with De Kalb and Battle of Camden. Sentimental and Gothic.

1826 [Cushing, Mrs. Eliza L.]. *Yorktown.* Gothic romance. Slight reference to battle.

1828 [Heath, J. E.]. *Edge-Hill; or The Family of the Fitzroyals.* Cornwallis, Lee, Lafayette in Virginia, 1781.

1830 [McClung, John A.]. *Camden; A Tale of the South.* After the fall of Charleston, Tarleton attacks Gates, DeKalb dies. Story patterned after Scott.

1831 [McHenry, James]. *Meredith; or, The Mystery of the Meschianza.* British in Philadelphia, 1778.
[Smith, Richard P.]. *The Forsaken.* Festival in Philadelphia for Howe on his departure.

1834 Anon. *Ambrose and Eleanor.* Melodramatic romance slightly connected with Battle of Brandywine.

1835 [Fay, T. S.]. *Herbert Wendall. A Tale of the Revolution.* New Jersey.
[Sedgwick, Catharine]. *The Linwoods.* Sentimental romance laid in New York and a New England village. Washington and Lafayette shown intimately.
[Tabb, T. T.]. *Rose-Hill.* Two families in West Virginia.

1838 [Ingraham, Joseph H.]. *Burton; or, The Sieges.* Battle of Quebec, Fall of Montcalm, retreat from Long Island and Siege of New York 1750–1812. Sensational defamation of Aaron Burr's early character. Washington, Putnam, Howe, Montgomery, Montcalm.

1841 [Willis, John R.]. *Carleton, A Tale of Seventeen Hundred and Seventy-six.* Washington, Howe; Battle of White Plains.

1842 Smith, Elizabeth O. (Mrs. Seba Smith). *The Western Captive*. Tecumseh, about 1781–1812.

1844 Lippard, George. *Herbert Tracy*. Romance of Germantown battlefield. Washington, Wayne, Pulaski. Sensational.

1845 Barker, Benjamin. *Ellen Grafton, the Lily of Lexington*. Dime novel with little on the Revolution. Cf. *The Female Spy* (1846) by Barker.

1846 Lippard, George. *Blanche of Brandywine*. Washington in Pennsylvania. Legends of murder, seduction, and intrigue in dime-novel style.

    [Little, George]. *The American Cruiser*. Captured in English Channel. Dartmouth massacre. 1812.

    Simms, J. R. *The American Spy*. Paper back. Defense of Nathan Hale.

1847 Robinson, J. H. *The Boston Conspiracy*. Boston Tea Party, 1773, and following events.

    Sterling, Charles F. *Buff and Blue*. Long Island and privateers during the Revolution.

1848 Brisbane, A. H. *Ralphton; or, The Young Carolinian of 1776*. Juvenile.

1849 Peterson, Charles J. *Grace Dudley; or, Arnold at Saratoga*. Cheap novel of '77.

1850 Cobb, Joseph B. *The Creole; or, Siege of New Orleans*. Jackson, Lafitte, 1814–15. By a writer of sensation.

    [Kilbourn, Diana T.]. *The Lone Dove*. Washington at Valley Forge. Scenes crowded and confusing.

1851 Bennett, Emerson. *The Female Spy* and sequel *Rosalie Du Pont*. Arnold.

1852 Anon. *The Swamp Steed*. Marion, Jasper, Moultrie, Flora Macdonald, 1778–81.

1853 Jones, J. B. *The Monarchist*. Intrigues against Washington. Jefferson, Patrick Henry. Intimate.

1854 Dupuy, E. A. *Ashleigh*. New Hampshire and New York quarrel, 1775.

1856 [Shepherd, Daniel]. *Saratoga*. Indian warfare in the Hudson River valley, 1787.

1858 Stephens, Ann Sophia. *Mary Derwent*. A tale of the Wyoming Valley, Pennsylvania.

1860 Clemens, Jeremiah R. *The Rivals*. Burr and Hamilton. Slight fiction.

1861 Ellis, Edward S. *The Forest Spy*. Dime novel of battles of Thames and Tippecanoe. Tecumseh, Harrison, Proctor.

1862 Winthrop, Theodore. *Edwin Brothertoft*. Third edition. Battle of New York. Slight.

1867 Simms, William Gilmore. *Joscelyn*. Whigs and Tories in Georgia.

1876 [Morford, H.]. *The Spur of Monmouth*. Human portrait of Washington and Indian John. Valley Forge and Lee's treason at Monmouth. Romance dubious. Juvenile.

1877 Cooke, John Esten. *Canolles*. Hackneyed account of American outlaw. Lafayette, Wayne, Tarleton, Arnold glimpsed. 1781.

Harte, Bret. *Thankful Blossom*. Short tale laid in New Jersey, introducing Washington and Hamilton.

1883 Marks, Mary A. M. Hoppus. *A Great Treason*. Arnold and André.

1888 Riddle, A. G. *The Tory's Daughter*. Battle of the Thames. Rhetorical, puerile, sentimental.

1890 Catherwood, Mary H. *The Story of Tonty*. Montreal, Frontenac, St. Louis. Based on life of La Salle's famous aide.

1892 Bynner, E. L. *Zachary Phips*. Burr and War of 1812 in the West.

1896 Barnes, James. *For King or Country*. New York campaign, both sides. Juvenile.

1897 Rodney, George B. *In Buff and Blue*. Delaware troops during the Revolution.

1901 Catherwood, Mary H. *Lazarre*. Legend of lost dauphin, son of Louis XVI of France, found among Illinois Indians in 1795. Tecumseh, Johnny Appleseed.

Chambers, Robert W. *Cardigan*. Indian adventures when British sought alliance with the Six Nations, in 1775 in Mohawk Valley, Pittsburgh, Lexington. Johnson, Butler, Revere, Patrick Henry.

1902 Atherton, Gertrude. *The Conqueror*. Fictionized biography of Hamilton. Burr.

Chambers, Robert W. *The Maid-at-Arms*. Popular novel of the Revolution.

Crowley, Mary C. *The Heroine of the Strait*. Detroit between 1760 and 1780 during divided loyalties. Pontiac.

1903 Reed, Myrtle. *The Shadow of Victory*. Anti-English romance of massacre at Fort Dearborn, with emphasis on domestic life.

1904 Parrish, Randall. *When Wilderness Was King*. Fort Dearborn massacre, 1812, by the Potawatomi. Absurd love duel, but realistic scenes of garrison life.

Stoddard, William O. *The Fight for the Valley*. Siege of Fort Schuyler and Battle of Oriskany.

1906 Wiley, Richard T. *Sim Greene*. Whiskey Insurrection in western Pennsylvania, 1794.

1917 Stimson, Frederic J. *My Story: Being the Memoirs of Benedict Arnold*. Aristocrat favoring self-governing under British rule.

1919 Carter, Jefferson. *Madam Constantia*. Goddaughter of Marion risks life of lover for patriotic reasons. 1780. British view.

1921 Chambers, Robert W. *The Little Red Foot*. Tories versus colonists in northern New York in 1774–80. Sir William Johnson.

1925 Sabatini, Rafael. *The Carolinian*. Cloak-and-sword drama of dashing Cavaliers and damsels in distress, by Italian novelist.

1926 McNeil, Everett. *Daniel Du Luth*. French explorer on Great Lakes in 1678. Juvenile.

1930 McCants, Elliott C. *Ninety Six*. Breath-taking story of frontier post in South Carolina.

1932 Bacheller, Irving. *The Master of Chaos*. Washington's secretary loves daughter of ardent loyalists.

Lewis, Janet. *The Invasion*. Eighteenth century Michigan trader and Ojibway wife. Background authentic.

McIntyre, John T. *Drums in the Dawn*. Economic intrigue in France injected into rival families' sacrifice for colonial cause.

1933 Crownfield, Gertrude. *Mistress Margaret*. Stilted. Juvenile.

Dudley, Albertus T. *A Spy of '76*. Enoch Crosby's story. For older boys.

La Farge, Oliver. *The Long Pennant*. Rhode Island privateer harries British shipping in the Caribbean during War of 1812.

1934 Crownfield, Gertrude. *Where Glory Waits*. Following death of Wayne's wife, he goes to war against the Indians of Ohio.

Wilson, Margaret. *The Valiant Wife*. Dartmoor prison during War of 1812.

1935 Bell, Sallie. *Marcel Armand*. Intrigue of Lafitte's lieutenant with André.

Chambers, Robert W. *Love and the Lieutenant*. Rebel girl and New York aristocrat.

Crownfield, Gertrude. *Conquering Kitty*. Pallid romance of Maryland girl in War of 1812.

Safford, Henry B. *That Bennington Mob*. Hampshire Grants men and Indians.

Sterne, Emma G. *Drums of the Monmouth*. Huguenots, Quakers; Freneau. Juvenile.

1936 Key, Alexander. *Liberty or Death*. South Carolinians under Marion. Juvenile.

Morrow, Honoré W. *Let the King Beware!* Tory returns to England and becomes court adviser. New interpretation of George III, Franklin.

Safford, Henry B. *Mr. Madison's War*. Naval impressment, War of 1812.

1937 Adams, Marshall. *They Fought for Liberty*. Patriotic youth returns from England to fight. Juvenile.

Hawthorne, Hildegarde. *Rising Thunder*. Dashing ride to save Jefferson, Henry, and Lee from Tarleton. Kentucky marriage. Juvenile.

Minnigerode, Meade. *Black Forest*. Northwest Territory wrested from Indians, French, British, 1754–88. Digressions on land speculations.

1938 Forbes, Esther. *The General's Lady*. Wife of American general in love with British officer in last years of war. Slightly historical.

Haines, Edwin I. *The Exquisite Siren*. Tory wife of Arnold and her love for André. Fast-moving, poorly motivated.

Harris, Cyril. *Trumpets at Dawn*. Contrasts opposing war-disrupted families; Battle of Trenton; Arnold. Spirited. History better than fiction.

Shafer, Donald C. *Smokefires in Schoharie*. New York German settlement's conflict with Indians, 1713–82. Exciting chronicle of three generations.

Singmaster, Elsie. *Rifles for Washington*. Boy with Washington's troops throughout the war. Juvenile.

1939 Baldwin, Leland. *The Delectable Country*. Whiskey Insurrection; Ohio and Mississippi Valley. Hugh Brackenridge, Mike Fink.

Cormack, Maribelle and William Alexander. *Land for My Sons*. Surveyor with Washington and Indians.

Lancaster, Bruce. *Guns of Burgoyne*. Defeat at Bennington and Saratoga as told by a Hession officer. Formula story but vigorous.

Williams, Ben Ames. *Thread of Scarlet*. Nantucket privateer fights a British frigate during War of 1812.

1940 Coatsworth, Elizabeth. *A Toast for the King*. Three orphan Tories at Christmas. Slight.

Dodge, Constance W. *The Dark Stranger*. From Scotland to Carolina to the *Bonhomme Richard*.

Footner, Hulbert. *Sailor of Fortune*. Fictionized biography of Joshua Barney, Maryland privateer.

Graves, Robert. *Sergeant Lamb's America*. British soldier serves under Burgoyne. Irish author ably discusses causes of Revolution and debunks army life. Accurate idiom. Interesting counterblast to chauvenistic accounts of the Revolution.

Shaw, Margaret. *Inherit the Earth*. Romantic adventures of indentured girl before and during the war.

Sinclair, Harold. *Westward the Tide*. Reminiscent account of George Rogers Clark's saving Kentucky. Balanced.

1941 Beebe, Ralph. *Who Fought and Bled*. Ohio, Detroit, General Hull. Meager but authentic.

Forester, C. S. *The Captain from Connecticut*. Blockaderunning on Long Island during Jefferson's administration, by the English author of *Captain Horatio Hornblower*.

Graves, Robert. *Proceed, Sergeant Lamb*. Sequel to *Sergeant Lamb's America*. After imprisonment, following Burgoyne's surrender, British soldier serves under Cornwallis.

Gray, Stanley. *Half That Glory*. Young Virginian allies himself with Beaumarchais to secure French aid for colonies.

Harris, Cyril. *Richard Pryne*. American spy story based on S. Culper, Jr., notes.

Marshall, Edison. *Benjamin Blake*. Dashing hero, slightly connected with Revolution.

Pleasants, Henry, Jr. *Mars' Butterfly*. André, Peggy Shippen, Arnold juxtaposed and caricatured.

Pridgen, Tim. *Tory Oath*. Flora Macdonald and Tory Scotch at Battle of Guilford Courthouse, and defeat in Battle of Moore's Creek Bridge.

Schumann, Mary. *My Blood and My Treasure*. Struggle for Detroit and Battle of Lake Erie, War of 1812. Stock characters and incidents, except for Commodore Perry.

Seifert, Shirley. *Waters of the Wilderness*. George Rogers Clark's love for the sister of the Spanish governor at St. Louis.

1942 Allis, Marguerite. *The Splendour Stays*. Birth of the Monroe Doctrine. Daughters of Connecticut Captain marry Isaac Hull, Fitz-Greene Halleck, and almost marry Simón Bolívar.

Bryson, J. G. *Valiant Libertine*. Robust tale of profligate in Boston and Quebec.

Dodge, Constance W. *Weathercock*. Social conflicts in North Carolina. Battle of Alamance.

Raddall, Thomas H. *His Majesty's Yankees*. Fort Cumberland and Nova Scotia withstand colonial privateers. Lyric descriptions.

Safford, Henry B. *Tory Tavern*. Story of espionage ending on a notorious prison ship.

Sperry, Armstrong. *No Brighter Glory*. John J. Astor's fur outpost on Columbia, 1810, with Britain and United States tensing for war.

Turnbull, Agnes. *The Day Must Dawn*. West Pennsylvania family life; Indians with Simon Girty. Lively.

Wiener, Willard. *Morning in America*. Charles Lee debunked as fascist. Antidote to *Oliver Wiswell*.

1943 Beebe, Elswyth Thane. *Dawn's Early Light*. Williamsburg in the war. For teen-age readers.

Eaton, Evelyn. *The Sea Is So Wide*. Acadian refugee family adjusts itself to Virginia.

Forbes, Esther. *Johnny Tremain*. Revolutionary Boston, Hancock, Revere, seen by a silversmith's apprentice. Lively. Juvenile.

Jennings, John E. *The Shadow and the Glory*. Sequel to *Next to Valour*. Bunker Hill, Ticonderoga, Trenton. Overcontrived plot.

Lane, Carl D. *The Fleet in the Forest*. Shipbuilding for Perry on Lake Erie in the eighteen tens. Well re-created and engrossing.

McMeekin, Clark, *pseud. Red Raskall*. Platonic wanderings in Virginia, 1816.

Richter, Conrad. *Free Man*. Pennsylvania Dutch indentured servant becomes free. Juvenile.

Whitney, Janet. *Judith*. Life in Philadelphia just after the Revolution. President Washington, John Adams, Benjamin Rush, Gilbert Stuart. Spirited romance of star-crossed lovers.

1944 Allis, Marguerite. *All in Good Time*. Jefferson embargo, the home front, and difficulties of an early Connecticut clockmaker.

Gessner, Robert. *Treason*. Benedict Arnold in milieu of colonial selfishness as seen by an aide. Credible, though modernized.

Jacobs, Helen H. *Storm Against the Wind*. Conflicts in pre-Revolutionary society in tidewater Virginia. Formula fiction.

Lancaster, Bruce. *Trumpet to Arms*. Transmutation of scattered local militia into an American army. Marblehead, Concord. Turbulent.

McNeilly, Mildred. *Heaven Is Too High*. Alaska during Russian dominance, 1790–1810. Carefully documented.

Mudgett, Helen. *The Seas Stand Watch*. Sea life at Salem and New Bedford between Revolution and War of 1812. By a historian.

1945 Case, Josephine Y. *Written in Sand*. To suppress Barbary pirates, a Connecticut Yankee invades Tripoli, 1805. Short "desert movie."

Kroll, Harry H. *Fury in the Earth*. Earthquakes in Missouri and Tennessee, 1811–12, with resulting reversion to primitivism.

Swanson, Neil. *The Perilous Fight*. Washington, Baltimore, and Fort McHenry in War of 1812. Repetitious details.

1946 Ball, Zachary. *Down to New Orleans*. Rowdy romance of Mississippi and Ohio river life in 1802, designed for women's "slicks."

Jennings, John E. *Salem Frigate*. Adventures over Seven Seas, particularly against Barbary pirates, and over African desert.

Tomkinson, Grace. *Welcome Wilderness*. Hardships of pioneering by Tory refugees in Nova Scotia and Connecticut. Costume piece.

1947 Edmonds, Walter D. *In the Hands of the Senecas*. Fighting in Finger Lakes district of New York in the seventeen seventies. Credible but not major.

Feuchtwanger, Lion. *Proud Destiny*. Parisian society and closet diplomacy. Beaumarchais and Franklin.

Finlay, Lucile. *The Coat I Wore*. Carolinian settlers in Natchez under Anthony Hutchins exhibit pro-British sympathies.

Miller, Helen T. *Sound of Chariots*. Loyalists in Georgia flee from guerrilla troops to state of Franklin. John Sevier.

Morton, Stanley. *Yankee Trader*. Robust account of Connecticut trader who favors the Revolution for selfish reasons.

Roberts, Kenneth. *Lydia Bailey*. Maine lawyer in Haiti when Napoleon stirs Toussaint's uprising. Tripolitan war, Barbary pirates. "*Lydia Bailey* is the stuff that sells, but doesn't survive."

Stanley, Edward. *Thomas Forty*. Quietist boy, former bond servant, in Westchester County, becomes a lieutenant in Armand's partisan legion.

1948 Chidsey, Donald B. *Stronghold*. Connecticut friends opposed to Jefferson's Embargo Act.

Nutt, Frances. *Three Fields to Cross*. Melodramatic account of adventures of Staten Island family during the Revolution.

CHAPTER III. *The Westward Movement*

1826 [Flint, Timothy]. *Francis Berrian*. Old and New Mexico, 1815–25. Characterization poor, natural history closely observed.

Anon. *Lafitte; or, The Baratarian Chief*. Sentimental account of the pirate's life.

1836 [Ingraham, Joseph H.]. *Lafitte: The Pirate of the Gulf*. Glamorous and Byronic, most popular romance of Lafitte; ends with Battle of New Orleans.

1838 [Ingraham, Joseph H.]. *Burton; or, The Sieges*. Defamation of Burr.

1845 [Judd, Sylvester]. *Margaret. A Tale of the Real and Ideal*. Early transcendentalism, and backwoods manners in Massachusetts.

1848 Bennett, Emerson. *The Renegade*. Kentucky border life and Daniel Boone in 1781.

1850 [McConnel, John L.]. *Talbot and Vernon*. Battle of Buena Vista and other Mexican scenes by an observer; romance jeopardized by accusation of forgery. Brisk and lucid.

Weir, James. *Lonz Powers; or The Regulators*. Pioneer "justice" in Kentucky.

1852 Weir, James. *Simon Kenton; or, The Scout's Revenge*. Boone's companion in western North Carolina, 1790.

1854 Bennett, Emerson. *Viola; or, Adventures in the Far Southwest*. Dime novel.

Weir, James. *The Winter's Lodge; or, The Vow Fulfilled*.

Sequel to *Simon Kenton*. Includes Simon Girty of Kentucky.

1856 [Arrington, A. W.] *pseud*. Charles Summerfield. *The Rangers and Regulators of the Tanaha*. Early Texas.

1859 Stowe, Harriet Beecher. *The Minister's Wooing*. New England spiritual conflicts about 1800. Aaron Burr.

1860 Clemens, Jeremiah R. *The Rivals*. Alexander Hamilton and Aaron Burr.

1862 Winthrop, Theodore. *John Brent*. Adventures among the Mormons in Utah.

1864 Trowbridge, J. T. *Cudjo's Cave*. Underground Railroad in Tennessee. Popular.

1869 Stowe, Harriet Beecher. *Oldtown Folks*. Rambling local color story of Massachusetts about 1790.

1881 Paddock, Cornelia (Mrs. A. G. Paddock). *The Fate of Madame La Tour*. Violently anti-Mormon novel by a resident of Utah. 1847–71.

1887 Tourgée, A. W. *Button's Inn*. Joseph Smith and founding of the Mormons in New York state.

1891 Catherwood, Mary H. *The Lady of Fort St. John*. Novelette of French colonization period.

1893 Frederic, Harold. *The Copperhead*. Troubles of a New York farmer who opposed abolitionism.

1897 Munroe, Kirk. *With Crockett and Bowie*. From election of Santa Anna to Battle of San Jacinto. Juvenile.

1898 Brooks, Elbridge S. *A Son of the Revolution*. Effect of Burr conspiracy on national expansion.

Fox, John, Jr. *The Kentuckians*. Feud between mountaineer and Bluegrass orators.

1901 Venable, William H. *A Dream of Empire*. Burr's scheme and its collapse.

1902 Atherton, Gertrude. *The Conqueror*. Aaron Burr and Alexander Hamilton. Based on Hamilton papers, and favors his "incorruptible integrity."

Devereux, Mary. *Lafitte of Louisiana*. Privateer and smuggler in Louisiana.

Stevenson, Burton. *The Heritage*. Marietta, Fallen Timbers, and the defeat of senile General St. Clair.

Tarkington, Booth. *The Two Vanrevels*. Fiery Indiana abolitionist in Mexican War.

1903 Grey, Zane. *Betty Zane*. End of Revolution in West Virginia; Hamilton's Rangers, 1782; migration from Virginia
to Ohio; Simon Girty and frontier.

1904 Dillon, Mary. *The Rose of Old St. Louis*. Faithful on Louisiana Purchase.

1906 Gates, Eleanor. *The Plow-Woman*. Two Texas girls main-
tain Dakota claim against Indians and others.

Lewis, Alfred Henry. *The Throwback*. Ranching in Texas.
Indians, Mexicans.

Read, Opie. *By the Eternal*. Jackson in New Orleans. Con-
tains unpublished material.

1907 Eggleston, George C. *Long Knives*. Winning of the West.

Lyle, E. P. *The Lone Star*. Roster of Texas heroes, to Battle
of San Jacinto.

Templeton, Frank. *Margaret Ballentine; or, The Fall of the
Alamo*. Appendix lists members of the garrison.

1908 Lewis, Alfred Henry. *An American Patrician; or, The story
of Aaron Burr*.

Pittman, Hannah Daviess. *The Heart of Kentucky*. Famous
Sharpe murder, 1825.

1909 Dillon, Mary. *The Patience of John Morland*. Monroe, Jackson, Webster, Clay, Calhoun.

1910 Bonner, Geraldine. *The Emigrant Trail*. Missouri to California in 1848.

1911 Kester, Vaughan. *The Prodigal Judge*. Slocum Price and
Cavendish and western Tennessee wastrels. Slave insurrection, 1820.

1914 McCarter, Margaret H. *Winning the Wilderness*. Story of
early Kansas pioneers.

1915 Atkinson, Eleanor. *Johnny Appleseed*. Juvenile tale about
Jonathan Chapman, planter of orchards in Ohio Valley.

1916 Howells, William Dean. *The Leatherwood God*. Religious
excitement and credulity in early Ohio.

Sabin, Edwin L. *With Sam Houston in Texas*. Juvenile tale
on Texas independence.

1917 McCarter, Margaret H. *Vanguard of the Plains*. Expeditions from Kansas City to Santa Fé in the eighteen forties.

Owen, Caroline. *Seth Way*. Vivid account of New Harmony (Indiana) Owenites.

Parrish, Randall. *The Devil's Own*. Missouri in 1832.

1919 Hergesheimer, Joseph. *Java Head*. Salem seafarer brings home a Manchu wife from China.

1920 Fox, John, Jr. *Erskine Dale, Pioneer*. Juvenile of Kentucky mountaineers.

1922 Masters, Edgar Lee. *Children of the Market Place*. Stephen A. Douglas and his times.

1923 Strachey, Ray (Mrs. Oliver Strachey). *Marching On*. Garrison, John Brown, and backwoods Michigan in eighteen thirties.

1925 Cronyn, George W. *'49, a Novel of Gold*. California gold rush. Local color.

Marquand, J. P. *The Black Cargo*. New England slaver during clipper-ship period.

Sabin, Edwin L. *White Indian*. Oregon Trail in the eighteen thirties and beaver-hunting Englishman.

1926 Ellerbe, Rose. *Ropes of Sand*. Pioneer aligns himself with Catholics against Indians in California.

Forbes, Esther. *O Genteel Lady!* The Boston and London of Alcott, Holmes, Tennyson.

Moore, John Trotwood. *Hearts of Hickory*. Jackson and Crockett. Duel with Dickinson and Battle of New Orleans. Juvenile.

Sabin, Edwin L. *Rio Bravo*. Temptation of one of Taylor's lieutenants. Romantic, far-fetched.

Skinner, Constance. *The White Leader*. General Wilkinson's intrigue to join Tennessee and Louisiana under Spanish rule.

Young, Stark. *Heaven Trees*. Gracious plantation life in Mississippi before the Civil War contrasted with life of Vermont kinswoman.

1927 Lynn, Margaret. *The Land of Promise*. Abolitionists in Kansas in conflict with proslavery Missourians. Juvenile.

Scott, Evelyn. *Migrations.* Moral novel of a Tennessean who goes to California gold rush.

1928 Boyd, Thomas. *Simon Girty.* Fictionized biography of "The Great Renegade."

Cooper, Courtney. *The Golden Bubble.* Organization of people's court in lawless Denver of 1859.

Evarts, Hal G. *Fur Brigade.* Indians of Northwest, 1815–35.

Hargreaves, Sheba. *The Cabin at the Trail's End.* An Oregon family's life in 1843.

Le May, Alan. *Old Father of Waters.* Mississippi steamboating before the Civil War. Rousing tale.

1929 Clark, Ellery H. *The Strength of the Hills.* Scout friend of Jackson. Based on authorized accounts. Competent.

Lovelace, Maud H. *Early Candlelight.* Domestic realism on the Minnesota (Fort Snelling) frontier in the eighteen thirties.

Vestal, Stanley, *pseud.* of Walter S. Campbell. *'Dobe Walls.* Kit Carson at Brent's Fort on the Santa Fé Trail in the eighteen forties.

1930 Chambers, Robert W. *The Rake and the Hussy.* Jackson's defense of New Orleans. Less unrestrained than former works.

1931 Gordon, Caroline. *Penhally.* Struggle to keep a Kentucky estate. 1826f.

Morrow, Honoré W. *Beyond the Blue Sierra.* Overland Trail from Mexico to northern California. Establishment of missions.

1933 Fierro Blanco, Antonio de. *Journey of the Flame.* Mexican boy's journey through Spanish California. Shows understanding of the Mexican temper.

Sass, Herbert Ravenal. *Look Back to Glory.* Charleston, South Carolina, prior to Civil War.

1934 Birney, Hoffman. *Grim Journey.* Donner party trek from Missouri to California, 1846.

Charnley, Mitchell V. *Jean Lafitte.* Fictionized biography. Juvenile.

Coolidge, Dane. *The Fighting Danites.* Government struggle with Brigham Young. A western.

Hatcher, Harlan. *Patterns of Wolfpen.* Idyllic life in Kentucky Valley, 1785–1885, before industrialization.

Lovelace, Maud. *One Stayed at Welcome.* Pioneering in Minnesota after period of Mexican War.

Swanson, Neil. *The Phantom Emperor.* James Dickson's attempt in 1836 to form an empire after sailing the Great Lakes and going through the wilderness to Winnipeg.

1935 Colony, Horatio. *Free Forester.* Kentucky during times of Boone and Crockett.

Duffus, R. L. *Jornada.* Comanche attack on frontiersmen along Santa Fé Trail during Mexican War.

Sweeny, Sarah. *Harvest of the Wind.* Kentucky-Kansas migration during border warfare.

1937 Bristow, Gwen. *Deep Summer.* Emergence of Louisiana plantations, 1800.

Carhart, Arthur H. *Drum Up the Dawn.* Zebulon Pike in Santa Fé negotiating with the Spanish governor.

Davis, Julia. *No Other White Men.* Sacagawea and Lewis and Clark Expedition.

Field, Rachel. *All This, and Heaven Too.* Fictional account of a New York *salon* frequented by Bryant, Mrs. Stowe, Fanny Kemble, and S. F. B. Morse in the eighteen fifties.

Stong, Phil. *Buckskin Breeches.* Mississippi-Iowa trek, 1837.

1938 Cooper, Courtney. *The Pioneers.* Kit Carson races British emigrants to Oregon in 1842. Thriller.

1939 Aldrich, Bess Streeter. *Song of Years.* Iowa frontier, 1854–65.

Coolidge, Dane. *Gringo Gold.* Bandit Murieta and California gold rush.

Derleth, August. *Restless Is the River.* Austrian count in Wisconsin, 1839–50.

Engstrand, Stuart. *They Sought for Paradise.* Account of Janssonist cult in Illinois, 1846. Unsympathetic.

Hallet, Richard. *Michael Beam.* Black Hawk War from Illinois recruit's point of view.

1940 Coolidge, Dane. *Bloody Head.* Western story of Texas cattle.

Drago, Harry. *pseud.* Will Ermine. *Boss of the Plains.* A western of the pony express.

Gaither, Frances. *Follow the Drinking Gourd.* Slavery in

Georgia, Alabama; the Underground Railroad. Mellow story.

Jones, Nard. *Swift Flows the River*. Pioneering in Idaho in the eighteen fifties.

Lutes, Della. *Gabriel's Search*. Valuable social history of Michigan community in the eighteen thirties.

Putnam, Nina. *The Inner Voice*. Border ruffians in Kansas in the eighteen fifties.

1941 Jones, Nard. *Scarlet Petticoat*. Early nineteenth century fur trading on Pacific Coast. A good yarn.

Liddon, Eloise. *Some Lose Their Way*. Tangled love of an actress, when the Creeks threatened in Alabama in 1835.

Niles, Blair. *East by Day*. New England aroused over mutiny of slaves on *Armistad* in Cuba in the eighteen forties.

1942 Edmonds, Walter D. *Young Ames*. Story of cardsharps, labor troubles, and rival fire companies in New York in early eighteen thirties. Juvenile.

Street, James. *Tap Roots*. A Mississippi manor before the Civil War.

Weld, John. *Sabbath Has No End*. Negro life on South Carolina cotton plantation in 1815.

1943 Daniels, Harriet M. *Muller Hill*. French aristocrat marries into New York society, settles in Oneida wilderness, disappears.

David, Evan J. *As Runs the Glass*. Seafaring Maine adventurer during post-Revolutionary period.

Derleth, August. *Shadow of Night*. Life among French *émigrés* and German refugees in Wisconsin in the eighteen fifties.

Dowdey, Clifford. *Tidewater*. West Tennessee frontier after 1837.

Fisher, Vardis. *The Mothers*. Donner party disaster on way to California in 1846, from point of view of mothers in the party. Veracious.

Foreman, Leonard. *The Road to San Jacinto*. Romance of Texas War for Independence. For young adults.

Kroll, Harry H. *Rogue's Companion*. Murrell's gang near Natchez, Mississippi.

Schachner, Nathan. *The Sun Shines West*. Abolitionist triangle in "bleeding Kansas," 1854–61. Vivid history.

Seifert, Shirley. *Those Who Go Against the Current*. Odyssey of Manuel Lisa, Spanish American who opened Missouri River to whites.

Shaftel, George A. *Golden Shore*. Conquest of California in 1840, imprisonment in Mexico. Romance and adventure.

Sublette, Clifford, and Harry H. Kroll. *Perilous Journey*. Natchez and New Orleans in the eighteen twenties. Robust and fast-moving; good social history.

1944 Barrett, Monte. *Sun in Their Eyes*. Mexico versus Texas in the eighteen twenties. Stirring.

Best, Herbert. *Young'un*. Fur trading around Lake Champlain after Revolution.

Buckmaster, Henrietta. *Deep River*. Mountain Georgians opposed to planter class. Prolix.

Gordon, Virginia. *A Man Should Rejoice*. Illinois trading post and Black Hawk War, eighteen thirties.

Pridgen, Tim. *West Goes the Road*. Overplotted novel of Indian fighting and secession from Aaron Burr's scheme.

Robertson, Constance. *Fire Bell in the Night*. Underground Railroad in Syracuse, New York. Tiresome heroine in phony situation.

Strabel, Thelma. *Storm to the South*. Swashbuckling story of California and Peru in early nineteenth century. Monroe Doctrine.

Wilson, Charles. *A Man's Reach*. Archibald Yell leaves North Carolina for Arkansas frontier and becomes governor. Women shadowy.

1945 Caldwell, Janet T. *Wide House*. Racial and religious intolerance in upstate New York in the eighteen fifties.

McLean, Sydney. *A Moment of Time*. Episodic novel about a godly Scotswoman on a Massachusetts farm, 1770–1838.

Van Every, Dale. *Westward the River*. Spain loses Louisiana Territory to France. Lewis and Clark. Natchez, Philadelphia.

1946 Ainsworth, Edward M. *Eagles Fly West*. Adventures of one of James G. Bennett's newspapermen at Monterey, California, in 1846.

Barrett, Monte. *Tempered Blade*. Romanticized story of Jim Bowie from the time when he was a broker for Lafitte in Louisiana to his death in the Alamo.

Emerson, Elizabeth. *The Good Crop*. Quakers in Illinois in the eighteen thirties break with some traditions.

Fuller, Edmund. *Star Pointed North*. Story of Frederick Douglass, who rose from slave to abolitionist orator and journalist.

Williams, Mary F. *Fortune, Smile Once More!* Australian gambler in San Francisco in early eighteen fifties. Fast-paced costume piece.

Yerby, Frank. *The Foxes of Harrow*. Plush romance of New Orleans gambler, 1825, with slight reference to history.

1947 Adams, Samuel H. *Banner by the Wayside*. Theatrical troupe tours Erie Canal country in 1846. Setting better than trite plot.

Allis, Marguerite. *Water Over the Dam*. Canalboat life in Connecticut in the eighteen twenties.

Bedford, Donald F., *pseud.* of Donald Friede, H. Bedford Jones, and Kenneth Fearing. *John Barry*. "Rollo among the Argonauts," 1846–50.

Breslin, Howard. *Tamarack Tree*. Vermont political rally in 1840 addressed by Daniel Webster. Well constructed, fast-moving.

Edmonds, Walter D. *The Wedding Journey*. By packet boat on Erie Canal in 1835. Inconsequential plot; clear picture.

Hall, Rubylea. *The Great Tide*. Florida plantation life in the eighteen thirties and forties: boom, yellow fever, and hurricane. Detailed background.

Janet, Lillian. *Touchstone*. San Francisco after the gold rush. Two brothers love the same woman.

Kenyon, Theda. *That Skipper from Stonington*. Connecticut shipbuilder's life after he helped beat the British in 1812.

Kroll, Harry H. *Darker Grows the Valley*. More than a century of Tennessee Valley life, 1778 to TVA. Competent.

Myers, John. *The Wild Yazoo.* Zestful yarn of pre–Civil War Mississippi frontier.

O'Dell, Scott. *Hill of the Hawk.* March on Los Angeles with Kit Carson, 1846–47. Authentic.

1948 Blake, Forrester. *Johnny Christmas.* Restless kid roams from Bent's Fort to California, 1836–46, for adventure.

Clark, Howard. *The Mill on Mad River.* Industrial revolution in Connecticut during early decades of nineteenth century.

Crabb, Alfred L. *Home to the Hermitage.* Genre painting of Andrew and Rachel Jackson to 1829, when he left alone for Washington.

Forbes, Esther. *The Running of the Tide.* Salem ship captains and merchants during the early decades of the last century. Good romance.

Gabriel, G. W. *I Thee Wed.* Romance of Marie Antoinette's double in Pennsylvania forest.

Hamele, Ottamar. *When Destiny Called.* Couple with Colonel Doniphan's Missouri Mounted Volunteers to Santa Fé and northern Mexico.

Jennings, John. *River to the West.* The Astor adventure in the Pacific Northwest.

Laughlin, Ruth. *The Wind Leaves No Shadow.* Santa Fé mixed society, 1821–46, from period of liberation from Spain to early American occupancy.

Slaughter, Frank. *Sangaree.* Land tenantry in post-Revolutionary Georgia.

Wilder, Robert. *Bright Feather.* Seminole war under Osceola in Florida during the eighteen thirties. Gusty, sympathetic romance; authentic; weak characterization.

1949 Davis, Harold L. *Beulah Land.* Travels of four whites and Indians from North Carolina to Natchez and to the Indian Territory. Well informed.

Gaither, Frances. *Double Muscadine.* Exciting trial of attractive yellow slave in Mississippi in the eighteen fifties. Compassion for race relations.

Laird, Charlton G. *Thunder on the River.* The Black Hawk War in Illinois.

Lewis, Sinclair. *The God-Seeker*. Presbyterian missionaries in Minnesota in the eighteen forties influence the money-making hero to favor labor unions.

Poole, Ernest. *The Nancy-Flyer*. Stagecoach epic laid in New England after 1835, and later in the West.

Putnam, George P. *Hickory Shirt*. Pioneer life in Death Valley in 1850.

Stanley, Edward. *The Rock Cried Out*. Blennerhassett's island, idyllic until guilty Aaron Burr appears.

Summers, Richard. *Vigilante*. Crooked politics in San Francisco in 1856.

Wilson, William E. *Abe Lincoln of Pigeon Creek*. Frontier boyhood, love affair, and experiences on a river boat.

CHAPTER IV. *The Civil War and Reconstruction*[1]

1870 Falconer, William. *Bloom and Brier*. Defense of plantation life in Alabama and account of Southern campaigns.

1873 Avery, M. A. *The Rebel General's Loyal Bride*. Plantation life; Battle of Bull Run, Libby prison, Seven Day's Battles; incidental passages of pious sentiment.

1880 [Benham, George C.]. *A Year of Wreck*. Reconstruction problems on a Mississippi plantation, as seen by a Northern immigrant.

[Goff, Harriet Newell Kneeland]. *Other Fools and Their Doings*. Weak retort to Tourgée's *A Fool's Errand*. Injuries inflicted on freedmen by landowners.

Meriwether, Elizabeth Avery. *The Master of Red Leaf*. New England governess in Louisiana in conflict with aristocrats.

1881 Bryan, Mary Edwards. *Wild Work*. Carpetbag rule and Klan violence in Louisiana. Conventional romance, dedicated to Alexander H. Stephens.

---

[1] Rebecca W. Smith, in *The Civil War and Its Aftermath in American Fiction, 1861–99*, University of Chicago dissertation, 1932, includes numerous short stories. See also her bibliography in *Bulletin of Bibliography*, Vol. XVI (1939), 193–94; Vol. XVII (1940), 10f.

1882 Ingraham, Ellen M. *pseud*. Grace Lintner. *Bond and Free*. Slightly disguised experiment in educating free folk of color in Georgia.

Thompson, Maurice. *A Tallahassee Girl*. Won from a former Union soldier. "Prosperity is the cure for the South."

1883 Roe, Edward P. *His Sombre Rivals*. Sentimental account of Union officer's love affair after First Battle of Manassas.

1884 Beard, Oliver. *Bristling with Thorns*. Rabid account of fire-eating Mississippian; Negro intimidation; Chickamauga; Andersonville prison.

Cable, George W. *Dr. Sevier*. New Orleans in wartime brings out courage and tenderness. Weak plot.

King, Charles. *Kitty's Conquest*. Kellogg-McEnery riots in New Orleans. Gallantry and adventure in Alabama. First of King's military novels.

Oldham, Henry. *The Man from Texas*. Kansas-Missouri conflict at end of war. Written in professional hack style.

[Robinson, Stephen T.]. *The Shadow of the War*. Father and daughter converted to Southern point of view. Reconstruction in South Carolina.

1885 Magruder, Julia. *Across the Chasm*. Faithful Negroes in Southern town after the war help reconcile sections. Good dialect.

Roe, E. P. *An Original Belle*. Battle of Gettysburg; New York draft riots; Northern coquette and suitors.

Tracy, J. P. *Shenandoah*. Sheridan's Ride. Paper back.

Winslow, William H. *Cruising and Blockading*. Annapolis graduate in Florida and elsewhere scorns Southerners.

1886 Townsend, George A. *Katy of Catoctin; or, The Chainbreakers*. Harpers Ferry; Quantrill; Lincoln's assassination. Pennsylvania. Credible.

1887 McGovern, John. *Daniel Trentworthy*. Rise of speculator to time of Chicago Fire, October, 1871. Lively.

1888 King, Charles. *Between the Lines*. Union officer nursed by one of the F. F. V. Skirmishes and escapes, but no battle scenes. Similar in plot and style to *A War-Time Wooing*.

Le Cato, N. J. W. *Tom Burton*. Norfolk blockade; abolitionist returns, marries aristocrat.

1889 [Gilmore, James R.] *pseud*. Edmund Kirk. *A Mountain-White Heroine*. Northern partisan in border warfare around Asheville, North Carolina.

MacKnight, James A. *Hagar*. Evils of rebellion and Mormonism in Ohio, Utah.

1890 [French, Alice] *pseud*. Octave Thanet. *Expiation*. Guerrilla warfare in Arkansas as backdrop for romance. Nonpartisan.

Anon. *Robert Warren, the Texan Refugee*. Strongly partisan account of Southern Unionist's gallant career, 1861–70, in Texas, Louisiana, and Kentucky.

Tiernan, Mary. *Jack Horner*. Southern heroine and Union lover in Richmond. Nonpartisan.

[Wood, Lydia Cope]. *The Haydocks' Testimony*. Quaker pacifism without rancor in North Carolina.

1891 Keenan, Henry F. *The Iron Game*. Lincoln, Sherman; plot to capture Jefferson Davis.

Kirkland, Joseph. *The Captain of Company K*. Camp life and battle experiences of a private Illinois soldier at Donelson, Corinth, Shiloh. Conventional plot. Veterans pushed aside by politicians.

1892 Bowles, John. *The Stormy Petrel*. Former Kentucky slaveholder fights with John Brown in Kansas.

Frederic, Harold. *The Return of the O'Mahoney*. Union privates before Richmond. Estate in Ireland.

1893 De Leon, T. C. *John Holden, Unionist*. Southern Unionist and bushwhackers in northern Alabama. General Forrest; President Johnson.

Frederic, Harold. *The Copperhead*. New York farmer, opposed to abolition, reconciled by son's marriage to daughter of abolitionist.

1894 Gardener, Helen. *An Unofficial Patriot*. Late echo of prewar prejudice against manumission of Negroes. Virginian frees slaves and becomes abolitionist in Middle West. Effective character study.

1895 Harte, Bret. *Clarence*. Union officer shields Confederate spy who had been his wife in California. Lincoln exonerates him personally.

1897 De Leon, T. C. *Crag-nest*. Romantic days of Sheridan's ride told in the manner of Charles King.

King, Charles. *The General's Double*. McClellan in Virginia and Gettysburg campaign. Spies, intrigue; improbable plot.

Mitchel, F. A. *Sweet Revenge*. Pro-Union account of bushwhacking and wooing in the Cumberland. Stereotyped melodrama.

1898 [Jones, Alice] *pseud*. John Alix. *The Night-hawk*. Blockaderunning and efforts to secure Napoleon's recognition of the Confederacy.

1899 [Cox, Millard F.] *pseud*. Henry Scott Clark. *The Legionaries*. Rambling adventures of Southern sympathizer, Northern sweetheart. Morgan's raid.

1900 Brown, Caroline. *Knights in Fustian*. Conspiracy of Knights of the Golden Circle thwarted by wartime Governor Morton of Indiana.

Orpen, Adela. *The Jay-Hawkers*. Quantrill's raid on Kansas. Dialect.

1901 Norris, Mary Harriott. *The Grapes of Wrath*. Virginia romance and home life during campaign of 1864. Well-informed, balanced. Lee.

Stephenson, Nathaniel. *They That Took the Sword*. Cincinnati, center of espionage among divided families. President Lincoln.

1902 Babcock, William H. *Kent Fort Manor*. Claiborne. Maryland. Veracious.

Benson, B. K. *Bayard's Courier*. Cavalry campaigns; McClellan, Morgan, Stuart, Stonewall Jackson. Virginia, Maryland; Confederate maps.

Eggleston, George C. *Dorothy South*. Slavery in Virginia, and romance of a nurse.

Morris, Gouverneur. *Aladdin O'Brien*. Romantic treatment of Gettysburg.

1903 Bentley, Robert T. *Forestfield*. Northern Alabama, 1850–65. Sentimental tribute to gracious home life.

Brady Cyrus T. *The Southerners*. Farragut at Mobile Bay; rivals from opposite sides vie for a girl.

Eggleston, George C. *The Master of Warlock*. Innocuous Virginia romance.

1904 ———. *Evelyn Byrd*. Romance in ante-bellum Virginia.

Floyd, C. J. *The Last of the Cavaliers*. Pro-Southern novel.

Morgan, George. *The Issue*. Plantation life near Charleston.

1905 King, Charles. *A Broken Sword*. Spy romance and military maneuvers of New York regiment in Potomac campaign.

1906 Howard, John H. *In the Shadow of the Pines*. Tidewater Virginia.

Thurston, Lucy M. *Called to the Field*. A Virginia woman's defense from foraging parties.

1907 Bogue, Herbert E. *Dareford*. Vermonter's experience in battles of Gettysburg and the Wilderness.

1908 Eggleston, George C. *The Warrens of Virginia*. Story of Southern heroine and Northern lover, based on William Churchill De Mille's play of family life during the war.

1910 [Meriwether, Elizabeth Avery] *pseud*. Hannah Parting. *The Sowing of the Swords*. General Butler in New Orleans.

1911 Kennedy, Sara Beaumont. *Cicely*. Southern belle, Northern officer with Sherman in Georgia.

1914 Boyles, Kate and Virgil. *The Hoosier Volunteer*. Two lads in Vicksburg campaign.

Parrish, Randall. *The Red Mist*. Stonewall Jackson and romance of Confederate officer disguised as Union cavalryman in West Virginia.

1915 Allen, James Lane. *The Sword of Youth*. Struggle of youngest son to replace father and brothers on farm. Lee after Richmond.

1922 Fairbank, Janet. *The Cortlandts of Washington Square*. Experiences of a Northern nurse in New York and Washington during the war.

1925 Boyd, Thomas. *Samuel Drummond*. Decay of Ohio farm while husband serves in the war.

1926 Deland, Margaret. *The Kays*. Woman pacifist when conscientious objectors were few.

Minnigerode, Meade. *Cordelia Chantrell*. Charleston belle and Northern lover. Dramatic.

1927 Markey, Morris. *The Band Plays Dixie*. Activities in Fredericksburg, Richmond, and Savannah.

Montgomery, James S. *Tall Men*. Blockade runners for Confederacy.

1928 Moore, Virginia. *Rising Wind*. Romance in Virginia, with little historical perspective. Written from Rebel point of view.

1929 Hergesheimer, Joseph. *Swords and Roses*. W. L. Yancey and Albert Sidney Johnston appear.

1931 Scott, Evelyn. *A Calendar of Sin*. Klan activities during Reconstruction.

1932 Chambers, Robert W. *Whistling Cat*. Improbable romance of military telegrapher. Cross section of strategy; General Grant and a host of historical figures.

Fairbank, Janet. *The Bright Land*. Free-soil controversy and war recalled by bride who moved west. General Grant's return to Galena, Illinois, during Reconstruction.

MacLeod, Le Roy. *The Years of Peace*. Confederate sympathizer farming in the Wabash Valley.

1933 Bradford, Roark. *Kingdom Coming*. Plantation life, Negroes, and Underground Railroad.

Davis, Samuel H. *Separated by Mountains*. Border warfare and Battle of Rich Mountain, Virginia.

1934 Fleming, A. M. *A Soldier of the Confederacy*. Sam Houston and plantation life in Texas, 1836–65.

1935 Eckenrode, H. J. *Bottom Rail on Top*. Reconstruction minus romanticism. By a Virginia historian.

1936 Harris, L. F. and F. L. Beals. *Look Away, Dixieland*. Reconstruction on Mississippi plantation fostered by daughter.

Lytle, Andrew. *The Long Night*. A prose epic of Alabama feud, ending with Battle of Shiloh. Vivid.

1937 Bradford, Roark. *The Three-Headed Angel*. Soldiers and poor whites in Tennessee.

Brier, Royce. *Boy in Blue*. Chickamauga and thoughts of participants as observed by Union private. Cf. *None Shall Look Back*.

1938 Bristow, Gwen. *The Handsome Road*. Lament for lost cause in Louisiana. Sequel to *Deep Summer* (1937); followed by *This Side of Glory* (1940).

Burnett, William R. *The Dark Command*. Violence in Kansas and Missouri during early part of war.

Tate, Allen. *The Fathers*. Virginia plantation code of the eighteen fifties.

1939 Cheney, Brainard. *Lightwood*. Realistic story of eviction of Georgians from pine barrens during Reconstruction. Violence without drama.

Kelland, Clarence. *Arizona*. Fast-moving story of Arizona life during the war.

Shuster, George. *Look Away!* Favors South in divided family.

Smith, Chard P. *Artillery of Time*. Upper York state view of the war. Excellent social history; good characterization.

1940 Bechdolt, Frederick R. *Bold Raiders of the West*. Intrigue and fighting in New Mexico.

Hutchens, Jane. *John Brown's Cousin*. Missouri pacifist later testifies against Ku Klux Klan.

Jacobs, Thornwell. *Red Lanterns on St. Michaels*. Caste-consciousness in Charleston, South Carolina.

Kroll, Harry H. *The Keepers of the House*. Realistic novel about a rebellious Mississippian.

McMeekin, Clark, *pseud*. *Show Me a Land*. Gypsies, tobacco, politics, horse breeding, voodooism, romance in Kentucky. 1815–75.

Waldman, Emerson. *Beckoning Ridge*. Harried farmers of West Virginia.

Warren, Lella. *Foundation Stone*. Alabama planter's economic struggles and relations with Negroes, 1820–65.

1941 Blake, William J., *pseud*. of William James Blech. *The Copperheads*. Draft riots in New York affecting immigrant and three lovers. Profiteers and spies.

Bromfield, Louis. *Wild Is the River*. Conflict between Union soldiers and Creoles in New Orleans.

Corbett, Elizabeth. *Faye's Folly*. Political influence on an Illinois farm family.

Mason, Van Wyck. *Hang My Wreath.* Movie-plot of cavalry battles in Virginia and Maryland.

Schachner, Nathan. *By the Dim Lamps.* Louisiana during Civil War and Reconstruction. Melodramatic plot.

1942 Chevalier, Elizabeth P. *Drivin' Woman.* Postwar rise of tobacco industry. Colorful and lively.

Crabb, Alfred L. *Dinner at Belmont.* Nashville during Civil War.

Hutchens, Jane. *Timothy Larkin.* Missouri family in first year of war and decade preceding.

Robertson, Constance. *Salute the Hero.* Ironic. Pictures scoundrel, probably Daniel Sickles.

Sims, Marian. *Beyond Surrender.* Reconstruction in South Carolina.

Wellman, Paul. *Angel with Spurs.* Unreconstructed Confederates seek glory and power in Mexico.

1943 Crabb, Alfred L. *Supper at the Maxwell House.* Reconstruction days in Nashville.

1944 Bennett, John. *So Shall They Reap.* Battle of Corinth and the part played by poor whites in the war.

Kenyon, Theda. *Black Dawn.* Family conflict in Virginia during the war.

McNeilly, Mildred M. *Heaven Is Too High.* Russian days in Alaska.

Pettibone, Anita. *Johnny Printer.* Fast-paced folk narrative of Washington and Oregon during Civil War period.

Street, James. *By Valour and Arms.* Vicksburg opposed to Virginians. Sprawling narrative.

1946 Roberts, Richard. *The Gilded Rooster.* Indian scout in Wyoming, 1863, but essentially the psychopathic conflicts of four shut-ins.

1947 Havill, Edward. *Big Ember.* Sioux attack on settlement in Minnesota in 1862.

1948 Abrahams, R. D. *Mr. Benjamin's Sword.* Escape to England of Confederate Secretary of State Judah P. Benjamin, in 1865.

Branch, Houston and Frank Waters. *Diamond Head.* Confederate cruiser *Shenandoah* hunts New England whalers in North Pacific.

Ernenwein, Leslie. *Rebel Yell.* Five former Confederate soldiers ready for fights.

Kane, Harnett. *Bride of Fortune.* Love story of Varina and Jefferson Davis.

Lagard, Gerald. *Scarlet Cockerel.* Confederate surgeon with Mosby's Rangers loves Union general's daughter. Run-of-the-mill.

Lancaster, Bruce. *No Bugles Tonight.* Four major projects to sabotage the Confederacy in Georgia. Well informed, but conventional plot.

1949 Bourne, Peter *pseud. Flames of Empire.* A Louisiana planter and Confederate agent helps Maximilian's scheme in Mexico.

Crabb, Alfred L. *A Mockingbird Sang at Chickamauga.* Espionage by a Confederate officer and his sweetheart to help General Forrest.

CHAPTER V. *National Expansion*

1889 King, Charles. *"Laramie"; or, The Queen of Bedlam.* Sioux uprising in 1876.

1901 White, Stewart E. *The Westerners.* War with the Sioux on the Great Plains.

1902 Garland, Hamlin. *The Captain of the Gray-Horse Troop.* Cattlemen versus Cheyenne Indians in Montana in the eighteen nineties.

1905 Wright, James N. *Where Copper Was King.* Mining activity in northern Michigan during the eighteen sixties.

1906 Parrish, Randall. *Bob Hampton of Placer.* Annihilation of Custer's men by the Sioux Indians in Montana.

1907 Garland, Hamlin. *The Long Trail.* Hardship of a boy in the Klondike gold rush of 1898.

1909 White, William Allen. *A Certain Rich Man.* Growth of Kansas town, about 1865 to first decade of twentieth century.

1912 Grey, Zane. *Riders of the Purple Sage*. Melodrama of Utah and the Mormons in 1871.

1920 Maule, Mary Katherine. *A Prairie-Schooner Princess*. Mystery story of Ohio Quakers settling Nebraska.

1923 Evarts, Hal G. *Tumbleweeds*. Passing of the cattlemen; Cherokee run. A western.

1924 Hooker, Forrestine C. *When Geronimo Rode*. Defiant Apache leader in Oklahoma at time of land opening.

Marshall, Edison. *Seward's Folly*. Officer blocks attempt of Hudson's Bay Company and a Russian corporation to keep Alaska from the United States.

1925 Oskison, John M. *Wild Harvest*. Development of Oklahoma pasture land.

Ostenso, Martha. *Wild Geese*. Theatrical story of Scandinavian farmer's domestic struggle in Minnesota and his greed for land.

1926 Cooper, Courtney. *Oklahoma*. Homesteading rush with Pawnee Bill.

Ferber, Edna. *Show Boat*. Mississippi River entertainment, eighteen eighties and nineties.

Oskison, John M. *Black Jack Davy*. Oklahoma land-rush quarrels of 1889.

1927 Coolidge, Dane. *Ranger Two-Rifle*. A western.

Fergusson, Harvey. *Wolf Song*. Kit Carson and the Mountain Men.

Garrard, L. H. (W. S. Campbell, ed.) *Wah-To-Yah and the Taos Trail*.

1928 Benson, Ramsey. *Hill Country*. Swedish settlement of western Minnesota promoted by James J. Hill, railroader. The Farmers' Alliance in politics.

Cooper, Courtney. *Golden Bubble*. Lawless Denver in the eighteen sixties.

1930 Hughes, Langston. *Not Without Laughter*. Negro life in Kansas. By a well-known poet.

1932 McNally, William J. *House of Vanished Splendor*. Decay of Minnesota family in river town.

1933 Jones, Nard. *Wheat Women*. Three generations of wheat-growers near Walla Walla, Washington.

1934 Cunningham, Eugene. *Texas Sheriff*. A good western.

Pound, Arthur. *Once a Wilderness*. Michigan farm life in the eighteen nineties.

1935 Oskison, John M. *Brothers Three*. Ranch life in Indian Territory after 1873.

Schorer, Mark. *A House Too Old*. Degeneration of a Wisconsin family.

1936 Cunningham, Eugene. *Whistling Lead*. Another western.

McNally, William J. *The Roofs of Elm Street*. Faithful picture of Minnesota domestic and racial problems.

Marquand, J. P. *The Late George Apley*. Ironical presentation of code of Boston aristocrat during era of national expansion.

1937 Chevigny, Hector. *Lost Empire*. The Russian Rezanov lost Alaska to the more practical Yankees.

Coolidge, Dane. *Texas Cowboys*. A western.

Davis, Julia. *No Other White Men*. Sacagawea on Lewis and Clark Expedition.

Haycox, Ernest. *Trouble Shooter*. Construction of Union Pacific.

———. *The Deep West*. Wyoming cattle rustling during the eighteen eighties.

Masters, Edgar Lee. *The Tide of Time*. Jeffersonian liberal ruined by mediocrity of Illinois town. Cf. *Spoon River Anthology*.

Richter, Conrad. *The Sea of Grass*. Very good poetic narrative of cattle kings and nesters in New Mexico.

Waters, Frank. *Below Grass Roots*. Sequel to *The Wild Earth's Nobility* (1935). Colorado gold mining after 1875.

1938 Aydelotte, Dora. *Trumpets Calling*. Opening of Cherokee Strip, told with humor.

Cunningham, Eugene. *Texas Triggers*. Southwestern codes and characters.

Downing, J. Hyatt. *A Prayer for Tomorrow*. Ruin of Dakota cattle lands by ranchers, drought, and dust storms.

Haycox, Ernest. *Sundown Jim*. One who brought order to Northern and Southern ranchers.

Kohl, Edith. *The Land of the Burnt Thigh*. Dakota homesteading.

Miller, May Merrill. *First the Blade*. Civil war in Missouri, pioneering in California.

O'Connor, Jack. *Boom Town*. Robust story of Arizona mining camp in the eighteen nineties.

1939 Alexander, Holmes. *American Nabob*. West Virginia during "robber baron" period.

Boyd, James. *Bitter Creek*. Cowboy life and psychology in the Black Hills during the eighteen eighties and nineties.

Carson, Katharine. *Mrs. Pennington*. Homespun novel of farms and chautauquas in Kansas in the eighteen eighties.

Coolidge, Dane. *Gringo Gold*. Melodramatic story of bandit Murieta during California gold-rush days.

Drago, Harry. *Singing Lariat*. Nebraska shortly after statehood.

Harris, Bernice K. *Purslane*. North Carolina cotton farmers after 1900.

Haycox, Ernest. *Border Trumpet*. Arizona army post in the eighteen seventies.

1940 Coolidge, Dane. *Bloody Head*. Story of Texas cattlemen.

Downing, J. Hyatt. *Sioux City*. The 1880 boom period in this meat-packing center.

Matschat, Cecile Hulse. *Preacher on Horseback*. Circuit rider in Mohawk Valley and in lumber area of Michigan.

Train, Arthur. *Tassels on Her Boots*. Intrigues of Tweed, Gould, and Fiske during Grant's second administration.

1941 Pearson, Lorene. *The Harvest Waits*. Mormon life in Utah.

Smith, Chard P. *Ladies Day*. Sequel to *Artillery of Time* (1939). Blaine-Cleveland campaign, railroad strike, panic of 1893.

1942 Briggs, William H. *Dakota in the Morning*. Courageous battle of Michigan family against fire and drought in South Dakota.

Swain, Virginia. *The Dollar Gold Piece*. Early growth of Kansas City.

1943 Idell, Albert E. *Centennial Summer*. Philadelphia family and

257

social background of 1876. Sequel: *Brooklyn Bridge* (1944).

Ostenso, Martha. *O River, Remember!* Norwegian settlement in Minnesota in the eighteen seventies.

Schrag, Otto. *The Locusts.* Pioneer life in Utah and Kansas in the eighteen seventies.

1944 Haycox, Ernest. *Bugles in the Afternoon.* Custer and Battle of the Little Big Horn. A competent western.

McNeilly, Mildred Masterson. *Heaven Is Too High.* Alaska during Russian dominance, 1790–1810. Carefully documented.

Mally, Emma Louise. *The Mocking Bird Is Singing.* Blockade-running in New Orleans followed by railroad-building and cattle breeding in Texas. Ideology too recent.

1945 Downey, Fairfax. *Army Mule.* Campaign against Apaches in Arizona in the eighteen seventies.

Howard, Elizabeth Metzger. *Before the Sun Goes Down.* Prize scenario of a Pennsylvania town in 1880.

Parkhill, Forbes. *Troopers West.* Indian warfare in Wyoming after Custer's massacre. Slight.

Scowcroft, Richard. *Children of the Covenant.* Conflicts of Mormon families through changing generations.

Steele, Wilbur D. *That Girl from Memphis.* Arizona silver camp in the eighteen nineties; outlawry, evangelism, floods.

1946 Arnold, Elliott. *Blood Brother.* War against Cochise and his Apaches. Love plot incidental.

Caldwell, Taylor. *This Side of Innocence.* Upstate New York life from 1868 to 1888. Violent interaction in small family group.

Corey, Paul. *Acres of Antaeus.* Farm mortgage war.

Hinckley, Helen. *The Mountains Are Mine.* Mormon girl freed from polygamous marriage by Brigham Young. Sympathetic.

Houston, Noel. *The Great Promise.* Highly colored romance of Oklahoma Territory during land lottery.

1947 Hannum, Alberta. *Roseanna McCoy.* Hatfield-McCoy feud in Kentucky in the eighteen eighties.

1948 Cannon, Blanche. *Nothing Ever Happens Sunday Morning.*
Domestic conflict in Mormon community in 1900.

Gardiner, Dorothy. *Great Betrayal.* Indian encampment at
Denver wiped out in 1864 by cavalry.

Stevens, Louis. *Days of Promise.* Panoramic record of pro-
Union Virginia family in Kansas. Grant, Lee, Pulitzer,
Roosevelt.

Young, Agatha. *Light in the Sky.* Cleveland in the eighteen
seventies; steel empires.

1949 Foote, Shelby. *Tournament.* A Mississippi planter's success
and his decline. From 1887 to World War I.

Kennelly, Ardyth. *The Peaceable Kingdom.* Mormon family life during the eighteen nineties.

Street, James and James Childers. *Tomorrow We Reap.*
Fourth of the Dabney stories in Mississippi. Conflict with
Northern lumber company in the eighteen nineties.

Index

Abbott, Charles C.: 221
Abe Lincoln of Pigeon Creek: 246
Able McLaughlins, The: 201
Abrahams, R. D.: 253
Acres of Antaeus: 258
Action at Aquila: 174, 177
Adams, John: 234
Adams, John Quincy: 123
Adams, John T.: 41
Adams, Marshall: 231
Adams, Samuel: 70, 72, 85, 87, 108, 109
Adams, Samuel Hopkins: *The Gorgeous Hussy*, 120; *Canal Town*, 124
Age of Innocence, The: 206
Agnes Surriage: 50
Ainsworth, Edward: 243
Aladdin O'Brien: 249
Alamo, the: 129f., 238
Alcott, Bronson: 239
Aldrich, Bess Streeter: 241; *A Lantern in Her Hand*, 199
Alexander, Holmes: 257
Alexander, William: 232
Alice of Old Vincennes: 89
Alison Blair: 223
Alix, John (*pseud.* for Alice Jones): 249
All in Good Time: 234
All Ye People: 123
All This, and Heaven Too: 241
Allen, Ethan: 50–51, 96, 226
Allen, Hervey: 8, 17, 64 n.; *Anthony Adverse*, 63, 128; *Action at Aquila*, 174
Allen, James Lane: 117, 250
Allis, Marguerite: 224, 233, 234, 244
Altrocchi, Julia: 121
Altsheler, Joseph: 222
Ambrose and Eleanor: 227
American Cruiser, The: 228
American Nabob: 257
American Patrician, An: 238
American Spy, The: 228
American Years: 149, 205
Amulet, The: 222

And Never Yield: 144
And Tell of Time: 186, 187
Andersonville prison: 247
André, John: 75, 77–79, 83, 229, 231
Andros, Sir Edmund: 46
Angel with Spurs: 253
Anna Zenger: 225
Antietam, Battle of: 154
Appleseed, Johnny (Jonathan Chapman): 229
Arizona: 252
Army Mule: 258
Arnold, Benedict: 51, 73 ff., 79, 83, 85, 87, 111, 228, 232
Arnold, Elliott: 258
Arouse and Beware: 170
Arrington, A. W. (*pseud.* for Charles Summerfield): 237
Artillery of Time: 252, 257
Arundel: 19, 73, 101
As Runs the Glass: 242
Ashes in the Wilderness: 225
Ashleigh: 228
Ask No Quarter: 225
Astor, John Jacob: 121, 133, 233, 245
Astoria: 133
At the Moon's Inn: 224
Atherton, Gertrude: 141, 229, 237
Atkinson, Eleanor: 238
Audrey: 30
Austin, Jane G.: 221
Austin, Mary: 141
Austin, Stephen F.: 130, 131, 133
Avery, M. A.: 246
Aydelotte, Dora: 256

Babcock, Bernie: *The Soul of Ann Rutledge*, 149
Babcock, William: 249
Bacheller, Irving: *A Candle in the Wilderness*, 48; *In the Days of Poor Richard*, 84; *D'ri and I*, 100; *A Man for the Ages*, 149; *Father Abraham*, 149; *Eben Holden*, 159; *The Master of Chaos*, 230

Bacon, Delia: 46, 219
Bacon's Rebellion: 27 f., 220, 221, 223, 225
Baker, Karle Wilson: 131
Baldwin, Leland: 232
Balisand: 108
Ball, Zachary: 235
Baltimore, Lord: 34
Band Plays Dixie, The: 251
Banner by the Wayside: 244
Banvard, Joseph: 41
Barker, Benjamin: 228
Barker, Shirley: 226
Barnes, James: 229
Barney, Joshua: 232
Barr, Amelia: *Remember the Alamo!*, 129; *The Bow of Orange Ribbon*, 221
Barrett, Monte: 243, 244
Battle-Ground, The: 19, 162, 189 n.
Bayard's Courier: 249
Bay-Path, The: 41
Beach, Rebecca: 221
Beals, L. F.: 251
Beard, Oliver: 247
Beaumarchais: 235
Bechdolt, Frederick: 252
Beckoning Ridge: 252
Bedford, Donald (*pseud.* of Donald Friede, H. Bedford Jones, and Kenneth Fearing): 244
Beebe, Elswyth Thane: 234
Beebe, Ralph: 232
Before the Sun Goes Down: 258
Begum's Daughter, The: 221
Bell, Sallie: 231
Bellamy, Edward: *The Duke of Stockbridge*, 112
Below Grass Roots: 256
Benét, Stephen V.: *John Brown's Body*, 153; *Spanish Bayonet*, 223
Benham, George: 246
Benjamin Blake: 233
Benjamin, Judah P.: 253
Bennett, Emerson: 220, 228, 236
Bennett, John: 253
Benson, B. K.: 249
Benson, Ramsey: 255
Bentley, Robert: 249
Bernard Lile: 128, 129
Berkeley, Sir Edward: 36, 225
Berkeley, Sir William: 27, 34
Best, Herbert: 243
Betrothed of Wyoming, The: 62
Betty Alden: 221
Betty Zane: 238

Between the Lines: 157
Beulah Land: 245
Beyond the Blue Sierra: 240
Beyond Surrender: 253
Big Ember: 253
Big Sky, The: 137–38
Binns, Archie: *The Land Is Bright*, 139; *Mighty Mountain*, 140
Bird, Robert M.: *Nick of the Woods*, 116
Birney, Hoffman: *Eagle in the Sun*, 132; *Grim Journey*, 142, 240
Bitter Creek: 257
Blackbeard: 220
Black Cargo: 239
Black Dawn: 253
Black Forest: 231
Black Hawk (Indian chief): 94, 122–23
Black Hawk War: 243, 245
Black Jack Davy: 255
Black Thunder: 146
Bladensburg, Battle of: 101
Blake, Forrester: 245
Blake, William (*pseud.* of William James Blech): 252
Blanche of Brandywine: 228
Blech: *see* Blake, William
Blennerhassett: 119
Blennerhassett Island: 246
Blood Brother: 258
Bloody Chasm, The: 182
Bloody Head: 241, 257
Bloom and Brier: 246
Blossom Like the Rose: 224
Bob Hampton of Placer: 254
Bogue, Herbert: 250
Bojer, Johann: 196
Bold Raiders of the West: 252
Bolívar, Simón: 102, 233
Bond and Free: 247
Bonner, Geraldine: 238
Bontemps, Arna: 146
Boom Town: 257
Boone, Daniel: 58, 90, 114, 115, 117, 143, 224, 236, 241
Booth, John Wilkes: 160
Border Trumpet: 257
Boss of the Plains: 241
Boston Conspiracy, The: 228
Boston Tea Party: 148, 228
Bottom Rail on Top: 251
Bourne, Peter (*pseud.*): 254
Bow of Orange Ribbon, The: 221
Bowie, Jim: 129
Bowles, John: 248

Index

Bowyer, James T.: 221
Boy in Blue: 251
Boyce, Burke: 78, 79
Boyd, James: 17; *Drums,* 102, 166; *The Long Hunt,* 118; *Marching On,* 154, 166; *Bitter Creek,* 257
Boyd, Thomas: 91, 240, 250
Boyles, Kate and Virgil Boyles: 250
Brace, John P.: 220
Brackenridge, Hugh: 62, 232
Braddock: 62, 64, 94, 109, 220, 222, 223, 225, 226
Bradford, Roark: 251
Bradford, William: 39, 221
Brady, C. Townsend: 155, 157, 164, 249
Brainard, J. G. S.: 219
Brand, Anna: 130
Brandywine, Battle of: 227
Brazos: 211
Breslin, Howard: 244
Brewster, William: 39
Bricks Without Straw: 180
Bride of Fortune: 254
Brier, Royce: 251
Briggs, William: 257
Bright Face of Danger, The: 223
Bright Feather: 245
Bright Journey: 122
Bright Land, The: 251
Bright Shawl, The: 213
Brisbane, A. H.: 228
Bristling with Thorns: 247
Bristow, Gwen: 241, 251
Brock, General: 100
Broken Sword, A: 250
Bromfield, Louis: 203, 252
Brooklyn Bridge: 258
Brooks, Elbridge: 237
Brothers Three: 256
Brown, Caroline: 249
Brown, John: 150, 151, 163, 239, 248
Brown, Katherine: 148
Bryan, Mary: 246
Bryson, J. G.: 233
Buccaneers, The: 219
Buchan, John: 222
Buckmaster, Henrietta: 243
Buckskin Breeches: 241
Buff and Blue: 228
Bugles Blow No More: 173, 174
Bugles in the Afternoon: 258
Bull Run, Battle of: 163, 167, 246
Bulwark, The: 207

Bunker Hill, Battle of: 70–71, 87, 96, 234
Burgoyne, John: 51, 72–74, 80, 232, 233
Burnett, William: 252
Burr, Aaron: 79, 92, 109, 110, 115, 118–19, 120, 135, 227, 229, 236, 237, 238, 246
Burr, Anna R.: 132
Burr, Theodosia: 135
Burt, Katherine: 225
Burton, or The Sieges: 118
Butler, John: 229, 250
Button's Inn: 237
By the Dim Lamps: 253
By the Eternal: 238
By Valour and Arms: 253
Byles, Mather: 69–70
Bynner, E. L.: 50, 221, 229

Cabell, James Branch: 224
Cabin at the Trail's End, The: 240
Cable, George W.: 15; *The Grandissimes,* 127; *Kincaid's Battery,* 154, 155, 161; *John March, Southerner,* 181; *The Silent South,* 181; *Dr. Sevier,* 247
Caldwell, Janet: 243
Caldwell, Taylor: 258
Calendar of Sin, A: 251
Calhoun, John C.: 136, 238
Californians, The: 141
Call the New World: 101
Called to the Field: 250
Calvert: *see* Baltimore, Lord
Camden: 227
Camden, Battle of: 105, 227
Campbell, Walter S.: *see* Vestal, Stanley
Canal Town: 124
Candle in the Wilderness: 48
Cannon, Blanche: 259
Cannon, Le Grand: 72–73
Canolles: 229
Captain Caution: 100
Captain from Connecticut, The: 232
Captain of Company K, The: 248
Captain of the Gray-Horse Troop, The: 254
Captain Paul: 98
Cardigan: 229
Carhart, Arthur: 241
Carleton: 227
Carlisle, Helen: 38
Carmer, Carl: 92
Carolinian, The: 230

Carpenter, Edward C.: 128
Carpenter, William H.: 25, 220
Carson, Katherine: 257
Carson, Kit: 140–41, 196, 240, 241, 245, 255
Carter, Jefferson: 230
Caruthers, William A.: 27, 31, 146
Case, Josephine Y.: 235
Cassique of Kiawah, The: 36
Catch a Falling Star: 226
Cather, Willa: 8, 18; *Shadows on the Rock,* 53; *Sapphira and the Slave Girl,* 148; *O Pioneers!,* 193; *A Lost Lady,* 194; *My Ántonia,* 194; *Death Comes for the Archbishop,* 195–96
Catherwood, Mary H.: 15, 89, 221, 229, 237
Cavalier, The: 161
Cavalier of Tennessee, The: 120
Cavaliers of Virginia, The: 27, 45
Cease Firing: 155, 164
Centennial Summer: 257
Certain People of Importance: 206
Certain Rich Man, A: 254
Chainbearer, The: 59
Chambers, Robert W.: 129, 229, 230, 231, 240, 251
Champions of Freedom, The: 227
Chancellorsville, Battle of: 159, 166
Charleston: 104, 168–69, 240
Charming Sally: 223
Charnley, Mitchell: 240
Cheney, Brainard: 252
Cheney, Harriet V.: 11, 37–38, 219
Cherokee Strip: 256
Chevalier, Elizabeth: 253
Chevigny, Hector: 256
Chicago Fire: 206, 247
Chickamauga, Battle of: 155, 173, 175, 247, 251, 254
Chidsey, Donald: 235
Child, F. S.: 222
Child, Lydia Maria: 10, 42, 69
Childers, James: 259
Children of the Covenant: 258
Children of God: 145, 210
Children of the Market Place: 239
Chisholm Trail: 211
Choir Invisible, The: 117
Christian Indian, The: 219
Churchill, Winston: 16, 18; *The Crossing,* 90–91; *Richard Carvel,* 96; *The Crisis,* 149, 160–61
Cicely: 250
Cimarron: 212
Circuit Rider, The: 125

Citizen Tom Paine: 85
City of Illusion: 210
Claiborne the Rebel: 220
Clansman, The: 185
Clarence: 248
Clark, Ellery: 240
Clark, George Rogers: 88, 89, 90, 91, 94, 114, 117, 224, 232, 233
Clark, Henry S.: *see* Cox, Millard
Clark, Howard: 245
Clark, Walter Van T.: 208
Clay, Henry: 238
Clear for Action: 98
Clemens, J. R.: 128; *The Rivals,* 119; *Bernard Lile,* 128; *Mustang Gray,* 128
Cleveland, Grover: 157
Clinton, DeWitt: 124
Close Pursuit: 225
Coat I Wore, The: 235
Coatsworth, Elizabeth: 223, 232
Cobb, Joseph B.: 228
Cochran, Hamilton: 225
Code of Victor Jallot, The: 128
Colby, Merle: 123
Cold Journey: 49
Colonial Witch, A: 222
Colonial Wooing, A: 221
Colonials, The: 222
Colony, Horatio: 241
Colter, John: 136–37
Columbus, Christopher: 222
Conceived in Liberty: 85
Conquering Kitty: 231
Conqueror, The: 229, 237
Conquest, The: 135
Conspirator, The: 118–119
Conway Cabal, the: 83
Cooke, Jay: 206
Cooke, John Esten: 11, 14, 23, 146, 147, 221, 229; *My Lady Pokahontas,* 23; *The Virginia Comedians,* 23; *Henry St. John,* 32–33; *Surry of Eagle's Nest,* 154, 156; *Hilt to Hilt,* 155; *Mohun,* 156
Coolidge, Dane: 240, 241, 255
Cooper, Courtney: 208, 212, 240, 241, 255
Cooper, James Fenimore: 9, 10, 11, 12, 31, 35, 51, 54, 56–57, 106, 115, 219; *The Last of the Mohicans,* 43; *Satanstoe,* 59–60; *The Spy,* 68, 76, 78; *Lionel Lincoln,* 70; *Wyandotté,* 80; *Oak Openings,* 93; *The Pilot,* 95; *The Red Rover,* 95; *The Prairie,* 134

Index

Cooper, Kent: 225
Copperhead, The: 237, 248
Copperheads, The: 252
Corbett, Elizabeth: 252
Cordelia Chantrell: 250
Corey, Paul: 258
Corinth, Battle of: 253
Cormack, Maribelle: 232
Cornwallis, General Charles: 87, 104, 105, 107, 227, 233
Coronado: 226
Cortlandts of Washington Square, The: 250
Coryell, H. V.: 223
Costain, Thomas B.: 226
Cotton, John: 41, 49
Covered Wagon, The: 139
Cox, Millard (*pseud.* of Henry S. Clark): 249
Crabb, Alfred: 245, 253, 254
Crag-nest: 249
Crane, Stephen: 17, 85, 154, 158–59, 166
Creole, The: 228
Crisis, The: 149, 160–61
Croatan: 22
Crockett, David: 117, 129, 131, 239, 241
Cronyn, George: 239
Crosby, Enoch: 231
Crossing, The: 90–91
Crowley, Mary: 230
Crownfield, Gertrude: 223, 230, 231
Cruising and Blockading: 247
Cudjo's Cave: 237
Cunningham, Eugene: 256
Cushing, Eliza: 10, 227
Custer massacre: 191, 208, 209, 254, 258

Dakota in the Morning: 257
Dana, R. H., Jr.: 134
Daniel DuLuth: 230
Daniel Trentworthy: 247
Daniels, Harriet: 242
Dareford: 250
Dark Comes Early, The: 130
Dark Command, The: 252
Dark Sails: 225
Dark Stranger, The: 232
Darker Grows the Valley: 244
Dartmouth massacre: 228
David, Evan: 242
Daviess, Maria T.: 149
Davis, Clyde: 200
Davis, H. L.: 210, 245

Davis, J. Frank: 130
Davis, Jefferson: 162, 163, 171, 174, 254
Davis, John: 9, 23
Davis, Julia: 241, 256
Davis, Samuel: 251
Davis, William S.: 71
Dawes, Rufus: 220
Dawn's Early Light: 234
Day Must Dawn, The: 234
Days of Promise: 259
Death Comes for the Archbishop: 8, 195–96, 213
Deep River: 243
Deep Summer: 241, 252
Deep West, The: 256
Deerslayer, The: 59
DeForest, John W.: 47, 71; *Miss Ravenal's Conversion,* 156–57; *A Volunteer's Adventures,* 157 n.; *The Bloody Chasm,* 182
Degenhard, William: 112
DeKalb, Baron: 78, 105, 227
Deland, Margaret: 250
Delectable Country, The: 232
DeLeon, T. C.: 238, 249
Deliverance, The: 186
Delusion: 220
Derleth, August: 122
DeSoto: 224
Devereux, Mary: 237
Devil's Own, The: 239
DeVoto, Bernard: 146
Diamond Head: 253
Dickson, James: 241
Dillon, Mary: 238
Dinner at Belmont: 253
Dinwiddie, Robert: 226
Disinherited, The: 64
Dix, Beulah: 222
Dixon, Thomas, Jr.: 14, 149, 154, 181 n., 185
'Dobe Walls: 240
Dr. Sevier: 247
Dodge, Constance: 225, 232, 233
Dollar Gold Piece, The: 257
Dongall, Lily: 144
Donner party: 142, 240, 242
Don't You Cry for Me: 142–43
Doomed Chief, The: 44–45
Dorothy South: 249
Double Muscadine: 245
Douglas, Stephen A.: 161, 205, 239
Douglass, Frederick: 163, 244
Dowdey, Clifford: 7, 173, 178, 223, 242

Down to New Orleans: 235
Downey, Fairfax: 258
Downing, J. Hyatt: 256, 257
Drago, Harry (*pseud.* Will Ermine):
    208, 241
Drake, Sir Francis: 103
Dream of Empire, A: 237
Dreiser, Theodore: 206–207
D'ri and I: 100
Drivin' Woman: 253
Drum Up the Dawn: 241
Drums: 102–103, 166
Drums Along the Mohawk: 82
Drums in the Dawn: 230
Drums of the Monmouth: 231
Drums of Morning, The: 151, 175
Dudley, Albertus: 231
Dudley, Thomas: 48
Duffus, R. L.: 132, 241
Duke of Stockbridge, The: 112
Dunmore, Governor John Murray:
    32, 91, 110, 219, 224
Dupuy, Eliza A.: 119, 228
Dust on the King's Highway: 226
Dutchman's Fireside, The: 55–56, 60
Dye, Eva: 135

Eagle in the Sky: 99
Eagle in the Sun: 132
Eagles Fly West: 243
Early Candlelight: 240
Early, Jubal Anderson: 156
East Angels: 183
East by Day: 242
East of the Giants: 142
Eaton, Evelyn: 234
Eben Holden: 159
Eckenrode, H. J.: 251
Edge-Hill: 227
Edith; or, The Quaker's Daughter:
    221
Edmonds, Walter D.: 18, 81–82, 235,
    242, 244; *Drums Along the Mo-
    hawk,* 82; *Rome Haul,* 123
Edwin Brothertoft: 229
Eggleston, Edward: 15, 125, 149;
    The Circuit Rider, 125; *The End of
    the World,* 125; *The Graysons,* 125;
    The Hoosier Schoolmaster, 125;
    The Mystery of Metropolisville,
    125; *Roxy,* 125
Eggleston, George C.: 147, 238, 249,
    250
Ehrlich, Leonard: 7; *God's Angry
    Man,* 150
Eliot, John: 41, 45

Elkswatawa: 93
Ellen Grafton: 228
Ellerbe, Rose: 239
Ellis, E. S.: 229
Ellsberg, Edward: 98
Elva: 223
Emerson, Elizabeth: 244
Emigrant Trail, The: 238
Emigrants, The: 196
Emperor Brims: 224
End of the World, The: 125
Endicott, John: 38, 48–49
Engstrand, Stuart: 241
Erie Canal: 124, 200, 244
Ermine, Will: *see* Drago, Harry
Ernenwein, Leslie: 254
Erskine, John: 224
Erskine Dale: 239
Eutaw: 105
Evarts, Hal: 240, 255
Evelyn Byrd: 250
Evening Wolves, The: 226
Expiation: 248
Exquisite Siren, The: 232

Fairbank, Janet: 206, 250, 251
Fair Rebel, The: 220
*Fairfax; or, The Master of Greenway
    Court:* 221
Fairfax, Lord: 221
Falconer, William: 246
Fallen Timbers, Battle of: 89, 91, 94
Farm, The: 203–204
Farmers' Alliance: 255
Farragut, David: 154, 162
Fast, Howard: 18, 85, 188
Fate of Madame La Tour, The: 237
Father, The: 148
Fathers, The: 169
Father Abraham: 149
Fawn of the Pale Faces, The: 220
Fay, T. S.: 227
Faye's Folly: 252
Female Review, The: 227
Female Spy, The: 228
Ferber, Edna: 206, 255; *Saratoga
    Trunk,* 206; *Cimarron,* 212
Fergusson, Harvey: 255
Feuchtwanger, Lion: 235
Field, Rachel: 241
Fields, The: 124
Fierro Blanco, Antonio de: 240
Fifty-four Forty or Fight!: 136
Fight for the Valley, The: 230
Fighting Danites, The: 240
Financier, The: 206

Index

Fink, Mike: 117, 232
Finlay, Lucile: 235
Fire Bell in the Night: 243
First the Blade: 257
First Gentleman of America: 224
First of the Knickerbockers, The: 55
First Rebel, The: 63
First Settlers of Virginia, The: 9, 23
Fisher, Vardis: 142
Fitzpatrick, Richard: 138
Flames of Empire: 254
Fleet in the Forest, The: 234
Fletcher, Inglis: 103; *Lusty Wind for Carolina,* 103; *Men of Albemarle,* 103; *Roanoke Hundred,* 103; *Raleigh's Eden,* 103–104; *Toil of the Brave,* 104
Flint, Timothy: 115, 236; *The Shoshonee Valley,* 134
Floyd, C. J.: 250
Folded Hills: 143
Follow the Drinking Gourd: 241
Fool's Errand, A: 180
Foote, Shelby: 259
Footner, Hulbert: 232
For King and Country: 229
For Us the Living: 149
Forayers, The: 105
Forbes, Esther: 41, 47, 234, 239, 245
Forbidden Ground, The: 64
Ford, Paul Leicester: 16, 84
Foreman, Leonard: 242
Forest and the Fort, The: 64
Forest Spy, The: 229
Forester, C. S.: 232
Forestfield: 249
Forever Free: 160
Forever Possess: 226
Forge, The: 168
Forrest, Nathan B.: 173, 185, 254
Forsaken, The: 227
Fort Braddock Letters: 219
Fort Dearborn: 230
Fort William Henry: 58–59
Fortune, Smile Once More!: 244
'49, A Novel of Gold: 239
Forward the Nation: 19, 137
Foundation Stone: 252
Founding a Nation: 222
1492: 222
Fox, Charles: 97, 102
Fox, John, Jr.: 237, 239; *The Little Shepherd of Kingdom Come,* 163
Foxes of Harrow, The: 244
Francis Berrian: 236

Franklin, Benjamin: 72, 83, 84, 96, 97, 98, 226, 231, 235
Frederic, Harold: 81, 82, 237, 248
Frederick de Algeroy: 227
Free Forester: 241
Free Land: 199
Free Soil: 150
Freedmen's Bureau: 187, 188
Freedom Road: 188
Freeman, Mary Wilkins: 30
Frémont, General John C.: 141
French, Alice (*pseud.* Octave Thanet): 248
French, Allen: 222
French, James S.: 93
Freneau, Philip: 231
Frey, Ruby: 226
Frontenac, Count de: 229
Fugitive Slave Law: 163
Fuller, Edmund: 244
Fuller, Iola: *The Loon Feather,* 123; *The Shining Trail,* 123
Fur Brigade: 240
Furman, Garrit: 219
Fury in the Earth: 235

Gabriel, G. W.: 245
Gabriel, Gilbert: 133
Gabriel Conroy: 141
Gabriel Tolliver: 184
Gage, General Thomas: 70
Gaither, Frances: 241, 245; *The Red Cock Crows,* 147
Gallatin, Albert: 109
Gallows Hill: 48
Gamble's Hundred: 223
Ganilh, Anthony (*pseud.* A. T. Myrthe): *Mexico versus Texas,* 128
Gardener, Helen: 248
Gardiner, Dorothy: 259
Gardiner, Sir Christopher: 41, 221
Gardiner, Sir Philip: 38, 43
Garland, Hamlin: 125, 126, 254; *Trail-Makers of the Middle Border,* 155, 165; *A Son of the Middle Border,* 192–93
Garnett, David: 23
Garrard, L. H.: 255
Garrick, David: 97
Garrison, William Lloyd: 239
Gates, Eleanor: 238
Gates, General Horatio: 74, 105, 106, 107, 227
Gazer, Giles (*pseud.*): 227
General's Double, The: 157
General's Lady, The: 231

Genesee Fever: 92
Gentleman Ranker: 225
Germain, George Sackville: 87
Germantown, Battle of: 83, 228
Gessner, Robert: 234
Gettysburg, Battle of: 154, 157, 158, 161, 164, 169–70; 175, 250
Giant Joshua, The: 210
Giants in the Earth: 5, 196–97, 213
Gilded Age: 204
Gilded Rooster, The: 253
Gilman of Redford: 71
Gilmore, James (*pseud.* Edmund Kirk): 248
Girty, Simon: 224, 233, 236–37, 238, 240
Gitana: 129
Give Me Liberty: 224
Glasgow, Ellen: 15–16, 156; *The Battle-Ground,* 162; *The Voice of the People,* 185; *The Deliverance,* 186, 189n.
Glover, John: 103
God's Angry Man: 7, 150
God-Seeker, The: 246
Goff, Harriet: 246
Goffe, William: 45, 219
Gold: 143
Golden Bubble, The: 240, 255
Golden Feather: 225
Golden Quicksand, The: 132
Golden Shore: 243
Gone to Texas: 186
Gone With the Wind: 155, 156, 170, 171, 173, 176, 187, 189
Good Crop, The: 244
Goodwin, Maud W.: 25, 34
Gordon, Caroline: 173, 224, 240
Gordon, Virginia: 243
Gorgeous Hussy, The: 120
Gorman, Herbert: 131
Gould, Jay: 257
Grace Dudley: 228
Grandissimes, The: 127
Grandmothers, The: 202
Grange: 200
Grant, Dorothy: 226
Grant, Ulysses S.: 154, 155, 156, 158, 161, 164, 165, 167, 176, 251, 257, 259
Grapes of Wrath, The: 249
Graves, Robert: 232, 233
Gray, Stanley: 233
Gray Dawn: 143
Graysons, The: 125, 149
Great Betrayal: 259
Great Captain, The: 160

Great Meadow, The: 19, 117–18, 148
Great Promise, The: 258
Great Smith: 225
Great Tide, The: 244
Great Treason, A: 229
Great Valley, The: 33
Greeley, Horace: 159, 160
Green Centuries: 224
Green Mountain Boys, The: 50–51, 60
Greene, Nathaniel: 86, 104, 105, 106
Gregg, F. M.: 222
Grey, Zane: 208, 255
Greyslaer: 14, 80
Grierson, Francis: 149
Grim Journey: 142
Grimstead, Durward: 223
Gringo Gold: 241, 257
Griswold, Francis: 188
Growth of the Soil: 196
Guns of Burgoyne: 232
Guthrie, A. B.: 137–38

Hagar: 248
Hagedorn, Hermann: 213
Haines, Edwin: 232
Hale, Edward Everett: 119
Hale, Nathan: 86, 111, 228
Half That Glory: 233
Hall, James: 116
Hall, Rubylea: 244
Halleck, Fitz-Greene: 233
Hallet, Richard: 241
Hamele, Ottamar: 245
Hamilton, Alexander: 86, 108, 119, 229, 237
Hamilton, Harry: 226
Hamilton's rangers: 238
Hammand, Esther: 224
Hampshire Grants: 49, 72, 231
Hamsun, Knut: 196
Hancock, John: 72, 85, 87, 234
Handsome Road, The: 251
Hang My Wreath: 253
Hannum, Alberta: 258
Hansford: 28–29
Hargreaves, Sheba: 240
Harpers Ferry: 156, 247
Harpe's Head: 116
Harris, Bernice: 257
Harris, Cyril: 232, 233
Harris, Joel Chandler: 184
Harris, L. F.: 251
Harrison, William Henry: 89, 93, 94, 227, 229
Harte, Bret: 141, 142, 229, 248
Harvest of the Wind: 241

Index

Harvest Waits, The: 257
Hatcher, Harlan: 241
Hatfield-McCoy feud: 258
Havard, Aline: 223
Haverhill: 51–52
Havill, Edward: 253
Hawk of Detroit: 224
Hawkeye, The: 200
Hawthorne, Hildegarde: 231
Hawthorne, Nathaniel: 13–14, 38, 46;
    The Scarlet Letter, 39–40
Haycox, Ernest: 256, 257, 258
Haydocks' Testimony, The: 248
Hayne, Paul Hamilton: 169
Head of a Hundred, The: 25–26, 34
Heart of Kentucky, The: 238
Heart's Highway, The: 30
Hearts of Hickory: 239
Heath, J. E.: 227
Heaven Is Too High: 235
Heaven Trees: 147
Henry, Patrick: 32, 85, 87, 98, 109,
    224, 225, 228, 229, 231
Henry St. John: 32–33
Hentz, Nicholas M.: 60–61
Herbert, H. W.: 220
Herbert Tracy: 228
Herbert Wendall: 227
Hergesheimer, Joseph: *Balisand,* 108;
    The Limestone Tree, 202; *The
    Bright Shawl,* 213; *Java Head,*
    239; *Swords and Roses,* 251
Heritage, The: 91
Herkimer, General Nicholas: 80, 81,
    85
Heroine of the Strait, The: 230
Hersch, Virginia: 226
Hewes, Joseph: 104
Heyward, Dubose: 168–69
Hickory Shirt: 246
High Towers: 226
High Wind Rising, A: 225
Hill Country: 255
Hill of the Hawk: 245
Hilt to Hilt: 155
Hilton Head: 224
Hinckley, Helen: 258
His Majesty's Yankees: 233
His Somber Rivals: 157
History of Rome Hanks, The: 176
Hobomok: 42
Hoffman, Charles F.: 79–80
Hogan, Pendleton: 130
Holdfast Gaines: 110
Holland, J. G.: 41
Hollister, G. H.: 44

Holmes, Oliver Wendell: 50, 239
Home to the Hermitage: 245
Homestead Act: 191
Honey in the Horn: 210
Hood, General John B.: 156, 164, 175
Hooker, Forrestine: 255
Hoosier Schoolmaster, The: 125
Hoosier Volunteer, The: 250
Hope Leslie: 41, 42–43
Horse-Shoe Robinson: 107
Hotchkiss, Chauncey: 222
Hough, Emerson: 17; *The Mississippi
    Bubble,* 127; *The Magnificent Ad-
    venture,* 135; *Fifty-four Forty or
    Fight!,* 136; *The Covered Wagon,*
    139; *North of 36,* 211
Hough, Frank: 75, 78
House Divided: 150, 176–77
House of Vanished Splendor: 255
House Too Old, A: 256
Houston, Noel: 258
Houston, Sam: 130, 131, 175
Howard, Elizabeth Metzger: 258
Howard, John H.: 250
Howe, Sir William: 83, 85, 87, 227
Howells, William Dean: 15, 238
Hubbell, J. B.: 25 n., 33 n.
Hueston, Ethel: 136–37
Hudson's Bay Company: 133, 139, 255
Hugh Wynne: 83–84
Huguenots: 231
Hughes, Langston: 255
Hughes, Rupert: 224
Hull, William: 100, 232
Hunting Shirt: 223
Hutchens, Jane: 252, 253
Hutchinson, Governor Thomas: 69

I, James Lewis: 133
I Thee Wed: 245
Idell, Albert: 257
If Not Victory: 78
In Adam's Fall: 225
In Buff and Blue: 229
In Castle and Colony: 222
In the Days of Poor Richard: 84
In the Days of St. Clair: 91
In the Hands of the Senecas: 235
In the Shadow of the Pines: 250
In the Valley: 81
In War Time: 158
Indian Brother: 223
Inez, A Tale of the Alamo: 129
Ingraham, Ellen (*pseud.* Grace Lint-
    ner): 247

Ingraham, J. H.: 118, 220, 236;
  Burton, or The Sieges, 118, 227
Ingram's rebellion: 221
Inherit the Earth: 232
Inner Voice, The: 242
Insurgents, The: 112
Invasion, The: 230
Invisible Woman, The: 200
Iredell, James: 104
Iron Game, The: 248
Irving, Washington: 37, 54, 115, 133;
  Astoria, 133
Isadore: 220
Isidro: 141
Israel Potter: 96
Issue, The: 250

Jack Horner: 248
Jackson, Andrew: 91, 111, 120, 130,
  131, 227, 228, 238, 239, 240, 245
Jackson, Helen Hunt: 142
Jackson, Stonewall: 154, 156, 164, 165,
  249, 250
Jacobs, Helen: 234
Jacobs, Thornwell: 252
Janet, Lillian: 244
Janice Meredith: 84
Java Head: 239
Jay-Hawkers, The: 249
Jean Lafitte: 240
Jefferson, Thomas: 85, 98, 108, 109,
  110, 111, 114, 119–20, 126, 131, 135,
  137, 225, 228, 231, 233, 234, 236
Jennings, John E.: 224, 225, 234, 235,
  245; *Call the New World,* 101–102
Jewett, Sarah Orne: 97
John Barry: 244
John Brent: 237
John Brown's Cousin: 252
John Holden, Unionist: 248
John March, Southerner: 181
Johnny Appleseed: 238
Johnny Printer: 253
Johnny Tremain: 234
Johnson, Sir William: 52, 55–6, 80,
  81, 82, 222, 223, 229, 230
Johnston, Albert Sidney: 251
Johnston, Joseph E.: 161, 164
Johnston, Mary: 15, 17, 18; *Croatan,*
  22; *To Have and To Hold,* 26;
  Prisoners of Hope, 29; *Audrey,* 30;
  The Great Valley, 33; *Lewis Rand,*
  119, 120; *The Long Roll,* 154, 164;
  Cease Firing, 155, 164; *1492,* 222;
  Hunting Shirt, 223
Jones, Alice: *see* Alix, John

Jones, J. B.: 228
Jones, James A.: 51–52, 77
Jones, John Paul: 78, 95, 96, 97, 102,
  104
Jones, John Richter: 83
Jones, Nard: 242, 255
Jornada: 132, 241
Joscelyn: 229
Journey of the Flame: 240
Judah, Charles: 225
Judah, S. B. H.: 219
Judas Tree, The: 64
Judd, Sylvester: 236
Judith: 234

Kabaosa: 93
Kane, Harnett: 254
Kansas struggle: 148, 150, 242
Kantor, MacKinlay: 154, 169, 170, 178
Kate Bonnet: 222
Katherine Walton: 105
Katy of Catoctin: 247
Kays, The: 250
Keenan, Henry: 248
Keepers of the House, The: 252
Kelland, Clarence: 252
Kellogg-McEnery riots: 247
Kennedy, John P.: 11; *Rob of the
  Bowl,* 34; *Horse-Shoe Robinson,*
  107; *Swallow Barn,* 146
Kennedy, Sara: 250
Kennelly, Ardyth: 259
Kent Fort Manor: 249
Kenton, Simon: 90, 92, 117
Kentuckians, The: 237
Kenyon, Theda: 225, 244, 253
Kester, Vaughan: 238
Key, Alexander: 231
Kidd, Captain: 219
Kieft, Governor: 37, 55
Kilbourn, Diana: 228
Kincaid's Battery: 154–55, 161
King, Charles: 247, 249, 250, 254;
  Rock of Chickamauga, The, 155,
  157; *Between the Lines,* 157; *The
  General's Double,* 157
King Noanett: 221
King of the Hurons, The: 55
King Philip's War: 43, 45, 225
Kingdom Coming: 251
Kings Mountain, Battle of: 107
King's Passenger, The: 225
Kirkland, Joseph: 125, 149, 248
Kitty's Conquest: 247
Knickerbocker History of New York:
  54

Knight of the Golden Melice, The: 41
Knights in Fustian: 249
Knights of the Horseshoe, The: 31
Knox, Henry: 86
Kohl, Edith: 257
Koningsmarke: 56
Kramer, Horace: 200
Krey, Laura: 128, 131, 186, 187
Kroll, Harry: 235, 242, 243, 244, 252
Ku Klux Klan: 168, 179, 184, 185, 187, 189

Ladies Day: 257
Lady of Fort St. John, The: 237
LaFarge, Oliver: 231
Lafayette, Marquis de: 86, 227, 229
Lafitte, Jean: 111, 120, 128, 228, 231, 236, 240
Lafitte of Louisiana: 237
Lafitte; or, The Baratarian Chief: 236
Lafitte: The Pirate of the Gulf: 236
Lagard, Gerald: 254
Laird, Charlton G.: 245
Lamb in His Bosom: 147–48
Lancaster, Bruce: 149, 232, 234, 254
Land for My Sons: 232
Land Is Bright, The: 139
Land of the Burnt Thigh, The: 257
Land of Promise, The: 239
Lane, Carl: 234
Lane, Rose Wilder: 199
Lanham, Edwin: 212
Lantern in Her Hand, A: 199
"Laramie": 254
La Salle, Sieur de: 89, 222
Last Frontier, The: 208 (C. Cooper); 209 (H. Fast)
Last Full Measure, The: 160
Last of the Cavaliers, The: 250
Last of the Mohicans, The: 58–59, 61
Late George Apley, The: 256
Laughlin, Ruth: 245
Lawrence, James: 227
Lazarre: 229
Leatherwood God, The: 238
LeCato, N. J. W.: 247
Lee, Charles: 86, 227, 229, 231, 234
Lee, Eliza Buckminster: 40, 220
Lee, Robert E.: 4, 154, 156, 164, 165, 167, 170, 175, 250, 259
Legionaries, The: 249
Leisler: 220
Leisler's Rebellion: 220, 221, 226
Le May, Alan: 240
Leopard's Spots, The: 185
Let the Hurricane Roar: 199

Let the King Beware!: 231
Lewis, Alfred H.: 238
Lewis, Janet: 230
Lewis, Sinclair: 195, 246
Lewis and Clark Expedition: 111, 114, 133, 134, 135, 136, 137, 241, 256
Lewis Rand: 119, 120
Lexington, Battle of: 70–71, 229
Liberty or Death: 231
Liddon, Eloise: 242
Light in the Sky: 259
Lightwood: 252
Limestone Tree, The: 202–203, 204
Lincoln, Abraham: 125, 146, 148, 149, 150, 153, 158, 160, 161, 163, 167, 205, 247, 248
Lintner, Grace: *see* Ingraham, Ellen
Linwoods, The: 71
Lion, Hortense: 223
Lionel Lincoln: 70
Lions of the Lord, The: 145
Lippard, George: 228
Little, George: 228
Little Lower than the Angels, A: 144
Little Red Foot, The: 230
Little Shepherd of Kingdom Come, The: 163
"Lively Lady," The: 100
Lockridge, Ross: 204
Lockwood, Ralph: 112
Locusts, The: 258
Lofts, Nora: 224
Logan: 219, 224
Logan, A Family Chronicle: 219
Lone Dove, The: 228
Lone Star, The: 238
Lone Star Preacher: 175
Long Hunt, The: 5, 118
Long Island, Battle of: 87
Long Knives: 238
Long Night, The: 251
Long Pennant, The: 231
Long Remember: 154, 169–70, 177
Long Rifle, The: 143
Long Roll, The: 154, 164
Long Trail, The: 254
Lonz Powers: 117, 236
Look Away!: 252
Look Away, Dixieland: 251
Look Back to Glory: 240
Look to the Mountain: 19, 73
Loon Feather, The: 123
Lost Empire: 256
Lost Lady, A: 194
Louisiana Purchase: 90, 126, 238
Love and the Lieutenant: 231

Lovejoy, Elijah: 148
Lovelace, Maud: 223, 240, 241
Lover's Revolt, A: 71
Lusty Wind for Carolina: 103
Lutes, Della: 242
Lydia Bailey: 235
Lyle, E. P.: 238
Lynn, Margaret: 150, 239
Lytle, Andrew: 224, 251

McCall, Marie: 226
McCants, E. C.: 230
McCarter, Margaret Hill: 238
McClellan, General George B.: 249
McClung, J. A.: 227
McConnel, J. L.: 236
McCook, Henry C.: 222
Macdonald, Flora: 104, 228, 233
McFarland, Raymond: 223
McGovern, John: 247
McHenry, James: 10, 45, 62–63, 227
McIntyre, J. T.: 230
MacKnight, James: 248
McLean, Sydney: 243
MacLeod, Le Roy: 251
McLoughlin and Old Oregon: 135
McMeekin, Clark: 252
McNally, William: 256
McNeil, Everett: 230
McNeilly, Mildred: 235
McVeys, The: 125, 149
Madam Constantia: 230
Madison, James: 109
Magnificent Adventure, The: 135
Magnificent Ambersons, The: 206
Magruder, Julia: 247
Maid-at-Arms, The: 230
Making of Christopher Ferringham, The: 222
Mally, Emma Louise: 258
Mamselle of the Wilderness: 222
Man Cannot Tell: 225
Man for the Ages, A: 149
Man from Texas, The: 247
Man of the Storm, The: 136
Man Should Rejoice, A: 243
Manassas: 163
Mann, Herman: 227
Man's Reach, A: 243
Marcel Armand: 231
Marching On: 19, 154, 166, 174;
   (Strachey), 239
Margaret: 236
Margaret Ballentine: 238
Margaret Smith's Journal: 40
Marginal Land: 200

Marion, Francis: 104 f., 228, 230, 231
Markey, Morris: 251
Marks, Mary A. M. Hoppus: 229
Marquand, J. P.: 239, 256
Mars' Butterfly: 233
Marsh, George: 225
Marshall, Edison: 225, 255
Mary Derwent: 228
Mason, Van Wyck: 18; *Rivers of Glory*, 99; *Stars on the Sea*, 99; *Three Harbours*, 99; *Hang My Wreath*, 253
Master of Chaos: 230
Master of Red Leaf, The: 246
Master of Warlock, The: 250
Masters, Edgar Lee: 239, 256
Mather, Cotton: 41, 46, 47, 48, 220, 225
Matrix: 149
Matschat, Cecile: 257
Maule, Mary: 255
Meade, General George: 167, 170
Meigs, Cornelia: 209
Mellichampe: 105
Melville, Herman: 96
Men of Albemarle: 103
Meredith: 227
Meriwether, Elizabeth Avery (*pseud.* Hannah Parting): 246, 250
Merry-Mount: 38
Mexico versus Texas: 128
Michael Beam: 241
Miers, Earl: 225
Mighty Mountain: 140
Migrations: 240
Mill on Mad River, The: 245
Mill Stream: 223
Miller, Caroline: 147
Miller, Helen T.: 225, 235
Miller, May: 257
Minster's Wooing, The: 119, 237
Minnigerode, Meade: 231, 250
Mirror for Witches: 47–48
Miss Ravenel's Conversion: 156–57
Mississippi Bubble, The: 127
Mistress Margaret: 230
Mitchel, F. A.: 249
Mitchell, Margaret: 17; *Gone With the Wind*, 155–56, 170–73, 176, 187, 189
Mitchell, S. Weir: 15; *Hugh Wynne*, 83; *The Red City*, 108; *In War Time*, 158; *Roland Blake*, 158; *Westways*, 158
Mockingbird Is Singing, The: 258

Index

Mockingbird Sang at Chickamauga, A: 254
Moment of Time, A: 243
Monarchist, The: 228
Monroe, James: 101, 109
Montana Road: 208
Montcalm, General: 58, 227
Montgomery, General James: 73, 227
Montgomery, James S.: 251
Moore, John T.: 239
Moore, Virginia: 251
Morford, H.: 229
Morgan, George: 250
Mormon Prophet, The: 144
Mormons: 144–45, 259
Morning in America: 234
Morris, Gouverneur: 249
Morris, Robert: 92
Morrow, Honoré W.: *We Must March,* 139; *Forever Free,* 160; *The Great Captain,* 160; *The Last Full Measure,* 160; *With Malice Toward None,* 160; *Let the King Beware!* 231; *Beyond the Blue Sierra,* 240
Mortgage Your Heart: 198
Morton, Stanley: 235
Morton, Thomas: 37, 38, 43
Morton's Hope: 220
Mothers, The: 19, 142–43, 242
Motley, John L.: 13, 38, 41, 220
Mount Hope: 44
Mountains Are Mine, The: 258
Mountain-White Heroine, A: 248
Mr. Madison's War: 231
Mrs. Pennington: 257
Mudgett, Helen: 235
Muller Hill: 242
Munroe, Kirk: 237
Mural for a Later Day: 223
Murfree, Mary Noailles: 183, 222
Murgatroyd, Matthew: 77
Murray, W. W.: 220
Murrell's gang: 242
Mustang Gray: 128–29
My Ántonia: 193, 194
My Blood and My Treasure: 233
My Lady of the North: 163
My Lady Pokahontas: 23
My Story: 230
Myers, John: 245
Myers, Paul H.: 55
Mystery of Metropolisville, The: 125

Nameless Nobleman, A: 221
Nancy Lloyd: 65
Naomi: 40

Nathan Burke: 17, 129
Naylor, James B.: 91
Neal, John: 10, 37, 46, 219, 227
Nebraska Coast: 200
Neutral French, The: 220
Neutral Ground, The: 78
New Orleans, Battle of: 111, 120, 121, 228, 238, 239, 240
New Road, The: 123
Next to Valour: 224
Nicholson, Meredith: 120
Nick of the Woods: 116–17
Night-hawk, The: 249
Night of Decision: 226
Niles, Blair: 242
Ninety-Six: 88
Ninety Six: 230
Nix's Mate: 220
No Brighter Glory: 233
No Bugles Tonight: 254
No Other White Men: 241, 256
None Shall Look Back: 173
Norris, Kathleen: 206
Norris, Mary H.: 249
North of 36: 211
Northwest Passage: 52–53
Not Without Laughter: 255
Not Without Peril: 224
Nothing Ever Happens Sunday Morning: 259
Nutt, Frances: 236

O Genteel Lady!: 239
O Pioneers!: 193
O River, Remember!: 258
Oak Openings: 93
O'Connor, Jack: 257
O'Dell, Scott: 245
Oglethorpe, James Edward: 225
Oh Promised Land: 120
Oklahoma: 255
Old Continental, The: 78
Old Father of Waters: 240
Old Fort Duquesne: 220
Old Jules: 201
Old Kaskaskia: 89
Oldham, Henry: 247
Oldtown Folks: 237
Oliver Wiswell: 79, 81, 87
On the Long Tide: 128, 131
On the Plains with Custer: 208
Once a Wilderness: 256
One Stayed at Welcome: 241
Oregon Trail, The: 134
Original Belle, An: 157, 247
Oriskany, Battle of: 79–80, 81, 82

Orpen, Adela: 249
Osceola: 220
Oskison, John: 212, 255, 256
Ostenso, Martha: 255, 258
Other Fools and Their Doings: 246
Otis, James: 70
Owen, Caroline: 239
Ox-bow Incident, The: 208

Paddock, Cornelia: 237
Page, Elizabeth: 109–10, 226
Page, Thomas Nelson: 146, 147, 183, 186
Page, Walter Hines: 181
Paine, Tom: 85, 86
Paradise: 19, 41
Parker, Sir Gilbert: 52, 221
Parkhill, Forbes: 258
Parkman, Francis: 52, 89, 134
Parrish, Randall: *My Lady of the North,* 163; *My Lady of the South,* 163; *A Sword of the Old Frontier,* 222; *When Wilderness Was King,* 230; *The Devil's Own,* 239; *The Red Mist,* 250; *Bob Hampton of Placer,* 254
Parting, Hannah: *see* Meriwether, Elizabeth Avery
Partisan, The: 104–105
Pathfinder, The: 59
Patience of John Moreland, The: 238
Patriots, The: 164
Patterns of Wolfpen: 241
Paulding, James K.: 11, 55, 78, 115
Pawle, Kathleen: 223
Peace, My Daughters: 226
Peaceable Kingdom, The: 259
Pearson, Lorene: 257
Peattie, Donald: 137
Peder Victorious: 197
Peep at the Pilgrims, A: 37
Pemberton, John Clifford: 154, 165
Pendexter, Hugh: 223
Penhally: 240
Penn, William: 54, 56, 58, 66
Pennell, Joseph: 176
Peploe, Annie: 220
Perilous Fight, The: 235
Perilous Journey: 243
Perilous Night, The: 79
Perry, Admiral Oliver Hazard: 100, 234
Peter Ashley: 168–69
Peterson, C. J.: 228
Pettibone, Anita: 253
Phantom, Emperor, The: 241

Philip Nolan's Friends: 119
Phillips, Alexandra: 226
Phips, Sir William: 225
Pickett, George Edward: 170, 176
Pidgin, Charles F.: 119
Pike, Zebulon: 133
Pilgrims of New England, The: 220
Pilot, The: 94–95
Pinckney, Josephine: 224
Pioneers, The: 57, 241
Pittman, Hannah D.: 238
Pleasants, Henry: 233
Plow-Woman, The: 238
Plume Rouge: 137
Pocahontas: 23 f.
Pocahontas: 19, 23
Polk, James K.: 136
Pontiac: 64, 94, 222, 224, 230
Poole, Ernest: 246
Pound, Arthur: 224, 256
Powhatan: 24, 25
Prairie, The: 134
Prairie-Schooner Princess, A: 255
Prayer for Tomorrow, A: 256
Preacher on Horseback: 257
Pridgen, Tim: 233, 243
Priscilla: 41, 221
Prisoners of Hope: 29–30
Proceed, Sergeant Lamb: 233
Prodigal Judge, The: 238
Proud Destiny: 235
Pryor, Elinor: 144
Pulaski, Count Casimir: 228
Puritan and the Quaker, The: 221
Purslane: 257
Putnam, General Israel: 70, 86
Putnam, George P.: 246
Putnam, Nina: 242

Quaker Ben: 222
Quaker Soldier, The: 83
Quakers: 40, 41, 45, 61, 65, 66, 83, 207, 221, 222, 223, 225, 244
Quantrill's raid: 247
Quick, Herbert: 124, 199–200

Rabble in Arms: 73
Rachel Dyer: 46
Raddall, Thomas: 233
Railroad West: 209
Raintree County: 204, 213
Rake and the Hussy, The: 240
Raleigh's Eden: 103
Ralphton: 228
Ramona: 142
Ranchero: 143

Index

Ranger Two-Rifle: 255
Rangers, The: 72
Rangers and Regulators of the Tanaha, The: 237
Ransom, J. B.: 220
Rayner, Emma: 222
Read, Opie: 238
Rebel General's Loyal Bride, The: 246
Rebel Yell: 254
Rebels, The: 69
Red Badge of Courage, The: 154, 159, 166
Red City, The: 108
Red Cock Crows, The: 147
Red Lanterns on St. Michaels: 252
Red Mist, The: 250
Red Morning: 226
Red Raskall: 234
Red Road, The: 223
Red Rock: 183–84, 186
Red Rover, The: 94
Redfield: 219
Reed, Myrtle: 230
Refugee, The: 77
"Regicides, The": 46, 219
Regicide's Children: 223
Regulators, The: 112
Reluctant Rebel: 226
Remember the Alamo!: 129
Remembrance Rock: 19
Renegade, The: 236
Renown: 75
Restless Is the River: 241
Return of the O'Mahoney, The: 248
Revere, Paul: 72, 229, 234
Revolt on the Border: 132
Rezánov: 141
Richard Carvel: 96–97
Richard Pryne: 233
Richardson, Major John: 220
Richter, Conrad: 5, 124, 234, 256
Riddle, A. G.: 229
Riders of the Purple Sage: 255
Riedesel, Baron Friedrich von: 72
Rifles for Washington: 232
Rio Bravo: 239
Ripley, Clements: 98
Rising Thunder: 231
Rising Wind: 251
Rivals, The: 119, 229, 237
Rivals of Acadia, The: 219
River to the West: 245
Rivers of Glory: 99
Rivers out of Eden: 224
Road to Endor: 224

Road to San Jacinto, The: (J. F. Davis), 130; (L. Foreman), 242
Roanoke Hundred: 103
Rob of the Bowl: 34–35
Robert Warren: 248
Roberts, Elizabeth Madox: 117–18
Roberts, Kenneth: 52; *Arundel,* 73; *Oliver Wiswell,* 87–88; *The "Lively Lady,"* 100–101; *Captain Caution,* 101; *Lydia Bailey,* 235–36
Roberts, Richard: 253
Robertson, Constance: 243, 253
Robinson, J. H.: 228
Robinson, Stephen: 247
Rock Cried Out, The: 246
Rock of Chickamauga, The: 155, 157
Rodney, G. B.: 229
Roe, E. P.: 157, 247
Rogers, Major Robert: 52
Rogers' Rangers: 79, 224
Rogue's Companion: 242
Roland Blake: 158
Rolfe, John: 24
Rölvaag, O. E.: 5, 196 f.
Romance of the Charter Oak, The: 46
Romance of Dollard, The: 15, 89, 221
Rome Haul: 123
Roofs of Elm Street, The: 256
Roosevelt, Theodore: 213
Ropes of Sand: 239
Rose Dawn: 143
Rose of Old St. Louis, The: 238
Roseanna McCoy: 258
Rose-Hill: 227
Rough Riders, The: 213
Roxy: 125
Running of the Tide, The: 245
Ruth Emsley: 25
Ruth Whalley: 220

Sabbath Has No End: 242
Sabin, E. L.: 208, 238, 239
Sabatini, Rafael: 230
Sac Indians: 122–23
Sacagawea (Sacajawea): 135, 137
Safford, Henry: 231, 233
Sailor of Fortune: 232
St. Clair, General Arthur: 51, 91
St. Leger, General Barry: 80, 81
Saints and Tomahawks: 224
Salem Belle, The: 220
Salem Frigate: 235
Salem Witchcraft: 219
Salute the Hero: 253
Salute to Adventurers: 222
Samuel Drummond: 250

Sandburg, Carl: 19
Sandoz, Mari: 201
Sangaree: 245
Santa Anna: 129
Santa Fé: 132, 140, 239, 240, 241, 245
Sapphira and the Slave Girl: 148
Saratoga: 228
Saratoga, Battle of: 73, 74, 232
Saratoga Trunk: 206
Sass, Herbert: 224, 240
Satanstoe: 59–60
Scarlet Cockerel, The: 223, 254
Scarlet Letter, The: 39–40, 42
Scarlet Petticoat: 242
Schachner, Nathan: 225, 243, 253
Schofield, W. G.: 225
Schorer, Mark: 256
Schrag, Otto: 258
Schumann, Mary: 224, 233
Schurz, Carl: 209
Schuyler, Philip J.: 51, 81
Scott, Evelyn: 167, 178, 240, 251
Scott, Sir Walter: 5, 7, 8 n., 9, 11, 28, 35, 45, 56–57, 71, 77, 95, 106
Scout, The: 106
Scowcroft, Richard: 258
Scruggs, Philip: 225
Sea Is So Wide, The: 234
Sea Island Lady, A: 188
Sea of Grass, The: 256
Sea Panther, The: 223
Seaman, Augusta: 222
Seas Stand Watch, The: 235
Seats of the Mighty, The: 52, 221
Sedges, John: 205
Sedgwick, Catharine M.: 42–43, 69, 71, 227
Seifert, Shirley: 224, 233, 243
Separated by Mountains: 251
Sergeant Lamb's America: 232
Sessler, J. J.: 224
Seth Way: 239
Seton, William: 46
Seven Cities of Gold, The: 226
Seventy-Six: 227
Sevier, John: 90, 224
Seward's Folly: 255
Shadow and the Glory, The: 234
Shadow of the Long Knives, The: 91
Shadow of Night: 242
Shadow of Victory, The: 230
Shadow of the War, The: 247
Shadows on the Rock: 53
Shafer, Donald: 232
Shaftel, George: 243
Shakespeare, William: 6, 24

Shaw, Margaret: 232
Shays's Rebellion: 110, 112–13
Shenandoah: 247
Shepard, Odell: 110, 128
Shepherd, Daniel: 228
Sheridan, Philip: 155, 156, 167, 174
Sherman, General William T.: 155, 161, 164, 165, 171, 172, 178, 182
Shiloh, Battle of: 168, 171, 176, 251
Shining Trail, The: 123
Shippen, Peggy: 233
Shoshonee Valley, The: 134
Show Boat: 255
Show Me a Land: 252
Shuster, George: 252
Sign of the Prophet, The: 93
Silent Drum, The: 64
Silent South, The: 181
Silver Shoals: 225
Sim Greene: 230
Simms, J. R.: 228
Simms, William Gilmore: 12–13, 35, 36, 116, 169; *The Partisan,* 104–105; *Mellichampe,* 105; *The Forayers,* 105; *Eutaw,* 105; *Katherine Walton,* 105; *The Scout,* 106; *Woodcraft,* 106; *Joscelyn,* 229
Simon Girty: 240
Simon Kenton: 117
Sims, Marian: 253
Sinclair, Harold: 149, 205, 232
Sinclair, Upton: 154, 162–63
Singing Lariat: 257
Singmaster, Elsie: 225, 232
Sioux City: 257
Sir Christopher: 34
Skinner, Constance: 239
Slaughter, Frank: 245
Slave Ship, The: 223
Slogum House: 201
Smith, Captain John: 23 f.
Smith, Chard: 252, 257
Smith, Elizabeth: 228
Smith, F. Hopkinson: 146
Smith, Jedediah: 133
Smith, Joseph: 144, 145
Smith, R. P.: 227
Smiths, The: 206
Smokefires in Schoharie: 232
Snedeker, Caroline: 223
Snelling, Anna: 93
So Red the Rose: 170
So Shall They Reap: 253
Soldier of Manhattan, A: 222
Soldier of the Confederacy, A: 251
Some Lose Their Way: 242

Index

Son of the Middle Border, A: 126, 192–93
Son of the Revolution, A: 237
Song of the Susquehanna: 226
Song of Years: 241
Sorensen, Virginia: 144, 145, 145 n.
Soul of Ann Rutledge, The: 149
Sound of Chariots: 235
Southerner, The: 149, 181, 181 n.
Southerners, The: 155, 249
Sowing of the Swords, The: 250
Spanish Bayonet: 223
Spectre of the Forest, The: 45, 62
Spectre of Power, A: 222
Sperry, Armstrong: 233
Splendour Stays, The: 233
Spoon River Anthology: 202
Spotswood, Governor Alexander: 31
Spur of Monmouth, The: 229
Spy, The: 9–10, 68, 76–78
Spy of '76, A: 231
Standish, Miles: 38
Standish of Standish: 221
Stanley, Edward: 236, 246
Stanton, Edward: 158
Star of the West: 136
Star of the Wilderness: 131
Star Pointed North: 244
Stark, General John: 72
Stars on the Sea: 99
Stately Timber: 224
Steele, Wilbur D.: 258
Stephens, Alexander H.: 246
Stephens, Ann S.: 228
Stephenson, Nathaniel: 249
Sterling, C. F.: 228
Stern, Philip Van Doren: 151
Sterne, Emma: 231
Steuben, Baron von: 86
Stevens, Louis: 259
Stevens, Thaddeus: 160
Stevenson, Burton: 91, 237
Stewart, George: 142
Stimson, F. J.: 221, 230
Stockton, Frank: 222
Stoddard, William O.: 230
Stoic, The: 207
Stone, Grace: 49
Store, The: 168
Storm Against the Wind: 234
Storm to the South: 243
Stormy Petrel, The: 248
Story of Old Fort Loudon, The: 222
Story of Tonty, The: 89, 229
Stouman, Knud: 226
Stover, Herbert: 226

Stowe, Harriet Beecher: 13, 119, 237
Strabel, Thelma: 243
Strachey, Ray (Mrs. Oliver Strachey): 239
Street, James H.: 120, 242, 253, 259
Strength of the Hills, The: 240
Strength of the Weak, The: 222
Stribling, T. S.: 168
Strife Before Dawn: 224
Strong, Phil: 241
Stronghold: 236
Stuart, Jeb: 164, 176
Stuyvesant, Peter: 54
Sublette, Clifford: 223, 243
Summers, Richard: 246
Sumner, Charles: 160
Sun in Their Eyes: 243
Sun Shines West, The: 243
Sundown Jim: 256
Supper at the Maxwell House: 253
Surry of Eagle's Nest: 154, 156
Swain, Virginia: 257
Swamp Steed, The: 228
Swanson, Neil: 18, 63, 235
Sweeny, Sarah: 241
Sweet Revenge: 249
Swift Flows the River: 242
Sword of the Old Frontier, A: 222
Sword of the Wilderness: 223
Sword of Youth, The: 250
Swords and Roses: 251

Tabb, T. T.: 227
Tadeuskund: 61
Take All to Nebraska: 198
Talbot and Vernon: 236
Tall Men: 251
Tallahassee Girl, A: 247
Talleyrand: 101
Tamarack Tree: 244
Tap Roots: 242
Tarkington, Booth: 205–206, 238
Tarleton, Sir Banastre: 103, 104, 105, 107, 227, 229, 231
Tassels on Her Boots: 257
Tate, Allen: 169, 252
Taylor, Ross: 211
Taylor, Zachary: 129, 132
Tecumseh: 89, 92, 93, 111, 120, 227, 228, 229
Tempered Blade: 244
Templeton, Frank: 238
Terrell, John U.: 137
Texas Cowboys: 256
Texas Sheriff: 256
Texas Triggers: 256

Thackeray, William Makepeace: 221
Thanet, Octave: *see* French, Alice
Thankful Blossom: 229
That Bennington Mob: 231
That Girl from Memphis: 258
That Skipper from Stonington: 244
Their Father's God: 197
They Fought for Liberty: 231
They Sought for Paradise: 241
They That Took the Sword: 249
This Land Is Ours: 94
This Passion Never Dies: 198
This Side of Glory: 252
This Side of Innocence: 258
Thomas, Anna: 65
Thomas, General George Henry: 155
Thomas Forty: 236
Thomason, John W.: 175, 186
Thompson, Daniel P.: 13, 44, 50–51, 72
Thompson, J. Maurice: 15, 89–90, 182, 247
Those Who Go Against the Current: 243
Thread of Scarlet: 232
Three Fields to Cross: 236
Three Harbours: 99
Three-Headed Angel, The: 251
Throwback, The: 238
Thunder before Seven: 130
Thunder in the Wilderness: 226
Thunder on the River: 245
Thunder Shield: 208
Thurston, Lucy M.: 250
Ticonderoga: 51, 56, 72, 74, 222, 224, 234
Tide of Time, The: 256
Tidewater: 242
Tiernan, Mary: 248
Timothy Larkin: 253
Timrod, Henry: 169
Tinker, Edward L.: 146
Tippecanoe, Battle of: 89, 93, 94, 114, 229
Titan, The: 206–207
To Have and To Hold: 26–27
Toast for the King, A: 232
Toil of the Brave: 104
Tolstoy: 5
Tom Bone: 225
Tom Burton: 247
Tomkinson, Grace: 235
Tomorrow We Reap: 259
Tory Lover, The: 97
Tory Oath: 233
Tory Tavern: 233

Tory's Daughter, The: 229
Toucoutou: 146
Touchstone: 244
Tourgée, Albion W.: 14, 157, 180, 237
Tournament: 259
Toward the Morning: 65
Townsend, George: 247
Townsman, The: 205
Tracy, J. P.: 247
Trail-Makers of the Middle Border: 155, 165
Train, Arthur: 257
Traitor, The: 185
Traveler's Candle: 225
Treason: 234
Tree of Liberty, The: 109–110
Trees, The: 5, 124
Trenton, Battle of: 86, 232, 234
Troopers West: 258
Trouble Shooter: 256
Trowbridge, J. T.: 237
Trumpet in the Wilderness: 100
Trumpet to Arms: 234
Trumpets at Dawn: 232
Trumpets Calling: 256
Tucker, St. George: 28
Tumbleweeds: 255
Turnbull, Agnes: 234
Two Vanrevels, The: 238

Uncharted Ways: 223
Unconquered: 64
Underground Railroad: 163, 242
Unofficial Patriot, The: 248
Unvanquished, The: 85–86
Updegraff, Florence: 225
U. P. Trail, The: 208–209

Valiant Libertine: 233
Valiant Runaways, The: 141
Valiant Wife, The: 231
Valley Forge: 85, 104, 228, 229
Valley in Arms: 225
Valley of the Shadows, The: 149
Vandemark's Folly: 124, 199
Van de Water, Frederic: 208, 226
Van Every, Dale: 243
Vanguard of the Plains: 239
Venable, William H.: 237
Vestal, Stanley (*pseud.* of Walter S. Campbell): 132, 240
Vicksburg, Battle of: 154, 161, 164, 165, 171
Vigilante: 246
Viola: 236
Virginia Comedians, The: 32

Virginia Massacre: 25
Virginian, The: 207–208
Virginians, The: 221
Voice of the People, The: 185
Volunteer's Adventures, A: 157 n.

Wacousta: 220
Wah-To-Yah and the Taos Trail: 255
Waldman, Emerson: 252
Wallace, Lew: 15
Walpole, Horace: 97
Warner, Seth: 50, 51
Warren Joseph: 70
Warren, Lella: 252
Warrens of Virginia, The: 250
Washington, George: 4, 62–3, 69, 75, 77, 78, 79, 83, 84, 85, 86, 87–88, 98, 104, 108, 109, 220, 221, 226, 227, 228, 229, 234
Water Over the Dam: 244
Water Witch, The: 219
Waters, Frank: 256
Waters of the Wilderness: 233
Watts, Mary: 17, 129
Wave, The: 167
Way West, The: 138
Wayne, Mad Anthony: 91, 92, 116, 228, 229, 231
We Begin: 38
We Must March: 139
Weathercock: 233
Webb, Mrs. J. B.: *see* Peploe, Annie
Webster, Daniel: 70, 244
Wedding Journey, The: 244
Weir, James: 117, 236
Welcome Wilderness: 235
Weld, John: 142, 242
Wellman, Paul: 253
Wept of Wish-ton-Wish, The: 44, 45
Wescott, Glenway: 202
West Goes the Road: 243
Western Captive, The: 228
Westerners, The: 254
Westward Ho!: 115
Westward the River: 243
Westward the Tide: 232
Westways: 158
Whalley, Edward: 28, 45, 219
Wharton, Edith: 16, 206
Wheat Women: 255
When Destiny Called: 245
When Geronimo Rode: 255
When Wilderness Was King: 230
Where the Battle Was Fought: 183
Where Copper Was King: 254

Where Glory Waits: 231
Whipple, Maurine: 210
Whiskey Rebellion: 92, 110, 230, 232
Whistling Cat: 251
Whistling Lead: 256
White, Stewart E.: 143, 254
White, William A.: 254
White Aprons: 221
White Indian: 239
White Leader, The: 239
Whitefield, George: 70
Whitman, Marcus and Narcissa: 139
Whitney, Janet: 234
Whittier, John G.: 40
Who Fought and Bled: 232
Wide House: 243
Wiener, Willard: 234
Wigglesworth, Michael: 41
Wild Geese: 255
Wild Harvest: 255
Wild Is the River: 252
Wild Work: 246
Wild Yazoo, The: 245
Wilder, Robert: 245
Wilderness, The: 62
Wilderness Adventure: 226
Wiley, R. T.: 230
Wilkinson, James: 115, 118, 119, 239
Williams, Ben Ames: 150, 176–77, 232
Williams, Catherine R.: 220
Williams, Mary: 244
Williams, Roger: 45, 225
Willis, John R.: 227
Wilson, Augusta Evans: 129
Wilson, Charles: 243
Wilson, Harry L.: 145
Wilson, Margaret: 201, 231
Wilson, William E.: 246
Wind Blew West, The: 212
Wind Leaves No Shadow, The: 245
Wind Over Wisconsin: 122
Wine of San Lorenzo, The: 131
Winning the Wilderness: 238
Winslow, Edward: 37, 221
Winslow, William: 39
Winslow, William H.: 247
Winter's Lodge, The: 236
Winther, Sophus K.: 196, 198
Winthrop, John: 37, 39, 43, 49, 219
Winthrop, Theodore: 229, 237
Winwar, Frances: 48
Wister, Owen: 5, 207
Witch of Jamestown, The: 221
Witch of New England, The: 219
Witchcraft: 46 f., 220, 222, 223, 225, 226

Witching Times: 47
With Cradle and Clock: 226
With Crockett and Bowie: 237
With Malice Toward None: 160
With Sam Houston in Texas: 238
Wolf Song: 255
Wolfe, General James: 52
Wolves Against the Moon: 121–22
Wood, Lydia: 248
Woodcraft: 106
Woodworth, Samuel: 227
Woolson, Constance F.: 183
Wright, James N.: 254
Written in Sand: 235
Wyandotté: 80
Wyoming Massacre: 60, 62, 228

Yancey, William: 163
Yankee Trader: 235

Year of Decision: 146
Year of Wreck, A: 246
Years of Growth, The: 205
Years of Illusion: 205
Years of Peace, The: 251
Yemassee, The: 35–36
Yerby, Frank: 244
Yorktown: 87, 227
Yorktown: 227
Young, Agatha: 259
Young, Brigham: 144, 145
Young Ames: 242
Young Patroon, The: 55
Young, Stark: 147, 239
Young'un: 243

Zachary Phips: 229
Zara, Louis: 94
Zury: 125

UNIVERSITY OF OKLAHOMA PRESS

NORMAN